How to Build
BIG-INCH
MOPAR SMALL BLOCKS

JIM SZILAGYI

S·A DESIGN

CarTech®

Edited By: Josh Brown

ISBN-13 978-1-932494-57-0
ISBN-10 1-932494-57-X

Printed in China

CarTech ®
39966 Grand Avenue
North Branch, MN 55056
Telephone (651) 277-1200 • (800) 551-4754 • Fax: (651) 277-1203
www.cartechbooks.com

OVERSEAS DISTRIBUTION BY:

Brooklands Books Ltd.
P.O. Box 146, Cobham, Surrey, KT11 1LG, England
Telephone 01932 865051 • Fax 01932 868803
www.brooklands-books.com

Brooklands Books Aus.
3/37-39 Green Street, Banksmeadow, NSW 2019, Australia
Telephone 2 9695 7055 • Fax 2 9695 7355

Front Cover: The most popular Mopar small-block engines are made with a 4.000" stroke using a 340 or 360 engine block. These engines make from 402" to 408" with 360 blocks, and 410 to 418 cubes with a 340 block.

Title Page: The basic design of Mopar engines allow up to 476 cubic inches using aftermarket blocks that have thicker bore walls. Engines of this size do not require crazy options like deck plates, raised camshafts, or manifold spacers normally needed on other engines.

Back Cover, Upper Right: Magnum and most Mopar Performance stroker crankshafts have a larger diameter on the rear main seal area of the crank. The machining in the block for the seal groove is the same on all Mopar small-blocks, so these LA or Magnum cranks are interchangeable.

Back Cover, Lower Left: The basic design of the small-block Mopar is "made to be stroked" and is the easiest stroker engine to build using ordinary tools in your own garage.

Back Cover, Lower Right: A Holley 0-3310S 750-cfm carb is bolted on with a thin Edelbrock carb adapter plate. The carb plate is needed to fill a small gap at the edge of the carb surface (spread bore shape on intake, but used with square bore carb). The dyno test data for this engine is shown in Chapter 15.

TABLE OF CONTENTS

Dedication 5

Acknowledgments 5

Chapter 1:   Introduction 6
Hot Rod and Street Rod Engines 6
Production Small-Block Engines 7
Why LA and Magnum Engines
are Shown in the Same Book 7
Mopar Performance Parts 8

Chapter 2:   Made to be Stroked 10
Advantages 10
Potential Problem Areas 13
Stroker Kits 14

Chapter 3:   Cylinder Blocks 16
LA Engine Blocks (1964-'92) 16
360 Magnum Engine Block (1993-'03) . .17
340 Replacement Engine Block 19
R3 Engine Block 20
Aluminum A Engine Block 23
Block Preparation 25
Block Selection 29

Chapter 4:   Crankshaft 30
Crankshaft Basics 30
Types of Cranks 31
Stroke 32
Bearings 33
Internal and External Balance 34

Chapter 5:   Oiling System 38
Problems with the Stock Oiling System . . .38
Recommended Modifications 40
Optional Modifications 41
Conclusion 44

Chapter 6:   Connecting Rods 46
Rod Length 46
Rod Ratio 46
Stock LA Rods 46
Stock Magnum Rods 46
Fasteners 47

Block Clearance 48
Pre-Assembly 48
Conclusion 49

Chapter 7:   Pistons and Rings 50
Material and Processes 50
Forged 50
Dished, Flat Top, or Dome? 54
Valve Clearance 55
Compression Height 56
Weight 57
Rings 57
Conclusion 57

Chapter 8:   Camshafts 60
Production Cams 60
Cam Bearings 60
Cam Drive 61
Timing Chain Tensioner 62
HP Thrust Plate 62
Fuel Pump Eccentric 62
Problems with Flat Tappet Camshafts . .63
Stroker Cams 63
Roller Tappets on R3 Blocks 63
Aluminum Blocks 63
Used R3 Blocks 63
Conclusion 65

Chapter 9:   Cylinder Heads 66
Iron vs. Aluminum 66
Valve Angle 66
Valve Spacing 68
Ports & Chambers 68
Flow 68
Cylinder Head Selection 70
CNC Porting .80
Conclusion 80

Chapter 10:   Valvetrains 81
48-Degree Valvetrain 81
Valvetrain Oiling 82
Tappets 82
Pushrods 84
Rocker Arms – LA Heads 84

CONTENTS

Rocker Arms – Magnum Heads 85
Valvesprings .86
Retainers 88
Valves 89
Valve to Guide Clearance 89
Conclusion 89

Chapter 11:   Induction Systems 90
Manifold Types 90
LA 340/360 Heads 90
W2 Heads 92
W8, W9 Heads 93
Indy 360-2 Heads 93
Magnum Heads 93
Fuel Pump 96
Magnum Fuel Injection (MPI) Intakes . . .98
Magnum Intake – Oil Leaks 99
Distributor Clearance 99
Cross-Over Pocket 101
Conclusion .101

Chapter 12:   Exhaust Systems 102
Header Basics 102
Types of Headers 102
LA Heads 103
Magnum Heads 104
W2 Heads 104
W9 Heads 104
Exhaust System 105

Chapter 13:   Cooling Systems 106
Cooling Theory 106
Improved Cooling 107
Cross Drilling Block 109
Cylinder Head Modification 110
Radiator 110
Electric Cooling Fan 111
Oil Cooler 111
Water Pump .112
Radiator Cap 112
Airflow Through the Radiator 112
Overflow Bottle 112
Coolants 112
Conclusion .112

Chapter 14:   Building and Blueprinting 113
Block Preparation / Engine Mockup . .113
Disassembly and Cleaning 119
Final Assembly 120
Additional Information 123

Chapter 15:   Engine Packages 126

Appendix A: 132
Stroker Kits .132

Appendix B: 139
Source Guide 139
Source by Type of Product 141

Engine Build Sheet 142

DEDICATION

This book is dedicated to my father –
Alexander John Szilagyi (September 27, 1939—July 7, 2004).

Acknowledgments

I would like to thank the engine builders I have worked with over the last several years. These guys have taught me a great deal about the small-block Mopar engine: Gary Stanton, Ron Beauchamp, Joe Gaerte, Mark Petty, Guy Forbrook, Bill Hancock, Paul Kistler, and Bill Haenelt.

I would also like to thank my co-workers at Dodge Motorsports and Mopar Performance Parts: Larry Shepard, Greg Reeves, Lee Carducci, John Wehrly, Neil Loughlin, Pat Baer, Rudy Sayn, and Dave James.

Special thanks go to the following people who helped gather information, parts, and helped in many other ways while writing this book:

Jack McCormack at McCormack Motorsports
Oz Cheek at KB Pistons
Rob Cunningham at Mancini Racing
Denny Hummel at Booth-Arons, Inc.
My wife Julie

All photographs in this book were taken by Jim and Julie Szilagyi.

About the Author

Jim Szilagyi has worked at DaimlerChrysler since 1989 and currently works in the Dodge Motorsports engineering department. His primary responsibility is development of the small-block Mopar race parts used in "Grass Roots" racing programs like the NASCAR Dodge Weekly Racing Series, USAC Sprint Cars and Midgets, and World of Outlaws Sprint Cars.

Prior to joining the Motorsports group, Jim spent several years developing high-performance and racing parts in the Mopar Performance Parts group. The author and his co-workers at Mopar developed many of the high-performance and stroker Mopar engine parts shown in this book.

INTRODUCTION

If you want to make some serious power from your Mopar small-block, then this is the book for you. Big-inch stroker small-block Mopar engines have become very popular over the last several years. The big-inch Mopar craze really took off when the 4.000" stroke cranks were launched by Mopar Performance a couple of years ago. These new cranks made stroker engines affordable for most car guys who would never consider buying a $2,000 to $3,000 custom-made stroker crank.

The basic design of the small-block Mopar is "made to be stroked" and is the easiest stroker engine to build using ordinary tools in your own garage. See Chapter 2 for more details on the features that make these engines ideal for big-inch strokers.

This book's chapters cover the details of engine components like blocks, cranks, heads, cams, induction systems, and much more. Each chapter gives technical advice on what parts work best in big-inch engines and provides tips on areas for needed improvement or modifications.

Chapter 14 shows the major steps in building a typical Mopar small-block stroker engine. Chapter 15 ends with several engine packages and gives examples of what parts work together and how much power they make with dyno test data.

The basic design of Mopar engines allows up to 476 cubic inches using aftermarket blocks that have thicker bore walls. Engines of this size do not require crazy options like deck plates, raised camshafts, or manifold spacers normally needed on other engines.

Hot Rod and Street Rod Engines

The engines and general recommendations in this book are geared for street engines in hot rods and muscle cars. Many of the concepts and procedures can also be used for street and strip or entry-level racing. Some of the engine packages are a little more involved and costly than what is normally used in a street cruiser or show car.

In this book, I consider any small-block Mopar engine with 371 cubic inches

or larger a big-inch or stroker engine. The smallest stroker engine would be a 340 block using a 3.58" (360) stroke with a 4.060" bore size. Initially, the only way to make this combination was to take a 360 crank and turn down the main journals to the 340 size. This allowed the longer 360 stroke with the bigger bore 340 block. Today, this modification isn't necessary since new stroker cranks are available with the small 340 mains. Some of these cranks are cast and are less expensive than the cost to modify a "used" 360 crank.

A wide variety of stroker cranks are available for Mopar small blocks. Prices range from $325 for cast cranks to several thousand dollars for special one-off custom cranks.

Stroker kits in Appendix A show stroker 318 engines, but these are pretty rare since most stroker customers want an engine larger than the stock 360 size.

The most popular Mopar small-block engines are made with a 4.000" stroke using a 340 or 360 engine block. These engines make from 402" to 408" with 360 blocks, and 410 to 418 cubes with a 340 block. Bigger-inch engines require the use of aftermarket R3 blocks with more material in the bore and (on some versions of the R3), with thicker bore walls, can handle a bore up to 4.220".

Since you can buy a stroker short block, you don't need to know the ins and outs of engine building. These short blocks have all the details already worked out for you and are available from many sources.

Stroker engines can be used with either carburetors or multi-point fuel injection. The camshaft heads and intake options allow many options for just about any type induction system.

Production Small-Block Engines

Mopar Small-Block Production Engines		
Production LA Engines		
Model Year	ci Displacement	Bore x Stroke
1964-1969	273	3.630" x 3.310"
1967-1991	318	3.910" x 3.310"
1968-1973	340	4.040" x 3.310"
1971-1992	360	4.000" x 3.580"
Production Magnum Engines		
Model Year	ci Displacement	Bore x Stroke
1992-2001	5.2L (318)	3.910" x 3.310"
1993-2003	5.9L (360)	4.000" x 3.580"

Many people call the 1964-'92 small-block Mopar (273/318/340/360 ci) the "A" engine. This is a little confusing since the 1955-'66 (277/301/318 ci) Mopar engine is the original A engine. These early small-block A engines are not very popular for high-performance use and won't be covered in this book. To avoid any confusion, I call the 1964-'92 small-block the "LA" engine. LA stands for "Lightweight A" engine.

Mopar produced LA small-block engines from 1964 to 1992. Magnum small blocks were produced from 1992 to 2003. Magnum 5.9L engines were replaced by the new 5.7L Hemi® in mid-2003 and are no longer in production today. LA and Magnum small-block engines are ideal bases for big-inch stroker engines.

Why LA and Magnum Engines are Shown in the Same Book

The 1964-'92 LA engines and 1992-'03 Magnum engines are very similar and their parts are interchangeable. You can use the same basic principals, parts, and processes to build an LA or Magnum stroker engine. Chrysler marketed the Magnum engines as being totally new and different, but they are really an LA with several updates to the oiling system, valve train, and cylinder heads.

Each chapter of this book describes the differences between LA and Magnum engines. In many cases the parts are interchangeable, but sometimes a subgroup of parts must be changed all at once. For example, Magnum heads can be used on an LA block, but you must also use the Magnum rocker arms, valves, valve gear, intake manifold, and valve covers. In some cases,

Common Features in LA and Magnum Engines
Head Bolt Pattern
Oil Pan Bolt Pattern
Bell-Housing Bolt Pattern
Front Cover Bolt Pattern
Deck Height
Bore Sizes
Stroke Sizes
Tappet Angle
Tappet Diameter
Crankshaft Main and Rod Journal Size
Camshaft Journal Size
Block Length / Width / Height
Bearings

Very Minor Changes (interchangeable)
Crankshafts
Connecting Rods
Camshafts (some)
Cylinder Heads & Valvetrain (some)
Gaskets (some)
Oil Pumps
Pistons & Rings & Rods (may change balance)

Major Differences Between Mopar LA and Magnum Engines

1964-1992 LA Engines 273/318/340/360	1992-2003 Magnum Engines 5.2L/5.9L
5-Bolt Valve Cover	10-Bolt Valve Cover
Hydraulic Flat Tappet Camshaft (1964-'87)	Hydraulic Roller Camshaft
Standard Tappet Bores	Taller Tappet Bores
Shaft-Mounted Rocker Arms	Stud-Mounted Rocker Arms
Rocker Arms Oiled Through Rocker Shaft	Rocker Arms Oiled Through Pushrods
1.5:1 Rocker Arm Ratio	1.6:1 Rocker Arm Ratio
Standard Intake Manifold & Mounting	Vertical Intake Manifold Screws
Standard Rotation Water Pump	Reverse Rotation Water Pump
V-Belt Fan Belt	Serpentine Fan Belt

Stroker Cubic Inch Displacement

| | Stroke | | | | |
	3.580"	3.790"	4.000"	4.250"	4.500"
Bore Size					
3.910"	344		384		
3.940"	349		390		
4.000"		381	402	427	452
4.030"		387	408	434	459
4.040"	367	389	410	436	461
4.060"	371	393	414	440	466
4.070"	373	394	416	442	468
4.080"	374	396	418	445	471
4.125"		405	428	454	481
4.180"		416	439	467	494
4.200"		420	443	471	499
4.220"		424	448	476	504
4.250"		430	454	482	511

High-flow cylinder heads are one of the key factors in making big power. This W9 head comes with a CNC-machined chamber and large high-flow intake and exhaust ports that are very efficient without any porting.

like with the cylinder heads and pistons, using Magnum parts instead of LA parts gives you a performance advantage.

The two charts listed above detail some of the major similarities and differences between LA and Magnum engines.

Magnum engines are normally sized in liters (i.e., 5.2L and 5.9L), even though the bore and stroke of these two engines are the same size as the 318 and 360 LA engines.

Mopar Performance Parts

Many of the high-performance parts in this book are made by Mopar and marketed under the Mopar Performance Parts product line. These parts are called "P" parts since they start with the letter "P" (which stands for "performance"). Throughout this book, these Mopar parts are described by the part number beginning with "P." You can buy Mopar Performance Parts from the parts department of any Dodge, Jeep, or Chrysler dealer, or from high-performance parts distributors that sell the Mopar Performance product line (Mancini Racing, Summit Racing, Jegs, and many others).

Shop around for the best pricing and customer support on Mopar Performance Parts. The seller sets the pricing, creating quite a difference in prices. If you buy the parts from a local dealer or distributor and pick them up yourself, you won't incur any shipping cost. If

A wide variety of high-quality stroker pistons are available off the shelf for big-inch Mopar engines. These new forged pistons are available from KB.

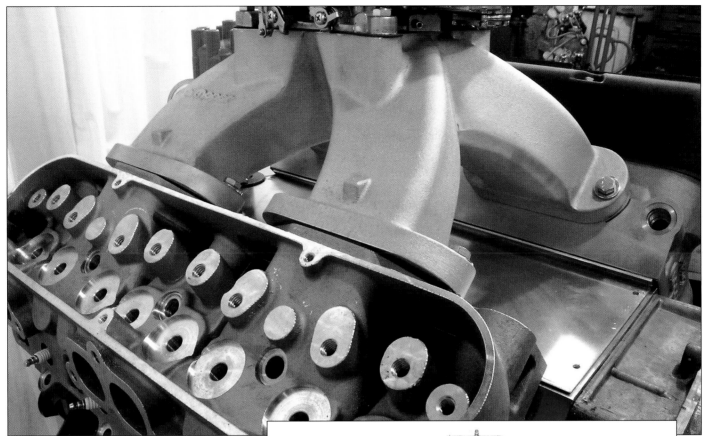

The camshaft and intake manifold are the other major components that must work together in harmony with the heads to produce good power. Note the raised intake ports and smooth transition from the carb to the chamber on this high-rise induction system.

you buy a heavy item like an engine block or short block by mail order, you may be charged for freight.

Consider technical support when you buy parts. Some retailers provide rock-bottom pricing but don't want to help you out after the sale. Other sellers provide great customer support, but need to charge a little more for the parts since good support staff can be expensive. Don't expect customer support from someone who did not sell you the parts. Retailers are busy and don't have time to help you out when you did not buy the parts from them in the first place.

The big-inch Mopar stroker is capable of making up to 800+ hp and weighing less than 500 lbs. The only limit is how much you want to spend. Once built, these engines are an easy "bolt-in" on any car or truck that originally came with a small-block.

MADE TO BE STROKED

The Mopar small-block engine seems as though it is made to be stroked. The engine is just a little bit larger than most other small-block engines, and this makes all the difference when building a stroker engine. The crankcase has so much room on the inside and so many other features that it works great on big-inch engines.

Advantages are listed below, followed by some potential problem areas. The last part of the chapter discusses the available completed stroker engines and short-blocks.

This is a typical Mopar 408-ci small-block stroker engine. This engine was built with an aftermarket R3 engine block, but it could be built using a stock 360 or Magnum 5.9L block. The tall deck height and high camshaft location allows the use of the 4.000" stroke crankshaft without any block clearancing at all.

Advantages

Tall Deck Height

All Mopar small-block engines have a relatively tall stock production deck height. The deck height is the measurement from the centerline of the crankshaft up to the top of the fire-deck on the block. The stock deck height varies slightly on different small-block engines, from about 9.585" to 9.599". Remember, when a block is milled on its deck, the deck height gets shorter by the amount machined away.

You can use long connecting rods and a long stroke on the crankshaft with this extra deck height. This is a big advantage since most other engines require a change to the length of the connecting rods when the stroke is increased.

When the stroke is increased on any engine, the distance from the top of the piston to the pin (compression height) must be reduced. With a shorter deck height block, sometimes the piston pin tries to take up the same space as the oil scraper piston rings. In this situation, the piston pin is made shorter and a special steel support ring is added to provide support for the bottom of the oil scraper ring. The special support rings increase the complexity, weight, and cost of the pistons.

Stock production deck height on a Mopar small-block has enough room for the stock 6.123" connecting rod with a 4.250"-long stroke and a piston compression height of about 1.327". This allows enough room to keep the piston pin out of the piston rings and still have enough extra room to allow a 0.020" clean-up cut on the fire deck of the block.

Extra deck height allows a longer stroke without moving the piston pin into the oil rings. This 4.000" stroker piston has a compression height of 1.404" (top piston to centerline of piston pin), and the piston pin is completely below the piston rings.

Connecting Rod

Stock length of the Mopar small-block connecting rod is 6.123". This is much longer than most other small-block rods, which range from 5.090" to 5.700" long. The extra length of the connecting rods provide clearance to the larger counterweights used on stroker crankshafts. The longer rod also

Extra deck height and long connecting rods allow the piston to clear the large counterweights on most stroker cranks. This piston has about 0.200" clearance to the counterweight.

improves the angle of the rod when used with a longer stroke crankshaft.

The rod journal size of 2.125" is larger and stronger than most small-block engines. This size is durable enough to handle big-block sized displacement.

Bore Size

The 360 and 340 engines have a standard bore size of 4.000" and 4.040". This size is common with most other small-block engines, making for a good choice of pistons and piston rings.

You can specially machine most flat-top piston castings and forgings offered for GM small-block engines to work in a Mopar engine. Intake and exhaust valves are in approximately the same location as GM engines, leaving enough material to allow special machining for the valve notches on the pistons. The piston pin size and location must also be specially machined for the use of the Mopar size and compression height.

When used with the 360 crankshaft, the 340 block is probably the easiest stroker Mopar small block to build. The 360 crankshaft's main bearing size is larger than the 340, so the main journals must be turned down to the 340 size. Another alternative is to buy a crankshaft made with the 340 main bearing journals size (2.500" journals) and the

360 stroke (3.580" stroke). A stock 0.040" to 0.080" oversize 360 piston can be used in the 340 engine block. This combination increases the displacement of the 340 engine from 367 to 375 cubic inches. It also requires no special machining except to turn down the main journal size on the 360 crankshaft (or buy Mopar P5007257 crankshaft with the 340 mains and 360 stroke). These stroker pistons are readily available, since they are really just an oversized 360 piston.

Bore Spacing

Mopar small-block engines have a bore spacing of 4.460". Bore spacing is the amount of space from the centerline of one bore to the adjacent bore. Most small-block engines have a bore center of 4.380" to 4.400". Larger piston sizes can be used with larger bore spacing and still have enough room between the cylinders to seal the head gasket between the bores. Special Siamese bore blocks are needed to really take advantage of this extra space, but these blocks available.

With a Siamese bore block, bore sizes of up to 4.250" are possible (4.220" are recommended). Most other brand Siamese bore blocks with smaller bore spacing limit bore size to about 4.155"

340 and 360 blocks use the same diameter pistons (4.040" and 4.000") as most other high-performance small-block engines. In most cases, GM piston cores can be specially machined for use in Mopar engines. The valve layout and valve notch on the piston is in the same place, so most manufacturers offer pistons with reasonable pricing.

The larger bore spacing on the Mopar block allows more room for the cylinder head gasket between the bores. This extra room also allows for better cooling with smaller bore sizes. This is typically the area in which head-gasket leaks are common on other brand engines.

or smaller. Larger piston bore sizes also un-shroud the valves at the edges of the bore, which increases airflow.

Tappet Size

Stock production tappet diameter on the Mopar is 0.904". This is a little larger than most other small blocks, which range from 0.841" to 0.875". A more aggressive flat tappet cam grind can be used with the larger diameter. The 0.904" size is the same size as a mushroom-style lifter in a GM engine.

High Camshaft Location

The height of the camshaft in stock Mopar small-block engines is 6.125" above the centerline of the crankshaft. This is much higher than on most other

All Mopar tappets are 0.904" diameter, and this allows for a more aggressive camshaft grind to feed a big-inch engine. This size is the same as a mushroom tappet on a GM engine, but it is completely stock.

small-block engines. The big advantage here is more room for longer strokes without the connecting rods hitting the camshaft. Most other engines require the camshaft to be raised to make extra room for the crankshaft and rods, but this comes standard on all small-block Mopar engines.

Another advantage of a high camshaft location is shorter pushrods. Shorter length makes the pushrods stiffer and lighter. This helps the valve-train to be more stable without as much pushrod flex.

Journal Sizes

Mopar 340 and 360 blocks have relatively large main bearing sizes. The 340 has a 2.500" and the 360 has a 2.810" main journal. Larger main size considerably strengthens the crankshaft.

Space Inside the Engine Block

The block has quite a bit of room inside to allow long strokes with very little, if any, clearancing. If the correct connecting rods are selected, no clearancing at all is required to build a stro-

Mopar small blocks have large journal sizes on the crankshaft, and this provides extra strength for big-block sized cubes on a stroker engine. The rod journals are 2.125" diameter, and the mains are 2.500" on 318/340 and 2.810" on 360s.

ker engine with a 4.000" stroke. When the stock LA or Magnum rods are used, a very slight amount of clearancing is needed at the bottom of the bores.

Shaft-Mounted Rocker Arms

All LA engines came from the factory with shaft-mounted rocker arms. Shaft-mounted rocker arms allow more pushrod offset in the rocker arms than stud-mounted units. This allows more

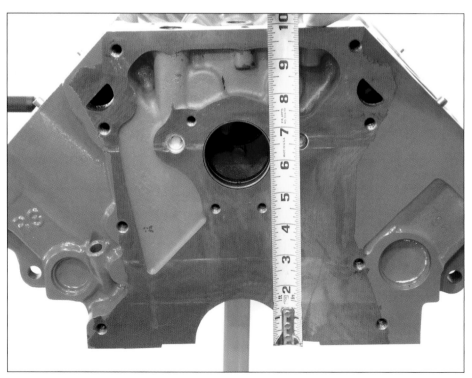

All Mopar blocks have the camshaft mounted up high in the block, and this provides more room for the connecting rods on a stroker engine. The high camshaft height (6.125" above the crank) also makes the pushrods shorter and stiffer than they would be if the cam were lower.

Mopar small blocks don't require any clearancing on the pan rail for the rods and crankshaft on strokes up to 4.000". If the correct rods are selected, then no clearancing is required for 4.000" stroker engines.

All LA engines come from the factory with shaft-mounted rocker arms. The shaft mounting allows more offset that moves the pushrod away from the centerline of the valve. The HP rocker arm set in the photo moves the pushrods over by 0.550" away from the very large intake ports on this W9 head. Stud-mounted rocker arms don't allow much, if any, offset.

room for larger intake ports. The more offset the pushrod, the farther you can get it away from the side of the intake port. Many racing engines convert from stud-mounted to shaft-mounted rocker arms for this very reason. The shaft mounting system is also stronger and more stable than stud-mounted rocker arms.

Low Cost

All the features discussed above reduce engine cost since mostly stock parts can be used to build a 408- to 418-ci stroker engine. The only special parts required to build a stroker engine up to this size is a 4.000" stroke crankshaft and stroker pistons.

The 4.000" stroke cast crankshafts from Mopar are also very reasonably priced at about $350. A complete 402- to

Only two parts are needed to build a Mopar stroker small block. A 402 to 418-ci stroker engine can be built using mostly stock used 340 or 360 parts for as little as $1,000. This stroker crankshaft is about $350.

418-ci stroker engine can be built for less than $1,000 by reusing most of the parts from a "used" 340/360 or 5.9L Magnum engine.

Potential Problem Areas

Mopar small blocks need some special care when building a high-performance stroker engine. The major issues are listed below and are discussed in detail in other chapters in this book.

Oiling System

The oil pickup on Mopar small-block engines is just adequate for production engines and is a restriction in a high-performance application such as a stroker engine. The pickup must be changed to allow more flow in any high-performance application. See Chapter 5 for details on how to overcome this problem.

Oil must follow a rather long and inefficient path to reach the cylinder heads. This causes problems in some engines. There are also several opportunities for leaks around the tappets. The oil path through timed passages in the camshaft may also restrict oil flow too much.

Head Bolts

There are only four bolts around each cylinder on the head, which is fewer than in most other small-block engines. Head gasket sealing is a problem at compression ratios of 11:1 or higher. See Cylinder Blocks (Chapter 3) and Cylinder Heads (Chapter 9) for details on how to overcome this problem.

Stock Mopars have a very small oil pickup tube that limits oil flow. This tube diameter should be increased on any HP engine.

Only four head bolts are around each cylinder, and this can lead to head-gasket leaks at high compression ratios. This is not a big problem for lower compression ratios of 11:1 or less, but special head gaskets must be used with higher compression ratios.

The tappet and pushrod angles are not in line, and this can cause valvetrain problems at high RPM. The stock system works fine unless the RPM is above 6,500 rpm for extended operation.

Valvetrain

Tappets and pushrods are not at the ideal angle for use in high-RPM racing and high-performance applications. Sustained operation over 6,500 rpm requires extensive modification to the valvetrain for best performance. Special cylinder blocks and cylinder heads are required to overcome this problem. This is not a big problem for most stroker engines since they are not well suited for high-RPM operation.

Stroker Kits

Several suppliers sell stroker kits for Mopar small-block engines. An extensive listing of these stroker kits appears in Appendix A. Not all the stroker kits include the same components, and some are not balanced. Take these two factors into account since balancing can cost $200 or more depending on the situation. Some kits come with the damper, bearings, and other parts, while others include just the pistons, rods, and crankshaft.

This stroker kit includes the Mopar cast crankshaft, Eagle rods, and KB pistons. This kit is not balanced, and it may take an additional $200 to balance the rotating assembly.

Stroker Short Blocks

Mopar Performance Parts also sells a stroker short-block engines (P5007840). This engine is 406ci with a 4.000" stroke and 4.020" bore size. The Mopar high-performance cast 4.000" stroke crankshaft is used in this short block.

The stroker short block reduces the complexity of building a stroker engine since the tough part of the job is already done. The engine is balanced and any needed clearancing is already done. Other suppliers also offer short blocks.

Stroker Crate Engine

If you don't want to go to the trouble of building a stroker engine, Mopar sells a complete 402-ci stroker engine

This complete 408 stroker engine makes 450 hp and 485 ft-lb of torque, and costs $3,000 to $7,000 to build.

402 Mopar stroker engines make about the same HP and torque as a production 426 Hemi® did when it was brand new in the late 1960s. The small-block stroker engine is about 300 lbs lighter and small enough to fit in most cars and trucks.

A stroker short block is the easy way to build a stroker engine since all the clearancing and balancing has been done. All the other parts can be swapped over from another used engine to save time and money.

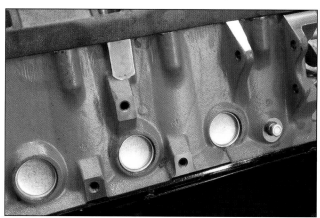

Production Magnum and aftermarket R3 blocks have two sets of motor mounts. The mounting ears on the front of the block are the same as the 1965-'92 LA, and the three-bolt mounts in the center of the block are for the 1993-'03 Magnum trucks.

(P5007647). It's made with all brand-new parts and includes a 360 Magnum block with big valve Magnum R/T cylinder heads, Eagle rods, Moroso oil pan, and cast 4.000" stroker crankshaft.

This engine sells for about $6,000 and makes 435 hp at 5,100 rpm and about 475 ft-lb torque at 4,400 rpm. The torque is over 400 ft-lb from 2,500 rpm to 5,700 rpm, so this engine has plenty of torque to accelerate any car very quickly.

These HP and torque numbers are about the same as a production 426 Hemi® when it was originally launched in the late 1960s in production cars. The really amazing difference is that this engine weighs about 300 or 400 lbs less than a 426 Hemi® and is much smaller. Because of this, it can easily be installed in just about any hot rod or high-performance vehicle.

The Magnum block fits easily into any vehicle that was originally available with a small-block Mopar. It has two sets of motor mounts (ears at front of block for muscle cars), and Magnum engine mounts for late-model trucks (three-bolt mount on the sides of the block). The HP R3 blocks also have the same dual motor mounts.

The remaining chapters get into more detail on the advantages and problem areas. Chapter 15 details several different common stroker engine packages complete with a parts listing for each engine.

CYLINDER BLOCKS

Engine block selection is the most important step in building a strong foundation for a stroker engine. The block selected determines how much HP the engine can handle and the maximum bore size and cubic inches of the stroker engine.

All Mopar (small-block) engine blocks have many features that make them ideal for use in stroker engines:

- High Camshaft Location – allows more room for longer strokes
- Short Pushrods – lighter and stiffer
- 4.460" Bore Spacing – allows larger bore sizes
- Wider Oil Pan Rails – more room for longer strokes and reduces windage
- Larger and Stronger Main Journals – (2.500" on 273/318/340 and 2.810" on 360) large diameter tappets (0.904" on cast iron blocks)
- Tall Deck Height – allows longer connecting rods and a longer stroke

This chapter will tell you which LA, Magnum, 340 replacement, R3, and aluminum blocks offer the best potential for use in stroker engines. These are all based on the basic LA design, and are for use with "Wedge"-style cylinder heads. The chapter follows up with tips on selecting the best block for your application and provides tips on block preparation.

Production Blocks

Mopar Production Blocks – LA Cast Iron

Year	CID	Bore (std)	Tappet Angle	Main Size	Main Caps	Deck Height	Approx. Weight (lbs)
1964-'69	273	3.625"	59 deg	2.500"	2-bolt	9.585"	160
1967-'91	318	3.910"	59 deg	2.500"	2-bolt	9.585"	160
1968-'73	340	4.040"	59 deg	2.500"	2-bolt	9.585"	160
1971-'92	360	4.000"	59 deg	2.810"	2-bolt	9.585"	160

Mopar Production Blocks – Magnum Cast Iron

Year	CID	Bore (std)	Tappet Angle	Main Size	Main Caps	Deck Height	Approx. Weight (lbs)
1992-'01	318	3.910"	59 deg	2.500"	2-bolt	9.585"	155
1993-'03	360	4.000"	59 deg	2.810"	2-bolt	9.585"	155

LA Engine Blocks (1964-'92)

All factory production LA engine blocks are cast iron, are made with two-bolt cast iron main caps, and have a full water jacket with water between each bore. The LA blocks weigh about 160 lbs. They are strong enough to handle output up to about 430 hp in high-endurance applications. Output can be slightly higher for low-endurance applications with lower RPM, but take special care to make sure they are not in detonation or have other tuning problems.

273 production blocks don't offer much potential for use in stroker applications. The bore size of 3.625" is too small, and this limits the valve sizes that fit into the bore and displacement. Additionally, the pistons and rings would have to be custom made for this bore

Production blocks have a full water jacket that allows water to pass between the bores. The full water jacket improves cooling but limits the bore size that can be used on a stroker engine. The best way to check the type of water jacket is by removing a freeze plug and inspecting the water jacket directly between the bores. This is a full water jacket block since I can fit a screwdriver blade between the bores.

This Siamese bore aluminum block has been sawed off just below the surface of the fire deck. A Siamese bore block allows use of much larger cylinder bore sizes for larger cubic inches in a stroker engine. The cooling system is not as efficient since the water in the cooling system does not go all the way around each cylinder bore. All Mopar aluminum blocks and some R3 blocks have a Siamese bore water jacket.

size since it is not common to build a stroker engine with this block.

318 production blocks offer a little more potential due to their larger 3.910" standard bore size, but they still would not be the best choice in most applications. A 340 or 360 production block allows a larger bore size and more displacement for about the same or a lower cost. 318-stroker engines also require custom pistons not readily available. Later 318 Magnum blocks have the same drawbacks and are not the best choice for use in a stroker engine.

One area the 318-stroker engine could be used in is racing applications with rules limiting the displacement to 350 cubic inches. A 360 stroke crankshaft can be used in the 318 block with a 0.030" overbore to achieve 349.2 cubic inches displacement. A stock production 360 crankshaft needs to have the main journals turned down to the 318/340 size and be re-hardened. An easy alternative is to buy a crankshaft that already has the 3.58" 360 stroke and the smaller 318/340 journals. This is available from Mopar under part number P5007253 (forged crank) or P5007257 (cast crankshaft).

The best factory production engine block for use in a stroker engine is the 340. The 340 has the largest stock bore

size of any production small-block Mopar. The stock bore size on the 340 is 4.040", and it can be overbored 0.030" or 0.040" on most blocks. A 0.020" to 0.040" overbore on a 340 block when used with a 4.000" stroke crankshaft makes 414 to 418 cubic inches displacement. The stroker 340 can also use 0.060" to 0.080" oversize 360-stroker piston and rings (actual bore size of 4.060" to 4.080"). These pistons are readily available in cast, hypereutectic, and forged versions.

The biggest drawback on the 340 block is a limited supply of original production blocks. Only about 199,000 production 340 engines were sold during its production run from 1968-'73. Most of these engines were used in racing and in muscle cars. Today, 340 engines are difficult to find and are expensive since they are used in collectable muscle cars. Most of the used 340 blocks are cracked or worn out. Mopar now has a block that offers an alternative to using a 30+ year-old used 340 block. See below for more details on this new 340 replacement block.

360 factory-production blocks are the most widely used blocks for Mopar stroker engines. Millions were made in production from 1971-'92 and prices are relatively low for a used 360 block or engine. The 360 has some important differences based on the year of production.

Early 1971-'74 360 blocks (casting #3870230) have more material in the cylinder bore and are heavier duty. These engines should allow up to a 0.040" overbore, but you should sonic check the block for enough material to allow this bore size. Most high-performance machine shops can do a sonic check on your block to check for enough stock for the desired overbore size.

In 1975 and later, the 360 blocks were made with a lighter engine block to improve fuel economy. This change removed some of the material in the cylinder bore on the water jacket side of the block. Most 360 blocks from 1975-'92 can only be bored to about 0.030" oversize, but again, you should sonic check the block to check for enough material to allow the desired bore size.

The 1988 and later 360 engines came with a production hydraulic roller tappet

camshaft. Changes were made to the block to add bosses in the valley of the block to bolt on the tappet retaining yoke. The tappet bores are also taller to accommodate the taller roller tappets. Other minor changes were made to the later blocks when electronic fuel injection was added to the production engines in 1989.

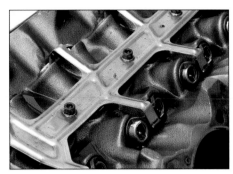

1987 and later LA and Magnum blocks have three extra tapped holes in the valley. These are used for the bolts that hold down the spider/retainer for the dog bones on the tappets. These three extra tapped holes are needed if you want to use the production-style hydraulic roller tappets.

360 Magnum Block (1993–'03)

Magnum blocks are very similar to LA blocks, but they have some important differences.

Similarity vs. LA Blocks

Magnum and LA blocks have similar bolt patterns and can use most of the same gaskets that meet up to the engine block (i.e., oil pan gasket, front cover gasket, head gasket, intake manifold end seals). The head gasket is slightly different since the Magnum blocks don't have an oil passage that leads from the camshaft up to the cylinder heads. LA head gaskets have a hole for this oil passage, but Magnum head gaskets do not. This means LA gaskets can be used on Magnum blocks, but Magnum head gaskets can't be used on LA blocks because they would block oil flow to the cylinder head.

Deck height is about the same at 9.585". This helps when swapping cylinder heads and intake manifolds between the two engines.

The bore and stroke of the 5.2L and 5.9L Magnum blocks are the same as the

All LA blocks have this oil passage between cylinders number 1-3 and 6-8. This is the oil passage that supplies oil to the cylinder heads. Magnum blocks don't have this oil passage, but it can be drilled by an experienced machine shop.

318 and 360 LA engines. Crankshafts are also interchangeable, but you will need to use a different rear seal and pilot bearing. You should also check the balance of the rotating assembly if switching the crankshaft.

Magnum and LA blocks have the same main bearing and cam bearing journal sizes and locations. The camshaft centerline to crankshaft centerline of 6.125" is also the same on both production blocks. The tappet diameter is also the same and relatively large at 0.904" as compared to other engines.

Machining for the distributor pocket is the same on both the Magnum and LA blocks. This means you can use the popular electronic ignition conversion kit on the Magnum block or upgrade the LA block with a stock Magnum distributor when converting to electronic fuel injection.

The bell-housing bolt pattern and location is the same as on all LA engine blocks. This allows Magnum blocks to be used with any small-block transmission that would normally be used with an LA block. On 360 engines, be sure to use the proper external balance on the damper and flywheel or torque converter. The external balance is different on the 1971-'92 360 LA as compared to the 1993-'03 5.9L Magnum engine. The major difference in the balance is the weight of the pistons, piston pins, and piston rings (Magnum parts are lighter weight).

Magnum blocks have two different types of motor mounts. The stock LA-style motor mounts with "ears" on each side of the front of the block are also on the Magnum blocks, but these motor mounts are not used on newer production vehicles. Newer production vehicles use motor mounts that bolt onto three tapped holes in each side of the block. This means it is easy to install the Magnum block in older vehicles (pre-1992), but more difficult to use the LA block in newer vehicles. When the LA is used in newer vehicles (1992 and up), custom fabricated motor mounts are needed.

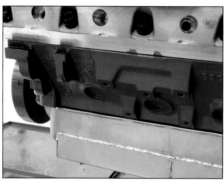

Note that R3 and Magnum blocks have the standard motor mount ears used on all LA engine blocks (front on each side of the block), and a second set of motor mount holes on each side of the block (three bolt holes on each side of the block). The dual motor mounts allow this block to be used in any vehicle that has small-block engine mounts from 1965-'03. R3 and Magnum blocks are the only ones that bolt in on 1993 and up production vehicles.

Differences vs. LA Blocks

The biggest difference in the Magnum block is it has no oil passage from the camshaft up to the cylinder head fire deck. Magnum engines use hollow tappets and pushrods to provide oil to the cylinder heads, so the LA-style oil passage is not there. This oil passage can be drilled in the Magnum block (if needed) by an experienced machine shop.

Magnum blocks have more material in the tappet bore area on the block. The tappet bores are about 0.400" taller to provide more support for the taller hydraulic roller tappets used on production engines. The valley in the block also has extra material for the tapped holes that are used by the tappet yoke retainer.

Magnum blocks are slightly lighter in weight than the LA blocks and should not be bored more than 0.020" oversize. A large number of stroker engines have been built using a 0.030" oversize bore with a 4.000" stroke crankshaft using the 360 Magnum block. This 408-ci engine package is common, but it has a pretty thin bore wall and this may lead to less than ideal piston ring sealing and bore distortion.

The timing cover is different from the LA engine and is set up for use with a reverse-rotation water pump driven by a serpentine belt system. Since the bolt pattern for the timing cover is the same on both Magnum and LA blocks, it is easy to use the LA front cover and the older-style standard rotation water pump with a V-belt pulley drive system. The LA-style front cover also has provisions for the mechanical fuel pump that can be adapted for use with the proper camshaft and fuel pump eccentric.

Magnum blocks have dowel pin holes in different places in the top of the china wall at the front and rear of the engine block. These dowel pinholes are used to hold the intake manifold end seals in place while installing the intake manifold. Be sure to fill any unused dowel pinholes in the block and intake manifold with RTV when installing the intake manifold or they may leak oil. This oil leak is very common, particularly at the back of the intake manifold when using HP intake manifolds with Magnum heads. The Mopar HP intake manifolds have the dowel pinholes for both the Magnum and LA blocks, and some are unused depending on which block is used.

The oil filter area of the block and the adapter that bolts onto the block is a different size on the Magnum blocks. The stock-style 1992-'03 Magnum oil filter must be used with Magnum blocks.

5.9L Magnum blocks are the best Magnum block to use when building a stroker engine. The 4.000" bore size and large main bearing journals make a combination that provides a good base for a high-performance stroker engine. Like LA blocks, this block can handle up to about 430 hp in extreme duty applications. With lighter usage and careful tuning, it can hold up for a little more HP.

Magnum blocks have two tapped holes on the passenger side rear of the block (just behind the cylinder head). These two holes are used to mount the electronic pickup for the production crankshaft trigger. The trigger is activated by gaps in the production flywheel or torque plate. Magnum blocks are suggested for use with a production fuel injection system and ECU, so that the crankshaft trigger can be mounted to the block.

Magnum blocks are probably the best choice when building a stroker engine for use in a late-model truck (i.e., 1993 and up Dakota, Durango, Jeep Grand Cherokee, Ram Pickup, or Ram Van). When used in a stroker engine, it is a bolt-in unit since it has the proper motor mounts, bosses for MPI sensors, and taller bosses for a stock-style hydraulic roller camshaft.

340 Replacement Engine Block

Mopar Performance Parts introduced the 340 replacement engine block in 2001. This new block provides a heavy-duty high-performance engine block at a relatively low price. This is the least expensive aftermarket heavy-duty engine block available for the small-block Mopar.

340 replacement engine blocks are cast from high-nickel cast iron and have the original 340 production casting part number "2780930" followed by a "-340-M." This block comes with the 340 main journal size and four-bolt ductile iron main caps on the center three caps. The block has thicker filled-in pan rails, main webbing, cylinder bore walls, and deck surface. The block comes with an unfinished bore size of about 3.900" and can be used with bore sizes from 3.910" to 4.080".

The design of the 340-replacement block is based on the design of the R3 engine block and is stronger and heavier duty than any previous racing blocks that were made prior to the R3 (i.e., X, T/A, and other special race blocks). This block is heavy duty and can handle 650+ HP.

A 340 replacement block comes with the hardware kit including the freeze plugs, oil plugs, dowels, and camshaft bearings. It is not stress relieved or painted. The bore must be bored and honed to the desired size prior to assembly. The oil filter mounting area is different on 340 replacement blocks and must be used with Mopar oil filter part number 05281090 or an equivalent filter.

When using 340 replacement blocks with a stock-style wet sump oiling system, a few special considerations need to be addressed. The tappet valley is cast solid and the drain holes are quite high – this traps oil in the valley. Several drain holes (4" or 5 1/2" holes) must be drilled in the valley to drain this oil. If these drain holes are not drilled, the valley can hold one to two quarts of oil before it drains back to the oil pan. These oil holes are drilled in the center of the valley so the oil drips on the camshaft for additional lubrication.

Roller tappet cams are not recommended for use with 340 replacement blocks (and 59-degree tappet bore R3 blocks). Most roller tappets have a guide bar that interferes with the wall of the block. The pushrods get into the tie bar toward the center of the block. In most cases, the outer wall does not have enough material to grind for guide-bar

Aftermarket Blocks

Mopar Performance Parts – 340 Replacement Engine Block (with 59-degree tappet bore)

Part Number	Min Bore	Max Bore	Tappet Angle	Main Size	Main Caps	Deck Height	Casting Number	Approx. Weight (lbs)	Motor Mounts
P5007552	3.910"	4.080"	59 deg	2.500"	4-bolt	9.595"	2780930	230	318

Mopar Performance Parts – R3 Engine Blocks (with 59-degree tappet bore)

Part Number	Min Bore	Max Bore	Tappet Angle	Main Size	Main Caps	Deck Height	Casting Number	Approx. Weight (lbs)	Motor Mounts
P4876791AC	3.910"	4.220"	59 deg	2.500"	4-bolt	9.200"	P4532907	230	318 & Magnum
P4876792AC	3.910"	4.080"	59 deg	2.500"	4-bolt	9.200"	P4532908	226	318 & Magnum
P4876793AC	3.910"	4.220"	59 deg	2.500"	4-bolt	9.560"	P4532909	232	318 & Magnum

Mopar Performance Parts – R3 Engine Blocks (with 48-degree tappet bore)

Part Number	Min Bore	Max Bore	Tappet Angle	Main Size	Main Caps	Deck Height	Casting Number	Approx. Weight (lbs)	Motor Mounts
P4876671AC	3.910"	4.220"	48 deg	2.500"	4-bolt	9.200"	P4532907	230	318 & Magnum
P4876672AC	3.910"	4.080"	48 deg	2.500"	4-bolt	9.200"	P4532908	226	318 & Magnum
P4876673AC	3.910"	4.220"	48 deg	2.500"	4-bolt	9.560"	P4532909	232	318 & Magnum
P4876674AC	3.910"	4.080"	48 deg	2.500"	4-bolt	9.560"	P4532910	230	318 & Magnum

Mopar Performance Parts – Aluminum A Engine Blocks (with 48-degree tappet bore)

Part Number	Min Bore	Max Bore	Tappet Angle	Main Size	Main Caps	Deck Height	Casting Number	Approx. Weight (lbs)	Motor Mounts
P5007580	4.100"	4.135"	48 deg	2.500"	4-bolt	9.000"	P4532711	90	Use Motor Plate
P5007581	4.100"	4.135"	48 deg	2.500"	4-bolt	9.100"	P4532711	92	Use Motor Plate
P5007582	4.100"	4.135"	48 deg	2.500"	4-bolt	9.600"	P4532711	100	Use Motor Plate

clearance. Grinding this area gets into the water jacket and creates a water leak that destroys the block. This block has more water around the bores, which pushes the inner and outer walls of the block farther away from the cylinder bores.

One option for roller tappets is to use Jesel tappets with special tappet bushings that have a keyway and don't use a tie bar. This option works great but is much more expensive than traditional tie-bar style tappets. Another option is to use special ISKY tappets that have the tie bar located below the seat for the pushrod. This allows the use of the tie bar on the inside without it getting in the way of the pushrod. These special roller tappets are available from ISKY on a special-order basis. ISKY tappets also require special shorter pushrods since the seat location is moved up higher than what is used on most other tappets.

340 replacement blocks can be used to build stroker engines up to about 418 cubic inches using readily available pistons and crankshafts (4.080" bore w/ 4.000" stroke). This block is the ideal choice for engines from 402 to 418 C.I.D. when output is over 430 hp.

340 replacement blocks have stock 318 LA-style motor mounts, so they can be used in any vehicle that was originally equipped with an LA small-block engine. The left-side 318 LA motor mount on this block is different from that on a stock 340 / 360 block. A mid-1970s 318 left-side motor mount must be used when installing this engine/block in a vehicle that was originally equipped with a 340 or 360 LA engine.

R3 Engine Block

R3 engine blocks are heavy-duty race blocks that were originally designed for use in NASCAR Craftsman Truck, NHRA Pro Stock Truck, and other racing applications. Mopar has made four separate castings and about 10 different machined versions for the R3. These blocks are available in tall and short deck heights and with Siamese bore and full water jacket versions (total of four different castings).

R3 blocks are easily identified by the logo on the passenger-side front of the engine block. Earlier R blocks have a similar logo in the same place w/ R, R1, R1a, or R2.

These blocks are heavy duty and can handle 750+ hp. The blocks are made from high-nickel cast iron and are stress relieved prior to machining. The tall-deck Siamese bore R3 engine blocks weigh about 230 lbs.

R3 blocks have stock 318 LA-style motor mounts and Magnum motor mounts, so they can be used in any vehi-

This block was modified by installing tappet bushings. These bushings can be used to repair a tappet bore, limit oil flow with a smaller oil passage, or for use with keyway and Jesel tappets to eliminate the tie bar normally used with roller tappets.

cle that was originally equipped with an LA or Magnum small-block engine. The left-side 318 LA motor mount on this block is different from that on a stock 340 or 360 block. A mid-1970s 318 left-side motor mount must be used when installing this engine in a vehicle that was originally equipped with a 340 or 360 LA engine.

The tall-deck Siamese bore version, casting number P4532909, is the best block for use in big-inch Mopar small-block engines. No water passes between the bores in Siamese bore blocks, and this allows for larger bore sizes. In Siamese bore R3 blocks, the maximum recommended bore size is 4.220" diameter. With a 4.220" bore size and 4.250" stroke, a small-block Mopar stroker engine can be built with up to 476ci.

476ci is a very large small block, but it may be better to start with a 4.180" bore size to allow for a better bore or piston ring seal and leave room for future rebuilds. The 4.180" bore size is tested to be bulletproof on the R3 block in racing applications. Pistons and piston rings with 4.180" bore sizes have a better selection.

This casting is available in two different machined versions from Mopar.

The first version, part number P4876793AC, is machined for use with a stock-style camshaft that uses the stock 59-degree tappet bores. The tappet angle is the angle measured from a vertical line that passes directly through the center of the block (looking at it from the end of the block) to the angle of the tappet as it extends outward from the centerline of the camshaft. The 59-degree tappet bore block is the least expensive big-inch stroker small block since it can use stock-style HP camshafts, rocker arms, valvetrain, and cylinder heads. The 59-degree tappet angle blocks work well for all applications up to about 7,000 rpm. Extended operation of the engine above 6,500 rpm requires the use of a 48-degree tappet block. Stroker engines are not well suited for high-RPM use, so this is not a big problem. The piston speed in a stroker engine is too high for extended high-RPM use.

The second version, part number P4876673AC, is machined with 48-degree tappet bores. When looking at a

Tappet Angle

All factory production blocks were made with a 59-degree tappet angle. When looking at the end of the block, the tappet angle is the angle at which the tappet bores downward from an imaginary vertical line that goes through the centerline of the block. This angle locates the top of each tappet very close to the outer edge of the valley in the block. This tappet angle forces the pushrods to be laid over at very steep angles to meet up with the rocker arms.

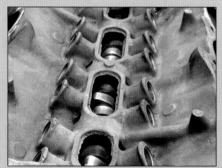

This 318 LA block has the standard 59-degree tappet angle. Note how close the tappets are to the wall of the block as compared to a 48-degree tappet bore block (shown in the next photo).

This steep pushrod angle works fine on production engines, but can be unreliable in high performance and racing applications at high RPM. The steep pushrod angle also requires slightly more camshaft lift to open the valve since some lift is lost due to the angled movement of the pushrod. In general, the valvetrain on a 59-degree block is not reliable for extended operation above 6,500 rpm.

In the 1990s, this problem was resolved on race blocks by changing the tappet angle to 48 degrees from vertical. The tops of the tappets are moved farther away from the outer edge of the valley and this straightens out the angle of the pushrods. The tappet angle cannot be changed on a block once it has been machined, so the only blocks with the 48-degree tappet angle are some versions of the R3 and all-aluminum A blocks. Some of the earlier R

Note the locations of the tappets are farther away from the cylinder bores on the 48-degree tappet bore blocks. The revised tappet angle straightens out the pushrods and improves valvetrain geometry for better reliability at higher RPM. 48-degree tappet bore blocks require special cylinder heads, camshaft, pushrods, and other parts.

blocks were also made with the 48-degree tappet engine, but these blocks are no longer available new.

When the tappet angle is changed, a special camshaft and cylinder heads are required to be changed at the same time. The heads must be changed since the now-straighter pushrods need to go through where the intake-mounting surface is located on the cylinder heads. The only cylinder heads designed to work with the 48-degree blocks are some versions of the W2 (P5007445AB and P5007708AB), W7, W8, and W9 cylinder heads. The valve angle on these cylinder heads is also changed to 15 degrees as part of the change (the stock production valve angle is 18 degrees).

The camshaft is also unique since the lobes must be moved to the new tappet angles. The locations of the lobes have also been moved forward and backward in the block to provide more room for pushrod clearance with larger intake ports.

A stock 59-degree camshaft cannot be used since the camshaft timing would be advanced on one bank of the engine and retarded on the other bank. Also, the lobes would not be in the proper location to match where the tappets have been moved away from the intake ports. The camshaft journals are all the same size on the 48-degree tappet bore blocks, and they are stepped with five different journal sizes on the 59-degree tappet blocks.

The tappet angle should be determined early in the process of planning for the engine since many other component parts must be selected to work together as a package (i.e., camshaft, cam bearings, cylinder heads, tappets, pushrods, rocker arms, etc.). Many engine builders don't realize this until they start to put the engine together and then cannot figure out why the parts don't fit together properly. Mistakes in this area can lead to the purchase of cylinder heads and camshafts that won't fit the engine block or a block that won't work with your existing heads. This is probably the most confusing area for engine builders with the small-block Mopar engine.

The 59-degree tappet angle works fine on many stroker engines since these engines are not really designed for high-RPM operation. On larger-displacement engines, the 48-degree tappet angle allows the use of larger intake ports since the tappets and pushrods are moved away from the intake ports. The larger intake ports allow higher output of the engine and are more reliable with an aggressive camshaft. The cost of the engine is quite a bit higher since an R3 block, special camshaft, and special cylinder heads are a little more expensive for the 48-degree engine.

48-degree tappet bore block, notice the tappets are not as close to the bores of the block. Also, the pushrods are not at as sharp of an angle as when they are installed. The 48-degree tappet bore blocks require special camshafts, camshaft bearings, pushrods, and cylinder heads.

Camshaft bearings in the 48-degree tappet bore blocks are all the same size and are not stepped like stock production cam journals. The tappets are also moved forward or backward in the block to provide more pushrod clearance for larger intake ports. The camshafts are also special since they have different size journals and the lobes are moved and changed to match the new tappet angle. On a stock-style camshaft, the lobes are not in the proper place. It also has valve timing that is advanced on one bank and retarded on the other bank. Special camshafts with un-ground lobes (UGL) are available from Mopar and Competition Cams for use in 48-degree blocks. These UGL camshafts must be taken to a camshaft grinder and ground to your specifications before they can be used.

The cylinder heads must be specially made to fit correctly on the 48-degree blocks. The only cylinder heads designed to work on a 48-degree block are Mopar W7, W8, W9, and special versions of the W2. Stock heads, Edelbrock Heads, Brodix Heads, Indy Heads, Magnum Heads, some W2, W5, and Commando heads cannot be used on a 48-degree block.

48-degree tappet bore blocks are one of the least understood areas with the Mopar small blocks. Care must be taken to use the proper parts so that the block works with all the other components (i.e., camshaft, valvetrain, and cylinder heads). If you want to build a 48-degree tappet bore engine, please carefully study the chapters on valvetrain, pistons, cylinder heads, and engine packages shown at the end of this book before buying the parts for the engine.

Siamese bore engine blocks do not operate as cool as a full water-jacket engine, so special care must be taken in the area of engine cooling. Siamese bore blocks should be cross-drilled between

This block has been cross-drilled to improve cooling on a Siamese bore block. Two small 0.125" holes are drilled from the deck on the block into the water jacket. These two small holes intersect in the middle between the bores and then extend down into the water jacket. These small passages allow some coolant between the bores and improve cooling. See Chapter 13 (Cooling Systems) for more information on cross drilling the block.

A special aluminum plug has been pressed into this R3 block to allow coolant to be fed from the water pump into the side of the block. This cooling method requires water pump modifications, and it significantly improves the cooling of a Siamese bore block.

the cylinder bores. Coolant should be fed into both sides of the engine block instead of the normal water path into the front of the block. See Chapter 13 for more information on cooling systems for stroker engines.

In most cases it may not be a good idea to buy a used R3 block. This is because most of them are short-deck Siamese bore blocks that have been specially machined for use in NASCAR Craftsman Super Truck or NHRA Pro Stock Truck. These used blocks are not

the correct R3 casting (P4532907 instead of P4532909) and have features that make them difficult to use in a stroker engine. Most used blocks are the short deck (9.000"-9.025" deck height) and have the motor mounts machined away to lighten up the block. The short deck height makes it difficult to use a long connecting rod and stroke without the piston pin getting into the piston rings. This is due to reduced compression height on stroker engines. A special motor plate, front cover, and water pump would have to be used to mount the engine when the motor mounts are machined away.

Additionally, most used R3 blocks are machined for use with 50mm roller

Most used R3 blocks are casting number P4532907. This casting is not the best choice for a stroker engine since it has the short deck height, roller camshaft bearings, wide spacing on the main cap bolts, and other modifications that make it difficult and more expensive to use.

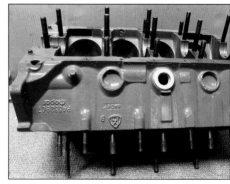

This used block had the motor mount ears machined away to reduce the weight of the block. Since this modification requires the use of a motor plate, it increases the cost of installation. The motor plate needs to be fabricated, and special mounts must be installed in the vehicle.

camshaft bearings. These 50mm roller camshaft bearings require the use of a special camshaft UGL and roller tappets. Once the block has been machined for the roller camshaft bearings, you cannot install Babbitt bearings since the journal is now too large. The camshaft journal in the block without the bearings installed should be 2.1293" to 2.1307" diameter for use with Babbitt camshaft bearings (48-degree block with all 5 journals the same size). Blocks machined for use with 50mm roller camshaft bearings only have the block machined to 2.2817" to 2.2822" diameter (all five journals). 59-degree R3 engine blocks have the stepped camshaft journals sizes (stock Mopar small-block sized journals).

The oil filter boss has been machined away on this used R3 block. This machining saves a slight amount of weight, but it makes the block unusable with a wet sump oiling system since you can't use an oil filter without the oil passages in and out of the filter base.

Most used R3 blocks and all-aluminum blocks (shown above) are machined for use with roller camshaft bearings. These 50-mm roller camshaft bearings must be used with a special un-ground lobe camshaft that has larger 50-mm journals. Once a block is machined for these camshaft bearings, the journals in the block are too large for use with Babbitt camshaft bearings.

Most used R3 race blocks were machined for use with dry sump oil systems only. Therefore, the oil filter base is not machined. They may also not have provisions for the stock-style oil pump to be mounted on the #5 main cap. Used race blocks usually have wider #2, #3, and #4 four-bolt main caps that do not fit inside most 340 oil pans.

Aluminum A Engine Block

Aluminum A engine blocks were originally designed for sprint cars, but they have also been used in Dirt Late Model oval track racing, the 24 Hours of Le Mans, and in blown-alcohol dragsters with up to 1,800 hp.

Aluminum blocks are cast in A356-T6 aluminum material. They weigh about 90 to 100 lbs., including the cast-iron cylinder sleeves and billet steel main bearing caps. Aluminum blocks are about 60 to 70 lbs. lighter than a production cast-iron block and 100-120 lbs. lighter than an R3 engine block. A complete stroker engine using the aluminum block weighs about 340 to 360 lbs. All aluminum A blocks are made with casting number P4532711 on the side of the block.

Aluminum block engines are more expensive due to several factors:
- Higher Cost of the Block – about $4,500
- Dry Sump Oiling System Only – no provisions for a stock-style wet sump oiling system
- Custom Motor Mounts Required – motor plate recommended
- Custom Oil Pan and Valley Tray is Needed
- Modifications are Required for the Cooling System – stock-style water pump will not fit and external cooling lines are needed.
- 48-degree Tappet Bore with 0.841" Diameter Tappets

- W7, W8, or W9 Cylinder Heads Only
- Gear Drive P5249988 is the Only Option – stock timing cover and timing chain will not fit.

Aluminum blocks have a wider oil pan rail that extends down beyond the centerline of the main bearing caps. The center three main bearing caps are cross-bolted through the sides of these "skirts" (extended oil pan rails). The skirted block design is very similar to the Chrysler 426 Hemi® production engine built from 1966 to '71. The oil pan skirt makes this block very strong as compared to most other aluminum blocks that have the oil pan rail at the parting line of the main caps.

Aluminum A blocks have a skirt that extends down beyond the parting line of the main caps. The center three main caps are cross-bolted through the side of the engine block. This design is much stronger than standard small blocks since it has more support at the bottom of the block. A special front cover and oil pan are required with the aluminum block.

In 2001, this block was used as a fully stressed member of the chassis in a prototype sports car that was run in the 24 Hours of Le Mans. The front of the block was bolted to the chassis and the rear suspension and transmission were bolted on the back of the engine. The only structure between the front and rear of the car was the engine itself. The valve covers, cylinder heads, and oil pan on this engine were also specially made to provide additional strength as part of the chassis. The car finished 4th overall in the race.

Cylinder Head Bolt Pattern

Factory-production blocks have only four bolts around each cylinder, so the bolts are pretty far apart. This can lead to head-gasket leaks (with most head gaskets) when the compression ratio is over about 11.5:1. New MLS head gaskets improve the head gasket sealing at higher compression ratios. MLS head gaskets are shown in another photo in this chapter.

All Mopar factory production small-block engines have four head bolts around each cylinder. Most other engines (i.e., GM, Ford, and Big-Block Mopar) have five or six bolts around each cylinder.

The four-bolt setup works fine for compression ratios up to about 11.0:1 (with a high-performance composition-style head gasket). When the compression ratio is higher than 11.0:1, often problems with head gasket sealing arise. The problem is because most head gaskets are flexible and the cylinder head gets a little distorted since quite a bit of space exists between each head bolt. In HP and racing applications with higher compression ratios, it was often required to o-ring the block or heads to obtain a reliable head gasket seal.

In the mid 1990s, the racing cylinder blocks and cylinder heads were modified to add two extra head bolts around each cylinder (for a six-bolt pattern).

The extra head bolts are added to the outer edge and valley side of each cylinder. The standard four bolts are still in the same locations, so a four-bolt head can be bolted onto a six-bolt block. The extra head bolts help to provide a good head gasket seal at compression ratios above 11.0:1. The two extra bolts are a smaller 3/8" size, and quite a bit smaller than the other 1/2" head bolts.

The only Mopar small-block "Wedge" cylinder heads that have provisions for the six-bolt pattern are the W7, W8,

This photo shows a four-bolt head gasket sitting on top of a six-bolt head gasket. Note that the four bolt holes are in the same location, so a four-bolt cylinder head and gasket can be used on a six-bolt block (by omitting the two smaller bolts or studs).

New Multi Layer Steel (MLS) head gaskets have three layers not bonded together. The middle layer is galvanized steel, and the upper and lower layers are spring steel coated with a special material to improve sealing. These gaskets provide a very good head-gasket seal on both six- and four-bolt blocks. Compression ratios of up to 15:1 are possible with these gaskets. MLS head gaskets are available from Cometic Gasket.

W9, and the aluminum 360 heads from Indy Cylinder Heads.

Recent developments in head gasket design have resolved the head gasket sealing problems with the four-bolt blocks and heads. New Multi-Layer-Steel (MLS) head gaskets are three-layer steel shim gaskets that provide good head gasket sealing for compression ratios as high as 15.0:1 (with the four-bolt blocks and heads). A wide variety of Mopar MLS head gaskets are available from Cometic Gasket.

See Chapter 9 for more information on the MLS head gaskets.

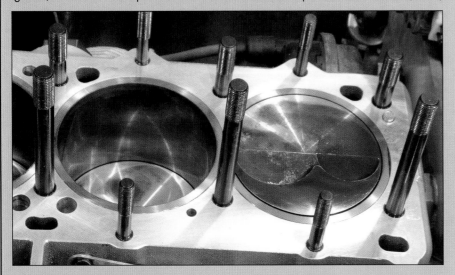

Some race blocks have six bolts around each cylinder to improve the head-gasket seal. The two extra bolts are added on the outer edge and on the valley side of the block. The two extra bolts are smaller 3/8" studs or bolts. The larger 1/2" studs are located in the same place as on four-bolt blocks. This block is a four-cylinder engine, but it has the same bolt pattern as the six-bolt V-8 engines.

The aluminum block must be used with a special gear drive set with a special front cover. Standard Mopar small-block timing sets and covers do not fit this block. Stock-style mechanical fuel pumps cannot be used since they normally fit into the timing cover. To use this block you need an electric fuel pump or a belt drive unit that can be bolted on the motor plate.

Aluminum blocks have a special shape to the front cover and cannot be used with a timing gear and chain set or with a stock-style front cover. The only option is a gear-drive set and special front cover. Note that the motor mounts require a motor plate, and a stock water pump and fuel pump cannot be used with this block. These changes increase the cost of the engine since many special parts are needed to complete an engine using the aluminum block.

Aluminum A engine blocks should only be used when a very light weight is desired and cost is not a factor, since this is by far the most expensive stroker small-block Mopar engine. This block is most often used in racing applications that require a very lightweight stroker engine (drag racing, sprint cars, and dirt late model). Custom-built aluminum A engines cost $25,000 to $40,000.

Block Preparation

340 replacement and R3 blocks are delivered with an approximate bore size of 3.900". They can be bored and honed to 3.910" to 4.080" bore size on the blocks with the full water jacket and up to 4.220" on the R3 Siamese bore blocks. The blocks should be bored and honed using a torque plate. Mopar and BHJ

All factory production LA and Magnum blocks have large holes in the valley. These holes allow the oil to drain back to the oil pan and allow oil to drip on the camshaft. These holes also allow breathing between the top and bottom of the engine. The area around the distributor is also quite open, and this allows more oil to drain back to the oil pan.

offer torque plates that have the four- or six-head bolt patterns.

Design of 340 replacement and R3 engine blocks has the valley area closed off without any holes allowing oil to drain on the camshaft. For dry sump applications, the closed-off valley tray allows for oil to be scavenged out of the valley to reduce windage. With less oil running past the crankshaft on its way back to the oil pan, windage is reduced. On wet sump engines (R3 and 340 replacement blocks), oil passages must be drilled in the valley to allow the oil to drain back to the oil pan. Four or five 0.500" holes should be drilled in the valley to allow the oil to drain back to the oil pan. These holes should be in line with the camshaft so that oil drips onto the camshaft, providing lubrication for the tappets and cam. Camshaft lubrication is extremely important on flat tappet camshafts. 340 replacement blocks have drain holes, but they are not located in a low part of the valley, and this allows about 1.5 to 2 quarts of oil to remain in the valley before it drains back to the oil pan.

Some early R3 engine blocks did not have the #5 main cap fully machined for use with a stock-style wet sump oil pump. The pump does not fit correctly into the #5 main cap on these blocks, since the hole in the cap is not large enough to allow the oil pump housing

The valley on the R3 block is cast solid without any holes in it. This works great for dry-sump engines, but holes must be drilled in the valley on wet-sump engines. Four or five 1/2" drain holes must be drilled in the valley to allow the oil to drain back to the oil pan on wet-sump engines.

into the cap (area around the oil pump drive). Most early blocks were used in dry sump applications, so the problem was not identified until after many blocks had been sold.

If the wet sump oil pump fits on the #5 main cap, no problem. If interference between the body of the pump and the cap where the intermediate shaft fits into the pump exists, then a modification to the #5 cap is needed. Remove the #5 main cap and enlarge the hole for the oil pump drive shaft with a 23/32" drill bit.

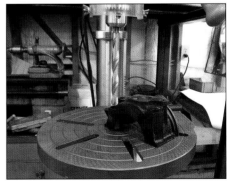

On some early R3 engine blocks, the #5 main cap was not fully machined. If the stock-style oil pump does not fit into the #5 main cap, then a minor modification is needed. Remove the #5 main cap and open up the hole where the pump fits into the main cap. Use a 23/32" drill bit in a drill press to open up the hole approximately 1/2" deep. Thoroughly clean any metal shavings before it is reinstalled.

This hole should be opened up about 0.500" deep on the oil-pump side of the main cap. Enlarge this hole using a drill press to make sure it is as straight as possible. Don't drill with the main cap attached to the block, since this gets metal shavings in the engine block. Be sure to fully de-burr and clean the main cap prior to reassembly.

Be sure to mock up the distributor drive shaft in the R3 block and check for enough clearance for the gear. The intermediate driveshaft fits between the oil pump and distributor. A few early R3 engine blocks do not have enough clearance for the gear, and in some cases it hits the block. Allow at least 0.060" clearance between the gear and the block casting. This problem was fixed on later blocks, but check for clearance when you are test fitting all parts prior to final cleaning of the block and final assembly. If needed, use a die grinder to grind on the block casting to provide clearance for the gear.

After final cleaning of the block, install two special oil plugs that are often overlooked. Two oil galley plugs are on the back of the block. The two that go on the rear face of the block are pretty simple, but sometimes it is easy to overlook the plug that goes in the back of the oil galley just in front of the distributor. This plug must be installed before the rear plug that goes on the rear face of the block and also before the distributor is installed.

R3 and aluminum blocks have an oil-feed passage on the top of the front china wall on the passenger side of the block. With most wet-sump oiling systems, this passage is not used and must be plugged with a thin pipe plug so that it does not interfere with the intake manifold (see upper right-hand corner of this photo).

Another frequently unnoticed oil galley plug is the one that leads from the oil pump up to the filter. This plug goes in from the bottom prior to installation of the #5 main cap (see photo). If this plug is omitted, then oil cannot pass through the oil filter and the engine will have very little oil pressure. Be sure to fully seat this plug so that it does not block the flow of oil to the oil filter. This plug should be replaced whenever an engine block is cleaned. The plug should

Be sure to install the oil galley plug that goes in front of the distributor pocket. It must be installed prior to installation of the distributor, and before the plug is installed in the back of the engine block. This plug uses a special square drive tool that can be made by grinding on a bolt to make a 5/16" square end on it.

Don't forget to install the cup plug that goes in the oil passage that leads from the oil pump up toward the oil filter. Without this plug the engine has very little or no oil pressure, and oil does not go through the filter. This plug must be replaced anytime the block is hot-tanked or cleaned.

also be replaced when a block is heated for a stress-relieving process or cleaning.

On R3 blocks with wet-sump oil systems, install a pipe plug in the front oiling passage on the block. This front oiling passage is located on the top passenger side of the front china wall of the block. This oil passage is normally only used with an external dry-sump oil pump to feed oil into the block. Be sure to use a thin pipe plug with an allen-head wrench so that the plug does not stick up beyond the top of the block. If a tall plug is used (i.e., hex or square head), then the plug may interfere with the intake manifold. This is generally a problem on most intake manifolds that have a cast-in valley tray and water neck in the front of the manifold.

On Siamese bore R3 blocks, water should be fed into the block with external lines from the water pump to each side of the block. See the cooling systems section (Chapter 13) for more information on this modification. Special machining is needed so that the fittings can be attached to the sides of the block.

If an external dry sump oil system is used, special machining is needed to add an oil scavenge fitting on the block. This requires machining of a tapped hole on the top of the rear china wall of the block (located midway between the distributor pocket and the oil pressure fitting passage).

The tappet bores intersect with the main oil galleys on all production blocks and 59-degree tappet bore R3 blocks. This allows oil for the tappets, and it can be used to lubricate the top of the engine via oil passages in the tappets and hollow pushrods. Before the R3 blocks were available, many engine builders would block off the oil passages to the tappets when a mechanical roller tappet was used. This modification is called "tubing the block." See Chapter 5 for more details on this modification.

The oiling passage between the main oil galley and the tappet bores was not machined on early 48-degree tappet R3 blocks. This eliminated the need to tube the block in order to block off oil to the tappets. About the same time this change was made, many high-quality racing rocker arms began using the tappet oil to lubricate the top of the engine

Tappet Oiling

All factory production blocks have an intersection between the tappet bores and the main oil galleys on each side of the engine block. This intersection provides oil to operate the hydraulic tappets on the 1965-'92 LA engine, and also provides oil to the top of the engine on the later 1992-'03 Magnum engines (through the tappets and hollow pushrods).

Most of the early 48-degree tappet bore R and R3 blocks did not have an intersection between the tappets and the oil galley. The 48-degree tappet angle no longer intersected with the main oil galley, so no oil passage provided oil to the tappets. This was done to dry up the tappet bores on racing engines that did not use hydraulic tappets. This change eliminated the need to "tube" the block to eliminate or limit oil flow to the tappets. See the oiling section of this book for more information on tubing the block.

About the same time the 48-degree R and R3 blocks were launched, most of the racing rocker arm systems began using tappet oil to lubricate the top of the engine. The tappet oil is fed

through passages in the tappets and hollow pushrods up to the rocker arms and valvesprings. Most Jesel and T&D racing rocker arms use the tappet oil to lubricate the top of the engine.

All AC-level 48-degree tappet bore R3 blocks have a 0.125" drilled oil passage from the main oil galley to the tappets (i.e., part numbers P4876671AC, P4876672AC, P4876673AC, and P4876674AC). This eliminates the problem of dry tappets when oil is needed in most cases to lubricate the top of the engine.

If you have an older 48-degree block (not AC-level block), and you want to run hydraulic tappets and/or oil the top of the engine though the tappets and pushrods, then these oil passages must be drilled in the block. These oil passages can be drilled with a hand-held drill motor using Mopar drill fixture tool P5007728. This tool includes the drill fixture tool and a 3/16" drill bit to add these oil passages. In most cases a 0.100" passage between the oil galley and each tappet bore is enough to lubricate the top of the engine, but it is easy to break off the drill bit while drilling these passages with a smaller drill bit.

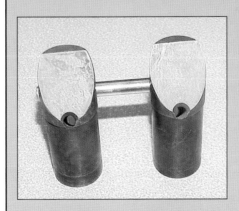

Early 48-degree tappet bore R3 blocks did not have an oil passage from the main oil galley to each tappet. In most cases this oil passage is needed, and it can be drilled with a special tool from Mopar P5007728. This tool is dropped into each pair of tappet holes, and the needed oil-passage holes are added by a hand-held drill motor and drill bit.

with oil passages in the tappets and hollow pushrods. Most racing rocker arms from Jesel and T&D Machine Products use this method for providing oil to the top of the engine.

Look for a small oil passage that leads from the main oil galleys to each tappet bore on 48-degree tappet bore blocks P4876671AC, P4876672AC, P4876673AC, and P4876674AC. All

Installing Distributer Drive Shaft Bushing

The Mopar small-block engine has an intermediate shaft that goes between the distributor and the oil pump. A gear that runs off the camshaft drives this intermediate shaft. It rotates on a special bushing that goes into the block.

This bushing must be installed using the Distributor Bushing Driver/Burnisher tool (C-3053). This special tool is available from Miller Special Tools.

The distributor drive shaft bushing is made slightly undersized and is burnished to the proper diameter with the special tool when it is installed. The bushing is placed on the tool and then driven into the block with a hammer. The tool is then used with a wrench to expand the bushing into the block and burnish it to the proper size at the same time.

If this tool is not used to install the bushing, it won't fit tightly in the block. Also, the hole inside the bushing will be too small for the distributor drive shaft.

Do not try reaming this bushing instead of using the tool. If you do not use the tool, the brushing will not fit tightly into the block.

Always test fit the distributor and drive shaft into the block prior to engine assembly to ensure this bushing has been installed correctly. This ensures easy distributor installation later when the engine is fully or partially assembled.

This special tool is used to install the distributor bushing in the engine block. If the special tool is not used, the bushing will not be burnished to the proper size and will not fit tightly in the block. This tool is available from Miller Special Tools – part number C-3053.

The bushing is hammered into the distributor pocket in the block using this special tool. After the bushing is pushed into the block, the nut and hub are tightened up to be level with the top of the block.

A wrench is used to remove the tool and burnish the inside diameter of the bushing to the proper size required for the intermediate shaft. If this tool is not used, the bushing will be too small to allow installation of the intermediate shaft. Always test fit the distributor and intermediate shaft when mocking up the engine to make sure it fits properly.

When a dry sump oiling system is used, an oil scavenge is normally added to the valley on an R3 or aluminum block. Oil is pulled out of the valley to reduce windage, since the oil cannot drip onto the camshaft and crankshaft. This scavenge is normally added to the rear china wall on the block (see the AN fitting).

Remove all freeze plugs and inspect inside the water jacket on any block being used in a HP engine. Often, casting sand is left inside the block, and this causes problems with the cooling system. This block was made in 1975, so sand has been inside this block for almost 30 years. The sand can be washed out using a garden hose and by chipping it out while washing inside the water jacket.

other 48-degree R and R3 blocks don't have this oil passage drilled (i.e., AB, and blocks without the AC at the end of the part number). This oil passage allows oil to flow from the oil galley to the tappet and then to the top of the engine through hollow pushrods (if this is the oiling method used in the engine).

Remove the freeze plugs on all blocks and thoroughly clean out the water jacket to ensure no sand is in the water jacket. Sometimes sand is left in the water jacket from the casting process when the block is made. I have seen a substantial amount of sand still left inside the water jacket on many used blocks. Any obstruction in the water jacket makes the cooling system less effective and can lead to other cooling problems. See Chapter 13 for more details. In some cases it may be necessary to install extra plugs and drill extra water passages through the deck of the block when preparing the engine block. These modifications depend on the type of block and how the water is plumbed into the block, out of the heads, and through the intake manifold. It is very important to make these modifications on Siamese bore blocks since they can run hotter without any water passing between the bores on adjacent cylinders.

Most blocks require a small notch at the bottom of the bore for clearance when using a 4.000" stroke crankshaft and stock connecting rods. The top part of the rod bolts is the part of the rod that gets into the block. Many aftermarket connecting rods have less material in this area, and this may eliminate the need for a notch at the bottom of the bore. See Chapter 6 (Connecting Rods) for more information.

Block Selection

If you want to use a production-style hydraulic roller camshaft, then a 1988 or later production block must be used (i.e., 1988-'92 360 block, or 1993-'03 5.9L Magnum block). Beginning in 1988, production blocks have provisions for the hydraulic roller tappets, dog bones, and the retainer that keeps the dog bones in place. The 1988-'92 LA and 1993-'03 Magnum blocks have the provisions for the dog-bone production-style tappets. The largest displacement that can be made from these blocks with a 4.000" stroke and 4.030"-bore size is 408ci. Used 360 blocks are readily available and probably the least expensive block when building a Mopar stroker engine. Keep in mind you may end up spending $300 to $500 refurbishing a used block since it needs to be cleaned, bored, honed, and maybe align bored.

If the vehicle is a late-model truck that was originally equipped with a Magnum V-8 (i.e., 1992 and up 5.2L or 1993 and up 5.9L), it is easiest to use a 360 Magnum block since the stock motor mounts are already there (production LA blocks do not have the Magnum motor mounts). R3 blocks also have Magnum motor mounts, so they can also be used in vehicles that have the stock Magnum motor mounts.

340 production and 340 replacement blocks allow a larger displacement of up to about 418ci with the larger 4.080" bore size and 4.000" stroke. Thoroughly and carefully check any used 340 block since it may be cracked, damaged, worn out, or already overbored to the maximum size. 340 replacement blocks are the least expensive aftermarket block with a cost of about $1,800 to $2,000.

Tall-deck Siamese bore R3 blocks (casting number P4532909) are the best option for engines above 418ci with the 4.000" stroke crankshaft. Any output above 430-500 hp should also use the R3 block since it is much stronger than any production block. 340 replacement blocks are another option for output above 430-500 hp, but they do not allow for bore sizes as large as Siamese bore blocks. The R3 blocks range from about $2,000 to $2,600, but they offer the most strength for very high-output and large-displacement stroker engines.

CRANKSHAFTS

Increasing the stroke is by definition the way an engine is made larger on a stroker engine. Fortunately, small-block Mopars have plenty of room inside the crankcase and a high camshaft location. This allows room for a longer stroke on the crank.

Crankshaft Basics

Three types of crankshafts are available for most engines. The difference is in how each crankshaft is made. This determines the cost and strength of the crank.

Today, most production engines use a cast crankshaft since it is less expensive to produce and strong enough for normal use. All production small-block Mopar crankshafts made since mid 1972 have been cast cranks.

LA and Magnum production crankshafts are very similar and can be interchanged as long as the proper rear main oil seal and pilot bearing are used. Most new stroker crankshafts offered by Mopar are made to the Magnum specifications. Be sure to use part numbers recommended in this chapter for the oil seal and pilot bearing with each of these crankshafts.

Early 273, 318, and 340 engines used a production-forged crankshaft. These cranks are preferred for racing, but they don't offer a long enough stroke (only 3.310") so they won't work in a stroker engine.

This is the most commonly used stroker crankshaft in Mopar small-block engines. This cast crankshaft is reasonably priced at about $300 to $400.

360 crankshafts have a larger main journal size than the 273/318/340. The larger main journal size (2.810" diameter) makes the 360 crankshaft slightly stronger than a 273/318/340 sized (2.500" diameter) crank. The 360 main journal is 0.310" larger in diameter than the 273/318/340 journal. This extra size makes the crank stronger since the distance between the rod journal and the main journal is less (about 0.150" closer). Unfortunately, most racers want the 2.500" journal size since the crankshaft is lighter and reduces bearing surface area and friction. Because of this, most of the R3 blocks are made for racing with the

All 360 LA and 5.9L Magnum crankshafts have a relatively large main journal size of 2.810". This is about 0.310" larger in diameter than the 2.500" journal on the 273/318/340 engines. The larger journal size makes the crankshaft stronger.

LA vs. Magnum Crankshafts

LA and Magnum crankshafts are almost the same and are interchangeable. The major difference is the machining for the pilot bushing.

LA 318/340 crankshafts have a rear main seal area that is .010" larger in diameter than the 5.2 Magnum cranks and must use a different seal. The seal groove in the block is the same, so the only difference is the part number for the seal. 1968-'98 318s and 340 should use oil seal part number 04397712, and 5.2 L Magnum engines should use seal 04778228. LA 360 and 5.9L Magnum don't have this difference and use the same rear seal 04798216AC.

All Mopar 3.580" and 4.000" stroker crankshafts with the small 318/340 main size are made for use with the Magnum seal 04778228. The only exception is Mopar crankshaft P5007253AB, which uses seal 04397712.

The pilot bushing is also a different size on the LA and Magnum crankshafts

5.2L Magnum and most Mopar Performance stroker crankshafts with the 318/340 mains have a slightly smaller diameter on the rear main seal area of the crank. These crankshafts must be used with seal # 04778228. The seal groove in the block and main cap are the same from LA and Magnum engines.

(see below for the proper part numbers). All Mopar 3.580" and 4.000" stroker crankshafts are made for use with the Magnum pilot bushing #P4876056.

The 360 LA and 5.9L Magnum crank specifications are shown below:

Model Year & Engine	1971-'92 360 Engine	1992-'03 Magnum 5.9L
Crankshaft Material	Cast	Cast
Stroke	3.580"	3.580"
Main Journal Size – std.	2.8095"-2.8105"	2.8095"-2.8105"
Rod Journal Size – std.	2.124"-2.125"	2.124"-2.125"
Rear Flange	Mopar 6-bolt	Mopar 6-bolt
Rear Oil Seal Surface-Diameter	2.962"-2.966"	2.962"-2.966"
Recommended Oil Seal	04798216AC	04798216AC
Externally Balanced	Yes	Yes, w/different balance
External Balance – Flywheel	19.79 in.-oz.	14.00 in.-oz.
Flywheel w/ External Balance	P4529110	P5249842
or		
Torque Converter Balance Weight Kit	P4120241	P5249843
Damper w/ External Balance	P5007301	P5007187
Pilot Bushing	4338876	P4876056

smaller 2.500" journal size. The 2.500" journal size is strong enough and not a problem for most stroker engines.

Types of Cranks

Cast Cranks

Most production engines are made with cast cranks. The base crank casting is made by pouring molten metal into a sand mold. Cast crankshafts have a few advantages and disadvantages as compared to forged cranks.

The cast crankshaft is less expensive and lighter than the same crankshaft made with a forging. The typical cost of a Mopar stroker cast crankshaft is $300 to $400. A cast crankshaft is about three to five lbs. lighter than the same crankshaft made in a forging. Cast iron or cast steel weighs less than forged steel since it is less dense. This lighter weight makes the rotating assembly lighter. The engine accelerates faster with less weight on the crankshaft. This lighter weight also makes the cast stroker crank more expensive to balance since the counter weights don't weigh as much and may be too light. When balancing the engine, it is always more expensive to add weight to the crank than to remove weight.

Cast cranks are not as strong as forged units and don't hold up as well in high-RPM applications. Cast cranks are suitable for engines that make up to about 450-500 hp and don't rev over 6,000 rpm. Since most stroker engines are not well suited for high-RPM applications, cast cranks can be used in many street and hot rod applications. Proper basic tuning to

Note the thin seam line on the edge of the rod throw at the parting line where the sand mould was put together. Cast crankshafts have a thin seam in this area, while forged cranks have a thicker seam.

minimize detonation also helps durability as you get close to these limitations.

Most cast cranks have a surface hardness depth of only about 0.015" to 0.030" deep. Since this surface hardness is not very deep, most cast cranks need to be hardened when the journals are machined undersize. Check with the manufacturer for recommendations when reworking their crankshaft.

Cast stroker crankshafts are available from Mopar and Eagle.

Forged Cranks

The next choice in strength is a forged crankshaft. A forging press forces high-quality steel bars into the shape of the crankshaft. The forging process allows the grain of the steel to be bent and forged into the shape of the part. Since the grains bend around corners when the part is formed, the grain is not cut, and this makes the crankshaft very strong. The forging process requires trimming to get to the net shape of the crankshaft, and this often leaves a thicker seam at the parting line. The thick seam is where the excess material is removed from the base forging with a trim die.

Most high-performance forged crankshafts are made from 4340 steel. This material is stronger than other materials often used in forged cranks (i.e., lower-cost 1053 steel).

Forged crankshafts should be used whenever possible in high-performance applications. Forged crankshafts must be used in applications over 500 hp and when RPM is over 6,000. A forged crankshaft should be used in racing applications where long-term durability and reliability is key.

Forged crankshafts are normally made in large quantities since it is expensive to make and set up the forging dies. Each forging is the same, so a large number of cranks must be made to spread out the high cost of the forging tools.

Forged stroker crankshafts are available from Mopar and Callies.

Billet Cranks

Billet crankshafts are most often used in custom applications in low volumes where the forging is not available. In situations with no suitable forging, it is less expensive to machine a billet into a crankshaft. Billet crankshafts are expensive to make since the entire crankshaft is fully machined starting

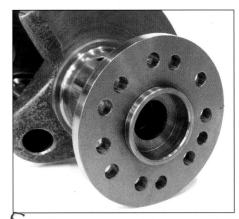

Most Mopar cast and forged stroker crankshafts have a full-round flange on the back of the crankshaft. This flange has six holes tapped with the Mopar six-bolt flywheel pattern. The extra six holes can be tapped and used with a generic GM bolt pattern. In some racing applications, it may be desirable to use the GM bolt pattern with an aftermarket racing clutch and transmission (i.e., T-10, Muncie, and Tex Racing). Special racing bell-housings and clutch systems are available from Mr. Gasket/Lakewood, QuarterMaster, or Tex Racing that allow the use of these racing transmissions on the Mopar small block.

from a round bar of high strength steel.

Billet stroker crankshafts are available from Mopar, Bryant, Callies, SCAT, Crower, LA Enterprises, and many other sources.

High-dollar racing engines usually use billet crankshafts since the engine builder wants a custom crank with special features (i.e., lightweight, special sizes for journals, knife edging, or a special stroke length).

Stroke

Increased stroke is the real reason why we need a special crankshaft in a stroker engine. The longer the stroke, the more cubic inches you can build in a small-block Mopar. Small-block Mopars have plenty of room in the crankcase, but the stroke length has limits. The largest stroke I have seen in a small-block Mopar is 4.250", but technically it can be larger. Joe Gaerte from Gaerte Engines, Rochester, Ind., tells me that he thinks he can get a 4.500" stroke into an

These parts are the most commonly used components for building a Mopar stroker engine. This photo features the Mopar cast 4.000" stroke crankshaft, Eagle SIR connecting rods, and KB hypereutectic pistons.

Stroker Crankshafts

Source

Part Number	Material	Stroke	Main Journal Size	Rod Journal Size	Crank Flange	Approx. Weight	Approx. Cost	Comments
Mopar Performance Parts								
P5007257	Cast Steel	3.580"	318/340	2.125"	6-bolt	53 lbs.	$379	Tap holes in flange for GM bolt pattern
P5007253	Forged 4340	3.580"	318/340	2.125"	6-bolt	57 lbs.	$700	Tap holes in flange for GM bolt pattern
P5007253AB	Forged 4340	3.580"	318/340	2.100"	Dual 6-bolt	50 lbs.	$1,200	Lt. Weight - Use Generic Rods
P5007903	Billet 4330	3.800"	318/340	2.000"	GM 6-bolt	47 lbs.	$3,200	Lt. Weight 410 Sprint Car Race Crank
P5007256	Cast Steel	4.000"	318/340	2.125"	6-bolt	57 lbs.	$400	Tap holes in flange for GM bolt pattern
P5007258	Cast Steel	4.000"	360	2.125"	6-bolt	58 lbs.	$400	Tap holes in flange for GM bolt pattern
P5007252	Forged 4340	4.000"	318/340	2.125"	6-bolt	59 lbs.	$700	Tap holes in flange for GM bolt pattern
P5007254	Forged 4340	4.000"	360	2.125"	6-bolt	60 lbs.	$700	Tap holes in flange for GM bolt pattern
Callies Performance Products								
Dragonslayer	Forged 4340	3.580"	318/340	2.100"	8-bolt	Call	$900	Use Generic 6.000" Rod
Dragonslayer	Forged 4340	3.790"	318/340	2.100"	8-bolt	Call	$900	Use Generic 6.000" Rod
Dragonslayer	Forged 4340	4.000"	318/340	2.100"	8-bolt	Call	$900	Use Generic 6.000" Rod
Magnum Plus	Forged 4340	Custom	318/340	1.888"-2.100"	8 or 6-bolt	Call	$1,931	Lt. Weight – Use Generic Rods
Magnum Plus	Forged 4340	4.250"	318/340	1.888"-2.100"	8 or 6-bolt	Call	$1,931	Lt. Weight – Use Generic Rods
Eagle Specialty Products								
103604000	Cast	4.000"	360	2.125"	6-bolt	Call	$305	
434040006123	Forged 4340	4.000"	318/340	2.125"	6-bolt	Call	Call	
436040006123	Forged 4340	4.000"	360	2.125"	6-bolt	Call	Call	
Ohio Crankshaft								
N3404000	Cast	4.000"	340	2.125"	6-bolt	Call	$295	
N3504000	Cast	4.000"	360	2.125"	6-bolt	Call	$295	
43404000	Forged 4340	4.000"	340	2.125"	6-bolt	Call	$595	
43604000	Forged 4340	4.000"	360	2.125"	6-bolt	Call	$595	

Custom billet crankshafts are also available from SCAT, Oliver, Bryant, Crower, and LA Enterprises (and many other sources).

aluminum-block Mopar racing engine, but he has not tried this yet.

Limitations on stroke length occur when the rods get too close to the edge of the bore, sides of the block, or into the camshaft area on the block. The longer the stroke, the more grinding or machining is needed to obtain clearance. The counter weights on the crankshaft also get close to the skirt on the piston. Long 6.123" connecting rods and a tall deck height help since the piston doesn't get as close to the bottom of the bores.

If you don't want to do lots of extra grinding or machining on the block for extra clearance, you should stick with the common 4.000" stroke crankshaft. With the proper connecting rods, a 4.000" stroker engine can be built without any extra grinding or machining.

Bearings

Most high-performance crankshafts are made with a large radius or smooth transition at the edge of the journal. This extra material makes the crankshaft much stronger than it would be with a sharp edge at the side of each journal.

Some bearings don't have enough clearance at the edge of the bearing and may interfere with this radius. The bearing fails when it does not fit correctly in this area. Most high-performance bearings have the edges machined for clearance to this radius. Carefully inspect each bearing while doing the engine mockup to make sure it fits correctly in this key area. Most V-8 rod bearings have the extra clearance on only one side since there are two connecting rods on each rod journal (only one side of the rod is at the edge of the crank journal).

Most main bearing sets have an oil groove in the upper main bearing shell or three quarters of the way around the bearing. One way to improve oil flow to the connecting rods is to use bearings that have a groove all the way around the main bearings (full groove bearings). This allows a constant uninterrupted flow of oil to the connecting rods. The easiest

Most high-performance and stroker crankshafts have a large radius at the edge of the journals. This makes the crankshaft much stronger than it would be with a sharp edge. Sharp edges and corners don't provide as much support and are prone to stress cracks in high-performance engines.

way to do this is to purchase two sets of main bearings and use the upper grooved bearings in both the block and main caps. This is more expensive, but it allows better oil flow and provides adequate oil flow to the rods.

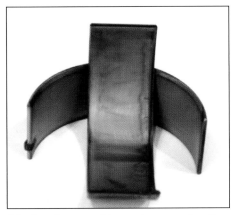

The bearings must have clearance to allow for the large radius at the edge of the journals. The rod bearing shell in the front has the clearance on the right side, and the shell in the back has it on the top edge.

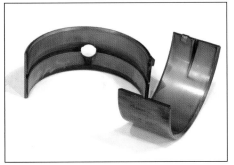

This Federal Mogul main bearing has a 3/4 groove around the bearing. The top shell has the full groove (shell with the hole in it), and the bottom has a partial groove at the ends. Mopar engines should use full groove bearings with the groove all the way around the main journals. Most bearing sets are not available with a full groove, so two sets of bearings can be combined to allow a full groove around the main journal. Use two top bearing shells on each of the main journals on the crankshaft. The full groove around the journal provides a constant supply of oil to the connecting rods through the oil passages in the crankshaft.

Internal and External Balance

The best way to balance an engine is to have a machine shop modify the crankshaft. The shop adds or reduces weight on the crank to balance the assembly. This is called internal balancing since the balance is all inside the engine on the rotating assembly. When the stroke is increased, the shop needs to add weight on the crank counterweights. To add weight, a portion of the crankshaft is drilled out and replaced with a heavy Mallory metal (by welding it into the counterweight). Mallory metal is very expensive and increases the cost of balancing.

In production engines, the high cost of using Mallory metal is avoided by adding some imbalance to the damper and flywheel or torque converter. This saves money in production, but causes confusion since many of the component parts are not interchangeable due to the imbalance.

From a performance standpoint, internal balancing is better than external balancing. The external imbalance at the ends of the crankshaft has a tendency to twist the crankshaft more. This problem is worse in high-RPM applications. Most racing engines use internal balance since it simplifies things when changing and trying different dampers, clutches, flywheels, and torque converters (they can all be neutral balance).

All 273 and 318 LA and Magnum 5.2L engines are internally balanced and do not have any imbalance weight added to the damper and flywheel or torque converter (neutrally balanced). All 340 LA engines with a forged crankshaft (1968-mid '72) are internally balanced. Midway through the 1972 model year, 340 engines began using a lighter-cast crankshaft. This required a production imbalance on the damper and flywheel or torque converter (externally balanced).

All 360 LA engines and Magnum 5.9L engines are externally balanced. They use a damper and flywheel or

360 LA and 5.9L Magnum engines use a damper built with an imbalance or external balance. The hollow top area on this damper is lighter and this makes the damper out of balance, but it makes the engine assembly balanced. The 360 LA and 5.9L Magnum dampers are not interchangeable since the amount of imbalance is different (the Magnum engines have lighter pistons, piston pins, rings, and connecting rods).

torque converter that has an imbalance (externally balanced). The external balance is not the same for the 360 LA and Magnum 5.9L engines. The dampers, flywheels, and torque converters are not interchangeable since the imbalance weight is different. The main difference in these engines is the weight of the pistons, piston pins, rings, and connecting rods, and this is the reason why the balance is not the same. Magnum 5.9L engines have lighter components, so the engine has less external balance.

If you want to reuse existing component parts like the damper and flywheel or torque converter, be sure you know what you have before you balance the engine. If you have parts from an

Production Engine Balance

Model Year	Engine	Crankshaft	Balance	Damper	Flywheel	Torque Conv. Weight Kit
1964-'69	LA 273	Forged	Internal	P4452816	P4529142	None
1967-'91	LA 318	Forged & Cast	Internal	P4452816	P4529142	None
1968-'72	LA 340	Forged	Internal	P4452816	P4529142	None
1972-'73	LA 340	Cast	External	Stock only	Stock only	N/A
1971-'92	LA 360	Cast	External	P5007301	P4529110	P4120241
1992-'98	Mag. 5.2L	Cast	Internal	P4452816	P4529142	None
1993-'97	Mag. 5.9L	Cast	External	P5007187	P5249842	P5249843
1998-'03	Mag. 5.9L	Cast	External	Stock w/ pulley	P5249842	P5249843

Note: These flywheels don't have provisions for a crank trigger (use stock Magnum flywheel or flex plate for use with Magnum MPI crank trigger).

Bearing Selection

Most high-performance and stroker crankshafts have large radii on the edge of the journals. This radius provides extra strength and requires the use of special bearings that have extra clearance for the edge of the journal. If the wrong bearings are used, the bearing rides on the edge and causes excessive heat and wear. This "fillet ride" can damage the crankshaft and cause premature failure of the bearings.

The recommended vertical bearing clearance on small-block Mopar engines is 0.0015" to 0.0025", with a maximum clearance of 0.0030". These numbers work well in high-performance and racing applications. Bearing clearances over 0.0030" lead to excessive leakage at the edges of the bearings as well as reduced oil pressure.

This rod bearing doesn't have enough clearance to work with this stroker crankshaft. The bearing does not clear the edge of the journal and does not fit correctly.

This rod bearing has more clearance at the edge where it is closest to the edge of the journal. Each rod bearing has the clearance on only one side since there are two rods on each journal of the crankshaft.

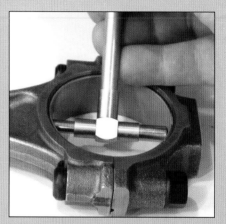

The bearing should be measured 90 degrees from the parting line in the main caps and rods (w/ bolts torqued to the proper specifications). Bearings are made with some taper and measurement at a different angle and may not provide accurate clearance calculations. Mopar small-block engines should have 0.0015" to 0.0025" oil clearance on the rods and mains (with a maximum oil clearance of 0.003").

Recommended Bearings:

Application	Manufacturer	Part Number	Journal Size
Rod Bearings	Clevite 77	CB-481H	2.125" (stock)
	Federal Mogul	7125CH	2.125" (stock)
Main Bearings	Clevite 77	MS-1344Z	2.500" (318/340 mains)
	Federal Mogul	120M	2.810" (360 mains)
	Mopar	P5249058 - Std	2.500" (318/340 mains)
	or	P5249056 - 0.001" oversize	2.500" (318/340 mains)
	or	P5249057 - 0.001" undersize	2.500" (318/340 mains)

internally balanced engine, you should internally balance the rotating assembly for your engine. The internal balance will cost more since it requires more Mallory metal than an external balance.

If you have externally balanced components that you want to reuse, you must balance the rotating assembly to work with these component parts. Be sure to work with an experienced machine shop since they need to take the external balance into account when balancing your engine. You need to bring these components to the machine shop when you are having the engine balanced.

The torque converter can be a problem (on 360 LA engines and 5.9L Magnum engines) since the external balance weights are welded to the converter. The torque converter is too large and cannot be attached to the crankshaft when balancing the engine. The easiest way to get around this issue is to use a B&M flexplate when balancing the engine. B&M flexplates have the external imbalance on the flexplate instead of on the converter. This special flexplate can be mounted on the crankshaft when it is being balanced. The same flexplate must be used on the engine, so grind the old weights off the torque converter. Be sure to use the proper external balance flexplate for your application:

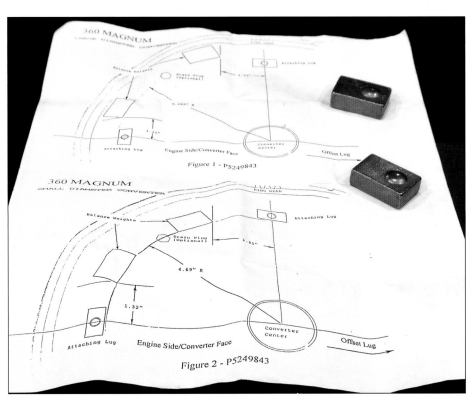

Weight can be added to a neutral balance torque converter to allow it to work on an externally balanced engine. Weights are welded onto the torque converter using a drawing provided with the kit to show where they should be installed for proper balance. Weight kit P4120241 is used on 360 LA converters, and P5249843 on 5.9L Magnum converters.

B&M Part Number	Transmission	Engine
10235	A-727	1972-'76 340 LA w/ cast crank
10234	A-904	1972-'76 340 LA w/ cast crank
10236	A-727	1971-'92 360 LA
10239	A-904	1971-'92 360 LA
10241	A-904	1993-'03 5.9L Magnum
10242	A-727	1993-'03 5.9L Magnum

If you have a neutrally balanced torque converter (no weights welded on it), it can be used on an externally balanced engine. The easiest way to use it is with the proper B&M flexplates mentioned above. The second option is to weld the external balance weights on the converter. These special balance weights are available from Mopar under part number P4120241 for 360 LA engines and P5249843 for 5.9L

This special B&M flexplate can be used on externally balanced engines. This one is for use with a 1971-'92 360 LA engine with an A-727.

Magnum engines. The balance weights come with a special template that shows where to weld them.

An experienced machine shop can modify a neutral balance flywheel for external balance by drilling holes in the backside of it (see the Mopar Crate Engine Installation Book P5007521

for instructions on this modification).

Selecting the proper crankshaft for a stroker engine is more complex than just getting one with the proper main bearing size and stroke. With research and planning, you can select the crank that meets your needs and budget as well as complements the rest of the engine package.

Bob Weight

Most manufacturers have a specified bob weight for each crankshaft. Care must be taken to select the crankshaft that is close to the desired bob weight or it could be expensive and difficult to balance the engine. If the counterweights of the crankshaft do not have enough weight, then expensive Mallory metal must be added to the crankshaft.

Mallory metal is installed in a hole drilled across the crankshaft counterweight. The Mallory metal is heavier than the material in the crankshaft, and this adds weight to balance the engine. This process can be expensive since the process of machining the hole takes labor, and the Mallory metal is expensive.

The major difference in the balance on the 360 LA and 5.9L Magnum engine is the weight of the pistons. A Magnum piston (with pin and rings) is 151.2 grams lighter than the LA piston. The Magnum connecting rod is also slightly lighter than the LA rod. See below for the detailed weight of the stock production parts.

Weight	1971-'92 360 LA Engine	1993-'03 Magnum 5.9L
Piston	584 grams	470 grams
Piston Pin	154.6 grams	134 gram
Connecting Rod - Small End	239 grams	225 grams
Connecting Rod - Big End	519 grams	519 grams
Ring Set	56.6 grams	40 grams
Rod Bearing	47.6 grams	47.6 grams
Reciprocating Weight	1,034.2 grams	869 grams
Rotating Weight	566.6 grams	566.6 grams
Weight Per Cylinder	1,600.8 grams	1,435.6 grams
Total Bob Weight	2,167.4 grams	2,002.2 grams

The total weight for each cylinder is 165.2 grams lighter in the Magnum engine. When eight cylinders are added together, this reduces the reciprocating and rotating weight by 1,321.6 grams or about 2.91 lbs. The reduction in weight allows the engine to accelerate faster since it is lighter.

Bob weight is calculated in the following manner. The reciprocating weight is the weight of the piston, piston pin, rings, pin locks (if used), and the small end of the connecting rod. The rotating weight includes the weight of the big end of the connecting rod with rod bolts and rod bearings.

On a V-8 engine like the small-block Mopar, where two rods connect to the same rod journal, the following formula is used (sample using 1971-'92 360 LA engine).

1/2 of the reciprocating weight x 2 (for two rods of the same rod journal) = 1,034.2 grams

Plus

2 x the rotating weight (for two rods on the same rod journal) = 1,133.2 grams

= 1,034.2 + 1,133.2 = 2,167.4 grams for one crank throw on a V-8 engine.

The best approach is to determine and calculate the bob weight of the desired components before buying them. That way you know how difficult and expensive it is to balance the engine. Another alternative is to purchase a pre-balanced stroker kit. Be sure you understand whether the stroker kit is balanced, since some come balanced and others do not. One potential pitfall – if any modifications or grinding is needed on these parts, it changes the balance of the engine.

OILING SYSTEM

The oiling system is the lifeblood of the engine, and it needs special care in a high-performance stroker engine. This chapter details the basic problems with the stock oiling system and provides solutions to overcome these issues. Optional modifications are also described in this chapter.

Problems with the Stock Oiling System

Restrictive Pickup

The stock production oil pickup tube does not flow enough oil to feed a high-performance engine. In the 1970s, Chrysler engineers tested the production oiling system when they were working on the Chrysler Kit Car. The Kit Car was an oval track racecar that was available in kit form from the Chrysler race group.

Engineers tested the volume of oil flow with a stock oil pump and then tested it again with a high-volume oil pump. With the stock pickup tube, the high-volume pump did not flow any extra oil (same volume as the standard volume oil pump). The only way they could get any additional oil flow was to add a second pickup tube (hose) between the pickup screen and the oil pump. The Kit Car system used a special bottom plate on the oil pump that had a second oil inlet into the pump. Since it had to be removable to allow assembly

of the original steel oil tube, the second line was a flexible hose with hose clamps.

The production oil tube is tapped on the end with a 3/8" NPT thread and screws into the oil pump. Most pumps do not have enough material to allow changing to a larger thread size and tube diameter.

Other Problems with the Stock Oiling System (LA Engine)

The main oil galley (passenger side of engine) intersects with eight tappets, allowing more chance for oil leakage around the tappets. It may reduce pressure to the rest of the engine. This situation is worse on older blocks with lots of wear in the tappet bores (a common problem on both LA and Magnum engines).

No direct constant flow of oil exists around the camshaft journal (#2 and #4 journals) to feed the cylinder heads. The camshaft has holes that allow oil flow when the holes are lined up, but these passages are blocked most of the time since the cam is turning.

Flow can be restricted if the wrong head bolts are used. Oil flows around two of the head bolts, and these bolts have a reduced diameter where the oil flows around them. Some head bolts and studs don't have the smaller diameter, and this can restrict oil flow. The two special head bolts are on the intake side

of the block – second one from the front on the driver's side and second from the back on the passenger side.

Flow can be reduced with some rocker shafts when larger 3/8" screws are used to hold them down (i.e., W2, W5, and Commando cylinder heads). These heads use larger 3/8" rocker shaft bolts, so the rocker shafts need a larger hole on the bottom to allow oil to flow around the larger bolt. This is the second rocker shaft bolt from the front on the driver's side and second from the rear on the passenger side.

Places for leaks in the system are plentiful (i.e., around the tappets, edge of cam bearings, rocker shaft to head, edge of rocker arms, around the head bolts, etc.).

With so many turns, changes in passage size, and opportunities for leaks, a long oil path to the heads leads to oil starvation. Another problem can be a lack of oil on the fuel pump eccentric.

Limited Oil Flow to the Connecting Rods

Most Mopar small-block main bearings have a groove around the bearing, but only in the upper bearing shell. This limits oil flow to the rod bearings as the crankshaft turns since the oil passage is reduced to half the bearing to journal clearance (about 0.0005" to 0.0015" passage). The reason the bearings are made

Differences in LA and Magnum Oiling Systems

The major difference in the LA and Magnum oiling system is the way the cylinder heads receive oil.

Cylinder Head Oiling on LA Engines

The stock LA block has passages in the block that feed oil from the #2 and #4 camshaft journals to the cylinder head deck surfaces. The oil then goes through an oil passage in the deck up into the head. This oil passage leads to the head bolt where the oil goes around the bolt and into another passage up to the rocker stand (second cast in rocker stand in head from the front on the driver's side, and second from the rear on the passenger side of the engine). The oil goes up around the rocker stand, and into the oversize hole in the bottom of the rocker shaft. The rocker shaft has holes in it that feed the oil to each rocker arm. The rocker arms splash the oil onto the valve tips and valvesprings.

The camshaft has holes in the #2 and #4 journals that allow some oil to pass up into the cylinder heads. There is no constant flow of oil since the oil passage in the camshaft is blocked most of the time as the camshaft turns.

Stock LA camshafts have oil passages drilled in the #2 and #4 journals, and this is how oil flow is restricted to the cylinder heads. These passages work fine on a stock engine, but they may not provide enough oil on a high-performance engine since oil only flows to the heads when these holes are lined up as the camshaft turns.

This oil path to the heads is really complicated compared to most engines. This situation creates many opportunities for leaks and other problems. Sometimes if the wrong head bolts are used, oil can be restricted to the cylinder heads. The head bolts have a reduced area to allow more oil flow around the bolt and up to the heads.

Stock LA heads have oil passages around the edge of the head bolts. These two bolts must have a reduced diameter where the oil flows around them. Be sure to use the proper bolts that have the reduced diameter or you could restrict oil flow to the heads.

Another common problem is when the rocker shaft is installed upside down or backwards. The rocker shaft has larger holes in the areas where the oil goes around the rocker hold-down bolts. If these larger holes are not installed in the proper location, then oil can be restricted to the heads.

Some cylinder heads use larger 3/8"

Two rocker shaft bolts must have a large hole around them for oil flow. If these rocker shafts are not installed correctly or larger-than-stock bolts are used, the oil flow can be restricted.

rocker shaft hold-down bolts, and this can restrict oil flow (stock heads use 5/16" bolts). W2, W5, and Commando cylinder heads use the larger 3/8" bolts to hold the rocker shaft on. The rocker shaft must have larger holes with enough oil flow when the 3/8" bolts are used.

Cylinder Head Oiling on Magnum Engines

Magnum engines have a much simpler path for the oil to reach the cylinder heads. The tappets and hollow pushrods have oil passages that allow oil flow to the heads. This oiling method is similar to the method used on GM small-block engines.

The oil passages from the camshaft to the deck and up into the heads are

Magnum tappets and pushrods have oil passages used to oil the heads. This oiling path is much shorter and has fewer restrictions.

not there on Magnum engines. Care must be taken to keep the oil as clean as possible since the 16 smaller oil passages in the tappets and pushrods could more easily become blocked with debris (as compared to two larger oil passages leading to the heads).

When Magnum heads are used on LA blocks, the tappets and pushrods must be changed to components that have the oil passages built in (tappets with oil passages and hollow pushrods). Many racing rocker arm systems are also set up to be oiled through the tappets and pushrods.

These bearings only have the oil groove in the top half of the bearing. Most bearings are made this way, but this limits oil supply to the connecting rods when the oil passage on the main journal is turning on the lower half of the bearing.

this way is so more bearing surface area can handle the high load on the lower half of the bearing.

Windage Tray

The windage tray sold by Mopar was designed for a crankshaft with a 3.310" stroke (stock 318 and 340 stroke). Many customers use the windage tray with the 3.580" 360 stroke. The windage tray fits, but it does not work as well with the longer 360 stroke. The crankcase pressure is increased when the windage tray is used with the 360-stroke crankshaft. The windage tray P4529790 is not recommended with a 360-stroke crank. This windage tray does not fit with a 4.000" stroke crankshaft (not enough clearance to the rods and crankshaft).

Recommended Modifications

High-Volume Oil Pump

The high-volume oil pump should be used on all high-performance LA and Magnum engines. With so many places for leaks in this system, the high-volume pump must be used.

Hardened Tip on Oil Pump Drive Shaft

When the high-volume oil pump is used, the distributor/oil pump drive shaft must have a hardened tip or it could break off. The extra force needed to drive the high-volume pump can cause the stock driveshaft tip to fail. These special drive shafts have two choices. P3690715 is recommended for use with cast cams and has a standard gear. P3690874 has an aluminum-bronze

This oil pump is a high-volume pump made by Melling – part number M72HV. This pump increases oil volume by about 25 percent as compared to the stock pump.

An oil pump drive shaft with a hardened tip must be used with the high-volume oil pump. The hex-shaped tip in the bottom of the shaft is the hardened area. This tip can break off if a standard drive shaft is used with a high-volume oil pump.

gear for use with billet steel roller camshafts. Both of these drive shafts have the hardened tip.

Larger Diameter or Dual Pickup

A pickup tube with a larger-than-stock diameter must be used to allow enough flow to feed the high-volume oil pump. The best pickups come with a new bottom plate for the oil pump and have a larger-than-stock tube. The stock oil pickup passage in the pump is blocked with a pipe plug when the larger bottom-feed pickup is used. The bottom-plate style pickup provides more clearance to the connecting rods on a stroker engine. With this style pickup, the tube does not come out the side of the pump and is located farther away from the connecting rods and crankshaft with the longer stroke.

Some pickups use a precision-machined thin wall tube where the pickup screws into the pump. These pickups screw into the pump in the standard location and allow more oil flow while using the stock 3/8" NPT tapped hole in the pump.

This oil pickup is a bottom-feed style pickup with a larger-than-stock pickup tube that can provide enough oil for a high-volume pump. This pickup includes a new bottom cover for the pump, and the pickup is mounted on the bottom plate. A pipe plug blocks the stock pickup location since it is not used (note the plug in the lower left-hand corner of the pump). The bottom-feed style pickup provides more room for the stroker crankshaft and rods, since the pickup is not mounted on the side of the pump.

This Moroso oil pickup has a thin-wall tube made to allow more oil flow using the standard pickup mounting location. Always check for interference from the connecting rods to the oil pickup on a stroker engine. The longer the stroke, the closer the connecting rods are to the pickup (worse on front-sump oil pans and pickups like this one).

Since no source for a dual pickup currently exists, one must be custom fabricated by using a modified pickup with a special oil pump bottom plate. The special bottom plate for the oil pump is available from Milodon (included with the pickup sold with their oval track oil pan).

Full Groove Main Bearings

Most main bearings only have oil grooves in the top bearing shell (in block) and no groove on the bottom half of the bearing (in main caps). The best way to provide constant oil flow to the connecting rods is to use fully-grooved main bearings. The grooves go all the way around the crankshaft, and the oil flow is not reduced when the passage to the rods is passing over the lower bearing shell. The easiest way to get fully grooved main bearings is to buy two sets of bearings and use the upper-grooved bearings in both the block and main caps. An extra hole in the second set of upper shells is not used, but this doesn't hurt anything. A new bearing tang receiver needs to be machined in the #5 cap since the tang is located in a different spot on the upper and lower bearing shells.

These main bearings have a groove all the way around the bearing on both the top and bottom shell. This oil groove provides a constant supply of oil to the connecting rods, but it reduces the bearing's surface area slightly. The easiest way to obtain fully grooved main bearings is to buy two sets of bearings and use the top-bearing shells in the block and main caps.

A compromise solution is to use Federal Mogul bearings that have a 3/4" groove around the crankshaft. This allows more oil flow and still provides more surface area in the highest load portion of the bearing (middle of the lower bearing shell).

Moly-Coated Fuel Pump Eccentric

All high-performance engines that use a mechanical fuel pump should use the Moly-coated fuel pump eccentric. This special coating provides improved protection where the fuel pump arm rubs on it. Many other coatings have been tried on this eccentric, but none have performed as well as the Moly. Some engine builders polish the Moly coating smooth since it is a bumpy coating.

Oil Squirter on Fuel Pump Eccentric

You should also drill a small hole in one of the front oil galley plugs so it

These Federal Mogul bearings have a groove three quarters of the way around the main bearing. The top bearing shell has the full groove, and the bottom shell has the grooves at the ends. This design is a compromise between load-carrying capability with more surface area and improved oiling to the connecting rods.

This fuel pump eccentric has been coated with a special Moly coating to reduce friction. This bumpy coating looks funny since it is not always smooth. Some engine builders polish the coating so that it is smoother in the area where the fuel pump arm rubs against it. All high-performance engines should use this fuel pump eccentric since it is a high-friction and high-wear area of the engine.

squirts oil onto the fuel pump eccentric. The hole is approximately 0.015", and a larger second hole must also be drilled in the camshaft thrust plate or timing chain tensioner plate to allow oil to squirt the eccentric. I normally use a 1/64" drill bit to drill the small hole in the plug. The small 1/64" drill bits are available from most tool stores or from Grainger. The small drill bits work well when mounted in a handheld rotary tool, like a Dremel.

A small 1/64" hole (about 0.016" diameter) can be drilled in one of the oil galley plugs in the front of the engine. This small hole squirts oil on the fuel pump eccentric to keep it lubricated. The easiest way to work with a tiny drill bit this size is to use a Dremel tool.

Another larger hole must also be drilled in the thrust plate that mounts in front of this plug, so that the oil can squirt on the fuel pump eccentric.

Optional Modifications

Pushrod Oiling

The best way to minimize the drawbacks in stock LA oiling systems is to feed oil to the top of the engine using oil passages in the tappets and hollow pushrods. The cylinder heads and rocker arms must also be the proper type to work with pushrod oiling. This modification provides a more direct path for oil to the heads and eliminates many of the problem areas on the LA oiling system.

Magnum engines use this oiling method in production, so pushrod oiling must be used when Magnum heads are used on an LA short block. The trick to converting to pushrod oiling is to use tappets with the oil passages and hollow pushrods. American Motors (AMC) tappets are used in LA blocks since they are the same diameter and have the needed oil passages. The AMC flat tappets are available in hydraulic or mechanical (solid) tappets. When using Magnum heads, hydraulic AMC tappets, and stock Magnum rocker arms on your LA block, the pushrods should be 7.625" long. Mopar Performance sells pushrod set P5007477 with these specifications for conversion to tappet oiling.

One caution – don't use stock production Magnum tappets in your LA block. These tappets are too tall and LA blocks do not have enough material to support them (tappet bores are shorter in the LA block).

Most modern Jesel and T&D racing rocker arms are designed for use with oiling through the tappets and pushrods. The T&D rocker arms are also available with a special passage that squirts oil on the valvesprings. This type of spring oiler is much simpler than ones that use a special spray bar in the valve covers. Valvesprings last longer when oil is sprayed on them to keep them cool. This is particularly critical on valvesprings used with high-lift camshafts and/or high spring loads.

LA Block Modifications With Tappet Oiling

When LA blocks are used with the tappet and pushrod oiling to the heads, there are two extra, unused oil passages

These T&D Machine Products rocker arms are designed for oiling through the tappets and pushrods only. W9 cylinder heads (shown) must have the oil fed to the head though the tappets and pushrods.

The oil galley should be plugged when the LA block is converted to oil through the tappets and pushrods. This oil galley is normally a 1/4" hole, so a 1/4" drill may not be necessary to prepare the hole for a tap and screw-in plug.

I recommend the use of a 5/16-18 tap since that tap size is designed to work with the 1/4" hole in the oil galley. Tap the hole deep enough so that the plug does not stick up above the deck surface and interfere with the head gasket.

Use a 5/16-18 allen-head set screw for the plug. Repeat this process on the other side of the engine. Fully clean and remove any metal shavings that get into the block when drilling and tapping this hole. If you ever go back to the stock oiling system, these plugs can be easily removed when changing cylinder heads.

in the block. You have three choices for blocking off these unused oil passages to the heads.

If the block is disassembled and the cam bearings are being replaced, the cam bearing can be rotated to block the unused oil passage to the heads. This method eliminates any possible leakage from the unused oil passages that were designed for the stock oiling to the heads.

The second and most simple method is to use the head gasket and head to seal off the unused passage. It blocks the oil passage since it doesn't have any oil passages in it (i.e., Magnum heads, W7, W8, and W9 heads). The head gasket seals the passage at the fire deck surface. The advantage of this method is that the engine doesn't need to be disassembled to change the oiling in the block.

A third method is to plug the unused oil passage in the block at the deck surface. I use a 5/16"-18 allen-head set screw to plug the oil passages in the block. This size works well since the oil passage is normally a 1/4" hole and this is the proper size for a 5/16"-18 tap without having to drill a pilot hole. With this method, if the short block is ever reused with heads that require these oil passages, the plugs can be easily removed before the new heads are installed. This method is less likely to leak and the engine doesn't have to be fully torn down to change the location of the oil holes in the cam bearings.

The first and third methods shown require that the engine be totally disassembled to install cam bearings, or to clean out the oil passages after tapping for the plugs. These two methods provide a better seal, but they require more cost and work if the engine is not already taken apart.

Oil Grooves on Camshaft

Some camshafts have an oiling groove around the #2 and #4 bearing journals. This allows continuous oil flow to the heads on LA engines. This groove allows the oil to flow around the camshaft journals at any point as it is turning. Without these grooves, the oil can only flow when the holes in the camshaft on these journals are lined up.

Most camshafts are made with inter-secting oil holes (#2 and #4 journals) that allow oil to flow to the cylinder heads only when the holes line up as the camshaft is turning. These holes are timed to restrict oil flow to the heads. The holes are not lined up most of the time, so it does not have a constant flow of oil to the heads. Do not restrict oil flow to the heads further since it is already restricted with this system.

This camshaft has a groove that goes all the way around the camshaft (on the #2 and #4 journals). This groove supplies continuous oil flow to the heads since the oil can go around the camshaft and flow while it is turning. Most camshafts are not made with this special groove.

The oil that flows to the cylinder heads should not be restricted with the stock LA oiling system. Since the passages in the #2 and #4 journals are already a restriction, any further restriction will not allow enough oil to the heads.

Synthetic Oil

Do not use synthetic oil until the engine has been run through its initial "break-in" cycle. This normally takes a couple hundred miles of usage. Synthetic oil does not allow enough wear to get the piston rings sealed properly. After the piston rings are sealed, synthetic oil has several benefits.

Windage

Windage is a loss in engine output due to excess oil getting in the way of the crankshaft and connecting rods. Windage is a major problem on a stroker engine since as the stroke gets longer, the crankshaft gets closer to the walls of the block and windage losses are increased.

In testing with a 408-stroker engine, the typical losses due to windage are about 42 hp with the stock oil pan (i.e., stock 360 oil pan).

The best way to minimize or eliminate windage losses is to use a deeper oil pan to get the sump farther away from the crankshaft. The Moroso street-and-strip oil pan is a good way to get the oil farther away from the crankshaft.

This oil pan has a forward sump and fits in most muscle car applications. Moroso also offers a rear sump pan designed for most trucks. The rear sump pan is pre-ferred from an acceleration standpoint, but does not fit in most production cars.

This Moroso Street and Strip oil pan is a deep sump pan that works with most muscle cars. This oil pan increases out-put of most stroker engines by about 42 hp by reducing windage (as compared to the stock 360 oil pan when used with a 4.000" stroker crankshaft).

This adapter can be used to relo-cate the oil filter for more clear-ance when it interferes with headers or part of the car. The part number for this kit is Mopar Perfor-mance P5249624.

Synthetic oil is less susceptible to aer-ation, or air bubbles mixed in with the oil. Aeration can cause a slight loss in valve lift when hydraulic tappets are used. The air mixed up in the oil compresses, and this causes the valve not to open as far as it would if the air was not there.

Synthetic oil holds up better in high-heat applications. If you don't have an oil cooler and experience high oil temperature, it is extra insurance to have synthetic oil.

The drawback with synthetic oil is that it is expensive at about $4 to $5 per quart.

Fixing the Stock LA Oiling System

Over the years many racers have had oiling system problems with the LA oiling system. These racers developed a couple of modifications to fix some of the problems with the stock LA oiling system.

Tubing the Block

One common modification is to "tube" the block. The purpose of this modification is to eliminate or restrict oil to the tappets. Tappet oil could also be blocked or restricted by installing tappet bushings, but this would cost more and must be done at a machine shop. The block can be tubed using a hand-held drill motor and ordinary tools.

One or both of the main oil galleys is drilled oversize and a copper tube is installed inside the oil galley. The tube eliminates oil flow to the tappets where it intersects with the tappet bores. A special peen tool is then driven into each tappet bore to force the copper tube out of the way of each tappet (this distorts the tube so the tappets fit back in). The oil passages from the main oil galley to the mains must be re-drilled through this tube since they are blocked by the tube.

Mopar sells a special drill and ream package P5249508 for installing the tube. Mopar also sells the tube and peen package P4120603. Two of these tube packages are needed to tube both sides of the block.

Some engine builders use this modification to minimize possible leakage in the oiling system. The block has 16 fewer places for oil leakage when it is tubed. Other engine builders use mechanical roller tappets that don't need any oil. Engine builders sometimes drill small oil passages in the tube to restrict oil to the tappets (hydraulic tappets or tappets that feed oil to the cylinder heads).

The 48-degree R blocks were originally designed with oil galleys that did not intersect with the tappets. This was done so that you did not have to tube the block on racing engines to control oil flow to the tappets. Initially, this worked well on engines that used mechanical tappets without oil. At about the same time these blocks were launched, most high-quality racing rocker arms started using tappet oil to lubricate the rocker arms and valvesprings. This oiling method requires a small oil passage from the main oil galleys to the tappets for head oiling. The 48-degree blocks now come with a 0.125" oil passage from the main galley to the tappets (for head oiling with mechanical tappets or for hydraulic tappets).

Oil Cross-Over Line

Some engine builders install a special oil cross-over line to provide a constant flow of oil (and more direct path) to the cylinder heads. This oil line supplies a continuous flow of oil since the flow is not restricted by the timed oil passages in the camshaft.

The first step is to drill an extra 3/16" hole in the #2 and #4 cam bearings before installation (drill in between any of the two existing holes in these bearings). Be sure to clean up any sharp edges or burrs on the new hole. Install these cam bearings (#2 and #4) with the new hole lined up with the oil passage that leads to the main bearings. These modified cam bearings now block off the oil passage to the heads.

The second step is to drill and tap two holes in the valley. These holes are drilled in the small oil galleys that lead from the #2 and #4 cam bearings up to the deck. Drill these holes near the bottom of the oil galleys just above the large main oil galley that feeds the tappets. Drill just deep enough to reach the oil passages and tap these holes for 1/8" NPT fittings. Drill a 0.050" hole inside the first hole that allows oil to flow from the main galley to the smaller galley (passenger side only). Install two 45-degree brake brass fittings (1/8" NPT on one end and 3/16" inverted flare on the other end) into the tapped holes. Bend up and install a 12" piece of 3/16" brake line between the two 45-degree fittings. Route this brake line in an "S"-shaped pattern and make sure it doesn't interfere with any tappets and pushrods.

This revised oil path to the heads now supplies a constant flow of oil to the heads in a much shorter and less restrictive path. This method should only be used on engines where the heads are oiled in the stock manner (don't use with Magnum, W7, W8, W9, and some W2 heads).

Right Angle Oil Filter Adapter

Mopar Performance sells an oil filter adapter that relocates the filter 90 degrees. This adapter is handy if you don't have enough room for the filter in the standard location. In some cases, the filter must be moved with some headers or in other applications like street rods. This adapter fits both LA and Magnum engines.

Conclusion

With careful planning, the small-block Mopar oiling system works well in most stroker engines. Many potential problems with the Mopar engine are minimized with a stroker engine since the RPM is normally lower than it would be in other HP racing applications.

I recommend using the tappet and pushrod oiling method whenever possible since it eliminates many of the potential problems with the stock LA oiling system. The most important recommendation is to use the high-volume oil pump and a large-diameter pickup that can supply enough oil to the pump.

Oiling System Modifications on R3 & 340 Replacement Blocks

Oil Drainback

The valley is cast solid or filled in on the R3 and 340 replacement blocks. This feature is desirable with a dry sump oiling system since the oil is sucked out of the valley by the dry sump pump before it can get on the crank and rods and increase windage losses.

R3 and 340 replacement blocks are cast with the valley area mostly filled. This feature is desirable with a dry sump oiling system since the multi-stage oil pump can suck oil out of the valley and reduce windage. On wet sump engines, the valley holds too much oil and needs more venting from the top to the bottom of the engine.

In a wet sump system, extra drain holes must be drilled through the valley to allow the oil to return to the oil pan. Five or six 1/2" diameter holes should be drilled in the valley so that the oil drips onto and provides lubrication to the camshaft on its way back to the oil pan. This is particularly important on engines that idle for a long time since this results in not much oil being thrown from the crank to the camshaft.

If these extra drain holes are not drilled in the valley, about two quarts of oil will be trapped in the valley and never return to the oil pan.

On wet sump engines, five or six 1/2" holes should be drilled in the valley to allow oil to flow back to the oil pan. These holes should be drilled in the low areas of the valley so that all the oil drains back to the oil pan. Be careful not to drill into the oil galleys or cam bearings.

Plumbing

R3 blocks have a tapped oil passage in the top of the front china wall of the block. This passage allows another way to feed oil into the engine. If an external oil pump or remote oil filter is used, the pressurized oil returning from the pump or filter can be fed into the engine with this oil passage. This is an optional way to feed oil in

R3 blocks have an optional oil passage that can be used to feed pressurized oil into the engine. This extra hole is located on the top wall on the front of the engine (passenger side). The return line from an oil cooler or remote oil filter can be connected here.

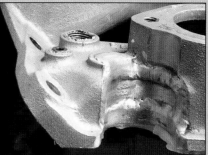

Most intake manifolds with a built-in valley tray may interfere with the oil feed passage. This passage can be plugged with a thin allen-head pipe plug when not used. When the intake doesn't have enough clearance it can be modified, or the other oil feed passage on the oil filter base can be used instead.

the engine instead of the normal inlet passage on the oil filter pad. In most cases, this oil passage is not used, and should be plugged with a thin allen-head style pipe plug.

Tappet Oiling on 48-Degree Blocks

The tappets are moved inward when the 48-degree R3 blocks are made. This revised machining moves the tappets away from the main oil galleys on the block. Small passages are drilled from the tappet bores on the R3 blocks to the oil galley. These small passages allow better oil control since the passage is smaller and less likely to leak. All AC-level R3 blocks have these oil passages drilled in the block when you receive it. Early R3 blocks (without the AC at the end of the part number) did not have these oil passages, and had to be drilled when needed. A special drill fixture tool (P5007728) is available from Mopar Performance to drill these oil passages. A photograph of this drill fixture tool is shown in Chapter 3.

CONNECTING RODS

Connecting rods are an area on the stroker engine worth spending a great deal of time planning to select the correct parts. Proper rod selection can make the engine more durable and much easier to build. Errors in this area create headaches from a clearance standpoint and increase the time and cost to prep the block.

Rod Length

When building a stroker engine, most engine builders recommend the use of a longer connecting rod to improve the rod angle when using a long-stroke crankshaft. On most Ford and GM small-block engines, the stock connecting rods are short, at about 5.400" to 5.700" long. All Mopar small blocks come from the factory with 6.123" connecting rods. This is a big advantage since the extra rod length also provides more clearance for large counterweights on a stroker crank. Most mild Mopar stroker engines can use the stock rods, avoiding the cost of aftermarket rods.

Rod Ratio

Rod ratio is the length of the rod divided by the crankshaft stroke. Many engine builders believe that a longer connecting rod makes more power and improves the angle of the rod with a

long stroke. The tall deck height on the Mopar block allows both a long rod and a long stroke.

The stock and common stroker rod ratios are listed below:

Engine	Rod Length	Stroke	Rod Ratio
273/318/340	6.123"	3.310"	1.85
360	6.123"	3.580"	1.71
4.000" Stroker	6.123"	4.000"	1.53

As the stroke gets longer, the rod ratio gets smaller (using the same rod length).

Stock LA Rods

All small-block Mopar rods are made from a steel forging.

The three basic types of LA production rods:

• 273/318/340 rods (1964-'73) – weight 726 grams
• 318 rods (1973-'91) and 360 rods (1971-'92) – weight 758 grams
• 3.9L V-6 rods (1986-'91) – weight 746 grams

The 1964-'73 273, 318, and 340 rods used a bushing in the small end of the rod

and a floating piston pin. All V-6 and 360 engines use a pressed piston pin. 1973-'91 318 rods also used a pressed pin.

The small end of the LA rod is 1.200" wide and is wider than the larger end of the rod. This extra width is too wide to work with Magnum and Keith Black (KB) pistons. The small end can be machined narrower to fit the Magnum-style pistons, but this changes the weight of the rods and requires the engine to be re-balanced.

All of these rods are very similar in size and are interchangeable except for weight (balancing). The only exception is the bushed piston pin on the early rods.

The stock rods can handle up to about 450 hp if the RPM is 6,000 or less. If production rods are used on a stroker engine, the 1973 and up 318 and 360 rods are preferred since they are a little heavier and stronger than the early rods.

Stock Magnum Rods

All Magnum rods are made from a steel forging.

The 5.2L and 5.9L Magnum rods are all the same size and weight. The small end of the Magnum rod is narrower than the LA rod. These rods are flat with the same width at both ends. The weight of the rods is also slightly less since they are narrower at the small end. Magnum rods are 744 grams and LA rods are 758 grams.

LA vs. Magnum Connecting Rods

Engine	1971-'92 360 LA	1993-'03 Magnum 5.9L
Length	6.123"	6.123"
Weight - Small End	239 grams	225 grams
Weight - Big End	519 grams	519 grams
Weight - Total	758 grams	744 grams
Width - Big End	0.9305"	0.9305"
Width - Small End	1.200"	0.9305"
Shape - Small End	Rounded	Squared-Off
Housing Bore - Small End	0.9829"-0.9834"	0.9819"-0.9834"
Housing Bore - Big End	2.2500"-2.2507"	2.2500"-2.2507"
Bolt & Nut Size	3/8"	3/8"
Forging Number	Various	53005798

The basic dimensions, other than the small-end width, are the same as LA rods. This makes them interchangeable, but requires re-balancing because of the difference in weight. Using heavier-than-stock pistons is one possible way of using Magnum rods without having to re-balance. This adds the extra 14 grams back.

The upper end of the Magnum rods have a squared-off area used to balance the rod. When the compression height is reduced in a stroker engine, the rod gets closer to the underside of the piston. This part of the rod needs to be machined to clear the piston on most stroker engines (i.e., with a 4.000" stroke crankshaft).

The rod at the top is an I-beam style rod similar to the ones used in production engines. The H-beam style rod is also readily available and is starting to become more popular.

Magnum Rods

Magnum rods (1992-'03) have a squared-off block at the small end of the connecting rod. This area needs modification to clear the piston on most stroker engines. The edges of the square block must be ground away or they hit the underside of the piston. This modification is mandatory on engines that use the 4.000" stroker crankshafts, since the reduced compression height puts the rod too close to the underside of the piston.

The rod should be machined to allow a 0.692" radius from the center of the small hole to the upper half of the rod.

Magnum rods are 14 grams lighter than LA rods (on the small end), and are interchangeable if the engine is re-balanced. Magnum rods are thinner at the small end and this is why they are slightly lighter. KB pistons are designed for use with the thinner-style Magnum rods. When these pistons are used, the magnum rods fit and don't require machining to make them thinner.

Magnum rods have a squared-off block on the small end of the connecting rod. This block gets into the underside of the piston on most stroker engines.

The small end of the Magnum rod can be machined to provide the clearance needed so it won't hit the piston. Use a 0.692" radius from the centerline of the piston pin as a guideline for how much material to remove.

Magnum rods require a small clearance notch to be machined in the bottom of the bore on the block. The rod bolt is the part of the rod that gets into the block.

Fasteners

All high-performance and stroker engines should use high-quality rod bolts. The connecting rod bolts are subject to the highest stress of any fastener in the engine. The weight of the reciprocating parts goes up on most stroker engines, especially when oversize pistons are used. The oversize pistons are one of the ways that additional cubes are added to the stroker engine. Most stroker engines don't turn high RPMs, but these bolts experience more load as the RPM increases.

The longer stroke also makes the piston and rod accelerate faster since it must travel farther in the same amount of time as a short-stroke engine. This increased speed combined with a heavier piston creates more stress on the rod bolts.

The rod on the top is using an ARP nut and bolt, and the rod on the bottom is using a cap-screw style fastener that does not use a nut. The cap-screw style rod usually provides a little more clearance to the block at the bottom of the bores on a stroker engine. The upper edge of the bolt-on stock style rods is the area that requires grinding on the block for clearance.

High-quality rod bolts are available from ARP and other sources. Most high-performance aftermarket rods come with ARP rod bolts. Don't just swap out the rod bolts with high-performance pieces and think you're done. All rods must be resized when new rod bolts are installed. Machine shops use a Sunnen rod machine to check and hone the large end of the rod after new rod bolts are installed.

Torque the high-performance rod bolts using the specifications recommended by the manufacturer. In most

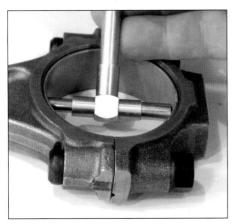

When measuring the rod for oil clearance, be sure to measure the clearance at the center of the rod away from the parting line. Bearings are tapered and have more clearance as you get closer to the parting line. This taper can lead to misleading measurements of vertical oil clearance.

cases, the torque procedure and torques are different from the production specifications. Most high-performance bolts require the use of Moly paste on the bolts.

Some manufacturers recommend that the bolt be torqued to a specific yield or stretched by a specific amount. A special tool is used to measure how much the bolt has been stretched.

Block Clearance

The area that usually needs clearancing on the block is at the bottom edge of the bores. The connecting rod bolt gets into the very bottom edge of the bore, and the block must be ground slightly for clearance in this area. I-beam style connecting rods with a cap screw (instead of a bolt and nut) generally have more clearance in this area.

Eagle SIR Mopar rods fit in most 4.000" stroker engines without any clearancing on the block or rods. The upper end of the Eagle rods is 1.060" wide and works with most Magnum-style pistons. This width is slightly wider than Magnum and narrower than LA rods. The rods come with ARP 8740 wave loc rod bolts and have clearance at the small end to avoid interference with the piston. These rods are economically priced and are cheaper than reworking stock rods. I don't think you could add ARP bolts and piston pin bushings to stock rods for less than the cost of buying new Eagle rods.

Pre-Assembly

Stroker engines need to be test fit before balancing. The engine should be pre-assembled with all parts to make sure no grinding or special fitting is needed. Remember that any grinding or machining on the rods and pistons changes their weight. Any changes require the engine to be re-balanced, so make sure everything fits up front.

This is the area in the block near the bottom of the bores where the rod bolt gets into the block. Mopar engines have much more room inside the crankcase, and the camshaft is so high that it allows enough room without much, if any, grinding on the block.

The rod shown in the front is the Eagle SIR rod. This rod is very reasonably priced (about $250 a set), and comes with ARP cap screws and a bushing in the small end of the rod.

The upper end of the Eagle rod (right) does not require any machining to clear the top of the piston. The thickness of the small end of the rods is 1.060" thick. It is thinner than LA rods and thicker than Magnum rods.

The cap screw used on the Eagle rod (bottom) makes all the difference when building a stroker engine. The extra clearance by eliminating the top of the bolt makes the rods clear the block with a 4.000" stroke crankshaft.

Viper Rods

Another option for connecting rods on stroker engines is 2000-'01 Viper V-10 connecting rods. This connecting rod is very similar to a Magnum rod, but is longer at 6.221". The piston pin bore size on the small end of the rod is slightly smaller at 0.9425" to 0.9440" (about 0.039" smaller). All of the other dimensions of this rod are the same as Magnum rods. The rod bearings are the same as the ones used in all LA and Magnum small blocks.

The Viper rods are made from the

Another option for rods is to use Viper V-10 (model year 2000-'01) rods. These rods are 0.098" longer than the stock rods (total length of 6.221").

same forgings as the Magnum rods, but are machined to be 0.098" longer. These rods come stock with ARP rod bolts when they are made. The small end of the rod has been machined

The Viper rods are made from the Magnum forging and have two machining changes on the small end of the rod. The squared-off portion of the small end is already ground away for piston clearance. The size of the piston pin is about 0.039" smaller, and it must be modified or used with pistons that use the smaller pin.

without the squared-off block and works with most stroker pistons.

The easiest way to accommodate the longer rod length and smaller piston pin bore is to custom order the pistons with the proper compression height and pin size. New pistons are

Another bonus of Viper rods is they have ARP rod bolts.

needed for any stroker engine anyway, so these features can be handled with custom forged pistons. Another option is to machine the small end of the rod and install bushings for use with full-floating piston pins.

Mopar sells these connecting rods under part number P5007504.

Viper rods require some machining on the block for most stroker engines. The rod bolt gets into the bottom edge of the bore on the block and requires grinding for clearance.

I usually install the pistons without piston rings for ease of assembly when mocking up the engine. Full-floater piston pins also make it easier to pre-assemble the engine, since the piston pins don't have to be installed by a machine shop prior to mock-up. If any machining is needed to the pistons or rods, these parts are easier to disassemble.

Conclusion

Rod selection can make the engine build a snap, or require extra grinding/machining for clearance. Eagle SIR rods have been used in many Mopar LA, Magnum, and R3 stroker engines without any block or rod machining (up to 4.000" stroke).

Generic GM Pistons and Rods

Aftermarket GM-sized rods can be used in a small-block Mopar engine. The trick to this modification is to turn down the rod journals on the crankshaft from 2.125" to 2.100". Any machine shop that grinds crankshafts can machine the crank to work with these rods.

The piston pin is a different size on generic rods, so the pistons must be made with the GM-sized piston pin. Stroker engines need new pistons anyway, so this is not a big deal. The pistons must be made with the valve notches in the proper location for the Mopar heads. The best way to get the proper pistons is to buy custom-forged pistons with the proper pin size, and dome or dish and valve notches to match your cylinder head. The basic bore sizes of the Mopar engines are close to the stock GM sizes, so plenty of

forgings are available. The valve layout is also the same, so most GM forgings have all the right stock in the right places to make these pistons. Piston rings are also readily available since both the GM and Mopar are based on a 4.000" bore size plus standard overbore.

One item to consider is the rod length when changing to generic GM-style rods. Most GM rods are shorter than Mopar rods, so the rod ratio gets smaller (going the wrong way). The longer stroke on your engine also makes this matter worse since the relative rod ratio gets smaller as the stroke increases. Consider using 6.123" or longer rods on any stroker engine. The rods should be as long as possible, but don't make the compression height so short that the piston pin gets into the piston rings.

PISTONS AND RINGS

Pistons are the second part of the one-two punch for big-inch small blocks. The pistons must be designed to work with the longer stroke and provide more cubes with a larger bore size.

Material and Processes

Most stock pistons are made from cast aluminum. In stock engines, cast pistons work fine as long as they have no tuning problems like detonation or a lean air-to-fuel mixture. For high-performance engines, use forged pistons since they are far superior to anything else available.

Hypereutectic pistons are stronger than standard cast pistons and are best suit-

The next step up from a cast piston is the hypereutectic piston (left). Hypereutectic pistons are cast from a special high-silicon-alloy material that makes them a little stronger than standard cast pistons. Other than the material, these two pistons are very similar.

ed for mild performance street cars and hot rods. Hypereutectic pistons are made the same way as normal castings, but the material includes more silicon than in a typical cast piston. This special alloy is stronger and harder than a stock cast piston, but more brittle than a standard cast piston.

Hypereutectic pistons cost more than cast pistons and less than forged pistons. KB sells hypereutectic pistons for Mopar stroker engines. These pistons work well in light-duty, lower-cost stroker engines.

Forged

Forged pistons are made from stronger and more dense material, but the biggest advantage is that they are

The lowest-cost stroker piston is a stock-style cast piston with the pin relocated for the longer stroke. This piston is available from Mopar.

The piston on the right-hand side is a forged stroker piston. It is made from a much stronger aluminum forging.

LA vs. Magnum Pistons

The LA and Magnum pistons have the same bore size and general dimensions.

The major difference in the LA and Magnum pistons is the weight. The Magnum piston (with pin and rings) is 151.2 grams lighter than the LA piston.

The shape of the dish on the Magnum engine is an oval shape, and this oval sits right under the smaller closed combustion chamber in the Magnum head. This dish shape helps to provide a more efficient combustion without interference from the valve notches. Any dome or irregular shape of the piston (like valve notches) makes the combustion time longer and less efficient. A flat-top or dished piston provides the most efficient combustion.

The piston rings are thinner and lighter on the Magnum engines.

Magnum pistons, pins, rings, and rods can be installed in an LA engine, and this is desirable in racing or high-performance applications since they weigh less than the LA parts. If this change is made, the Magnum piston pins and rings must also be changed as part of the assembly. Less rotating weight (360 engines only) changes the external balance of the engine. The easiest way to rebalance the engine is to use the Magnum damper and flywheel or torque converter. See Chapter 4 for more details on the differences in the Magnum and LA balance. Another alternative is to rebalance the entire rotating assembly at a machine shop.

The compression ratio is also changed when Magnum pistons are installed in an LA engine since the pistons are designed to work with a smaller 60cc combustion chamber. Most production Magnum cylinder heads have a 60cc chamber, and most production LA heads have a 70cc chamber.

Here are the same three pistons showing the underside or bottom view. Note the forged piston has a much smoother and stronger surface without any sharp edges to minimize high-stress areas prone to cracking.

for a stroker kit supplier listing. At this time, Diamond and KB have the best selection of forged Mopar stroker pistons. These pistons are shown in their catalogs and are shelf items. Mancini Racing also offers a wide selection of forged stroker pistons.

Custom-made stroker pistons are needed for most large-displacement stroker engines (i.e., 419ci or larger engines, or engines with a stroke longer than 4.000"). Custom pistons are available from Diamond, Wiseco, Ross, CP, and many other sources.

Most Mopar small-block pistons can be made from forgings designed for GM small-block engines. The valve layout and valve placement are very close

Engine Weight	1971-'92 360 Engine	1993-'03 Magnum 5.9L
Piston	584 +/- 2 grams	470 +/- 1 gram
Piston Pin	154.6 +/- 1 gram	134 +/- 1 gram
Ring Set	56.6 grams	40 grams
Compression Height	1.590"	1.622"
Approx. Compression Ratio	8.5:1 (w/ 70cc Chamber)	9.0:1 (w/ 60cc Chamber)
Piston Shape – Top	Standard Dish	Oval Shaped Dish
Valve Notches	Valve Notches	None
Piston Ring Thickness – top 2 rings	5/64" (.0781")	0.0600"
Piston Pin Diameter (OD)	0.984"	0.984"

This forged racing stroker piston is made by Bill Miller Engineering and it features a high-compression dome designed for W9 heads.

more ductile. If another component gets loose and is smashed by the piston, it won't usually break and fall apart. The foreign component gets stuck in the top of the piston and will not cause as much damage to the engine (or scatter broken pieces of piston throughout the engine).

Diamond, KB, Mopar, and many of the suppliers who sell stroker kits, stock forged stroker pistons. See Appendix A

Stroker Pistons

Source Part Number	Material	Bore	Stroke Size	Rod Length	Pin Diam.	Comp. Height	Dome/Dish	Dish/Package Volume	Ring Package	Weight w/Pin	Rec. Block	Rec. Cylinder Head
Arias Pistons												
E4671040	Forged	4.040"	4.000"	6.123"	.984"	1.460"	"D" Dish	17.5cc	5/64x5/64x3/16	Call	340 & R3	Any
Diamond Racing Products, Inc.												
50001	Forged	3.940"	4.000"	6.123	0.984"	1.457"	Flat Top	6.8cc	1/16x1/16x3/16	Call	318 & Mag 5.2L	Any
51005	Forged	4.040"	4.000"	6.123"	0.984"	1.457"	Flat Top	6.8cc	1/16x1/16x3/16	Call	340 & R3	Any
51007	Forged	4.070"	4.000"	6.123"	0.984"	1.457"	Flat Top	6.8cc	1/16x1/16x3/16	Call	340 & R3	Any
51008	Forged	4.070"	4.000"	6.123"	0.927"	1.457"	Flat Top	6.8cc	1/16x1/16x3/16	Call	340 & R3	Any
51009	Forged	4.080"	4.000"	6.123"	0.984"	1.457"	Flat Top	6.8cc	1/16x1/16x3/16	Call	340 & R3	Any
51010	Forged	4.080"	4.000"	6.123"	0.927"	1.457"	Flat Top	6.8cc	1/16x1/16x3/16	Call	340 & R3	Any
51025	Forged	4.020"	4.000"	6.123"	0.984"	1.457"	Flat Top	6.8cc	1/16x1/16x3/16	Call	360 & Mag 5.9L	Any
51026	Forged	4.030"	4.000"	6.123"	0.984"	1.457"	Flat Top	6.8cc	1/16x1/16x3/16	Call	360	Any
51027	Forged	4.030"	4.000"	6.123"	0.927"	1.457"	Flat Top	6.8cc	1/16x1/16x3/16	Call	360	Any
51028	Forged	4.060"	4.000"	6.123"	0.984"	1.457"	Flat Top	6.8cc	1/16x1/16x3/16	Call	340 & R3	Any
50010	Forged	3.940"	4.000"	6.123"	0.984"	1.457"	Flat Top	16.7cc	1/16x1/16x3/16	Call	318 & Mag 5.2L	Any
51450	Forged	4.060"	3.580"	6.123"	0.984"	1.665"	"D" Dish	11cc	1/16x1/16x3/16	Call	340 & R3	W2
51401	Forged	4.005"	4.000"	6.123"	0.984"	1.457"	"D" Dish	19cc	1/16x1/16x3/16	Call	360 & Mag 5.9L	Any
51402	Forged	4.005"	4.000"	6.123"	0.927"	1.457"	"D" Dish	19cc	1/16x1/16x3/16	Call	360 & Mag 5.9L	Any
51403	Forged	4.020"	4.000"	6.123"	0.984"	1.457"	"D" Dish	20cc	1/16x1/16x3/16	Call	360 & Mag 5.9L	Any
51404	Forged	4.020"	4.000"	6.123"	0.927"	1.457"	"D" Dish	20cc	1/16x1/16x3/16	Call	360 & Mag 5.9L	Any
51405	Forged	4.030"	4.000"	6.123"	0.984"	1.457"	"D" Dish	20cc	1/16x1/16x3/16	Call	360 & Mag 5.9L	Any
51406	Forged	4.030"	4.000"	6.123"	0.927"	1.457"	"D" Dish	20cc	1/16x1/16x3/16	Call	360 & Mag 5.9L	Any
51407	Forged	4.040"	4.000"	6.123"	0.984"	1.457"	"D" Dish	20cc	1/16x1/16x3/16	Call	340 & R3	Any
51408	Forged	4.060"	4.000"	6.123"	0.984"	1.457"	"D" Dish	21cc	1/16x1/16x3/16	Call	340 & R3	Any
51409	Forged	4.070"	4.000"	6.123"	0.984"	1.457"	"D" Dish	21.5cc	1/16x1/16x3/16	Call	340 & R3	Any
51410	Forged	4.070"	4.000"	6.123"	0.927"	1.457"	"D" Dish	21.5cc	1/16x1/16x3/16	Call	340 & R3	Any
51411	Forged	4.070"	4.000"	6.123"	0.984"	1.457"	"D" Dish	9.3 cc	1/16x1/16x3/16	Call	340 & R3	Any
51412	Forged	4.080"	4.000"	6.123"	0.984"	1.457"	"D" Dish	21.5cc	1/16x1/16x3/16	Call	340 & R3	Any
51413	Forged	4.080"	4.000"	6.123"	0.927"	1.457"	"D" Dish	21.5cc	1/16x1/16x3/16	Call	340 & R3	Any
Hughes Engines												
2036	Forged	3.940"	4.000"	6.123"	0.984"	1.465"	Stepped Dish	22.4cc	5/64x5/64x3/16	579g	318 & Mag 5.2L	Any
2024	Hypereutectic	4.030"	4.000"	6.123"	0.984"	1.377"	Stepped Dish	26.5cc	5/64x5/64x3/16	600g	360 & Mag 5.9L	Magnum
2024	Hypereutectic	4.070"	4.000"	6.123"	0.984"	1.377"	Stepped Dish	26.5cc	5/64x5/64x3/16	600g	340 & R3	Magnum
2020	Hypereutectic	4.030"	4.000"	6.123"	0.984"	1.465"	"D" Dish	26.5cc	5/64x5/64x3/16	610g	360	LA
2020	Hypereutectic	4.070"	4.000"	6.123"	0.984"	1.465"	"D" Dish	26.5cc	5/64x5/64x3/16	610g	340 & R3	LA
2030	Forged	4.030"	4.000"	6.123"	0.984"	1.457"	Flat Top	6.8cc	1/16x1/16x3/16	640g	360 & Mag 5.9L	Any
2030	Forged	4.070"	4.000"	6.123"	0.984"	1.457"	Flat Top	6.8cc	1/16x1/16x3/16	640g	340 & R3	Any
2030	Forged	4.030"	4.000"	6.123"	0.984"	1.457"	"D" Dish	21.5cc	1/16x1/16x3/16	647g	360 & Mag 5.9L	Any
2030	Forged	4.070"	4.000"	6.123"	0.984"	1.457"	"D" Dish	21.5cc	1/16x1/16x3/16	647g	340 & R3	Any

Other pistons can be custom ordered. Also see Stroker Kits – Appendix A

Source Part Number	Material	Bore	Stroke Size	Rod Length	Pin Diam.	Comp. Height	Dome/Dish	Dish/Package Volume	Ring Package	Weight w/Pin	Rec. Block	Rec. Cylinder Head
KB Performance Pistons												
KB356	Hypereutectic	4.020"	4.000"	6.123"	0.984"	1.465"	Stepped Dish	23.5cc	5/64x5/64x3/16	615g	360 & Mag 5.9L	Any
KB356	Hypereutectic	4.030"	4.000"	6.123"	0.984"	1.465"	Stepped Dish	23.5cc	5/64x5/64x3/16	615g	360 & Mag 5.9L	Any
KB356	Hypereutectic	4.040"	4.000"	6.123"	0.984"	1.465"	Stepped Dish	23.5cc	5/64x5/64x3/16	615g	340 & R3	Any
KB356	Hypereutectic	4.060"	4.000"	6.123"	0.984"	1.465"	Stepped Dish	23.5cc	5/64x5/64x3/16	615g	340 & R3	Any
KB745	Forged	4.030"	4.000"	6.123"	0.984"	1.465"	Stepped Dish	20.5cc	1/16x1/16x3/16	638g	360 & Mag 5.9L	Any
KB745	Forged	4.040"	4.000"	6.123"	0.984"	1.465"	Stepped Dish	20.5cc	1/16x1/16x3/16	638g	340 & R3	Any
KB745	Forged	4.060"	4.000"	6.123"	0.984"	1.465"	Stepped Dish	20.5cc	1/16x1/16x3/16	638g	340 & R3	Any
KB744	Forged	4.030"	4.000"	6.123"	0.984"	1.465"	Flat Top	5cc	1/16x1/16x3/16	628g	360 & Mag 5.9L	Any

Stroker Pistons

Source Part Number	Material	Bore	Stroke Size	Rod Length	Pin Diam.	Comp. Height	Dome/ Dish	Dish/ Pocket Volume	Ring Package	Weight w/ Pin	Rec. Block	Rec. Cylinder Head
KB744	Forged	4.040"	4.000"	6.123"	0.984"	1.465"	Flat Top	5cc	1/16x1/16x3/16	628g	340 & R3	Any
KB744	Forged	4.060"	4.000"	6.123"	0.984"	1.465"	Flat Top	5cc	1/16x1/16x3/16	628g	340 & R3	Any
KB741	Forged	4.040"	3.580"	6.123"	0.984"	1.675"	Flat Top	5cc	1/16x1/16x3/16	651g	340 & R3	Any
KB741	Forged	4.060"	3.580"	6.123"	0.984"	1.675"	Flat Top	5cc	1/16x1/16x3/16	651g	340 & R3	Any
KB742	Forged	4.040"	3.580"	6.123"	0.984"	1.675"	Stepped Dish	9.6cc	1/16x1/16x3/16	669g	340 & R3	Any
KB742	Forged	4.060"	3.580"	6.123"	0.984"	1.675"	Stepped Dish	9.6cc	1/16x1/16x3/16	669g	340 & R3	Any
KB743	Forged	4.040"	3.580"	6.123"	0.984"	1.675"	Domed 0.200"	−11.2cc	1/16x1/16x3/16	693g	340 & R3	Open Chamber
KB743	Forged	4.060"	3.580"	6.123"	0.984"	1.675"	Domed 0.200"	−11.2cc	1/16x1/16x3/16	693g	340 & R3	Open Chamber
Mopar Performance Parts												
P5007478	Cast	4.000"	4.000"	6.123"	0.984"	1.412"	Dished	19cc	5/64x5/64x3/16	Call	360 & Mag 5.9L	Any
P5007479	Cast	4.020"	4.000"	6.123"	0.984"	1.412"	Dished	19cc	5/64x5/64x3/16	Call	360 & Mag 5.9L	Any
P5007731	Cast	4.060"	4.000"	6.123"	0.984"	1.412"	Dished	19cc	5/64x5/64x3/16	Call	340 & R3	Any
P5007412	Forged	4.000"	4.000"	6.123"	0.984"	1.418"	Flat Top	5cc	1/16x1/16x3/16	Call	360 & Mag 5.9L	Any
P5007413	Forged	4.030"	4.000"	6.123"	0.984"	1.418"	Flat Top	5cc	1/16x1/16x3/16	Call	360 & Mag 5.9L	Any
P5007414	Forged	4.060"	4.000"	6.123"	0.984"	1.418"	Flat Top	5cc	1/16x1/16x3/16	Call	340 & R3	Any
Probe Industries												
13746-030	Forged	4.030"	4.000"	6.125"	0.984"	1.460"	Flat Top	5.5cc	1/16x1/16x3/16	599g	360 & Mag 5.9L	Any
13746-040	Forged	4.040"	4.000"	6.125"	0.984"	1.460"	Flat Top	5.5cc	1/16x1/16x3/16	605g	360 & Mag 5.9L	Any
13744-030	Forged	4.030"	4.000"	6.125"	0.984"	1.460"	"D" Dish	17.5cc	1/16x1/16x3/16	593g	360 & Mag 5.9L	Any
13744-040	Forged	4.040"	4.000"	6.125"	0.984"	1.460"	"D" Dish	17.5cc	1/16x1/16x3/16	605g	360 & Mag 5.9L	Any
Ross												
99789	Forged	4.030"	4.000"	6.123"	0.984"	1.459"	Flat Top	3cc	1/16x1/16x3/16	607g	360 & Mag 5.9L	Any
99788	Forged	4.070"	4.000"	6.123"	0.984"	1.459"	Flat Top	4.2cc	1/16x1/16x3/16	615g	340 & R3	Any
99787	Forged	4.030"	4.000"	6.123"	0.984"	1.459"	Domed	-21cc	1/16x1/16x3/16	598g	360 & Mag 5.9L	Any
99786	Forged	4.070"	4.000"	6.123"	0.984"	1.459"	Domed	-21cc	1/16x1/16x3/16	608g	340 & R3	Any
Wiseco												
PT060H3	Forged	4.030"	4.000"	6.123"	0.984"	1.460"	Flat Top	5cc	1/16x1/16x3/16	Call	360 & Mag 5.9L	Any
PT060H4	Forged	4.040"	4.000"	6.123"	0.984"	1.460"	Flat Top	5cc	1/16x1/16x3/16	Call	340 & R3	Any
PT060H6	Forged	4.060"	4.000"	6.123"	0.984"	1.460"	Flat Top	5cc	1/16x1/16x3/16	Call	340 & R3	Any
PT060H7	Forged	4.070"	4.000"	6.123"	0.984"	1.460"	Flat Top	5cc	1/16x1/16x3/16	Call	340 & R3	Any
PT036H3	Forged	4.030"	4.000"	6.123"	0.984"	1.460"	Dished	20cc	1/16x1/16x3/16	Call	360 & Mag 5.9L	Any
PT036H4	Forged	4.040"	4.000"	6.123"	0.984"	1.460"	Dished	20cc	1/16x1/16x3/16	Call	340 & R3	Any
PT036H6	Forged	4.060"	4.000"	6.123"	0.984"	1.460"	Dished	20cc	1/16x1/16x3/16	Call	340 & R3	Any
PT036H7	Forged	4.070"	4.000"	6.123"	0.984"	1.460"	Dished	20cc	1/16x1/16x3/16	Call	340 & R3	Any

Other Sources for Stroker Pistons:

Allied Motors	See Stroker Kits	Appendix A
CP Pistons	Custom order stroker pistons	
Flatlander Racing	See Stroker Kits	Appendix A
Mancini Racing	See Stroker Kits	Appendix A
Muscle Motors	See Stroker Kits	Appendix A
RPM Machine	See Stroker Kits	Appendix A
Speed-O-Motive	See Stroker Kits	Appendix A

to the GM engines, so only minor machining changes are needed to make Mopar stroker pistons. Most forged pistons cost about $60 to $80 each when custom ordered.

The piston manufacturer needs to know the desired compression height, compression ratio, valve angle, bore size, pin size, and stroke. Use a compression height that places the piston about 0.005" to 0.010" below the deck height on the block. The reason for this is that the machining tolerances on the rods, crank, block, and piston are likely to vary a few thousandths of an inch, and this could let the piston protrude above the deck on the block. It is much better to be on the short side than to allow the piston to stick slightly out of the block.

Dished, Flat Top, or Dome?

The shape of the top of the piston changes the compression ratio and the way the fuel mixture burns in the cylinder. The three basic types of piston shapes are dished, flat top, and domed.

Dished and flat-top pistons offer the best flame travel (efficient and quick combustion). Think of it this way: if you wanted to make a circular fire and burn fuel in the most efficient (quickest) manner, you would make a thin circular layer of fuel with most of the fuel in the center of the circle, and then start the fire in the middle of the circle. The fire would burn the fuel starting in the center and move outward toward the edges all at once. This is also the reason why many engines have the spark plug located in the center of the combustion chamber (i.e., Hemi® engines).

Flat-top pistons are lighter than domed or dished pistons since it takes less material to make them. The shape of the dish or dome also increases the surface area and runs slightly hotter than flat-top pistons. More surface area allows more heat buildup that must be transferred to the oil and cylinder bore walls to cool the piston.

Domed pistons increase compression but reduce the flame travel time and weigh more than flat-top pistons. A better way to increase the compression ratio without using a domed piston is to use a cylinder head with a smaller com-

Calulating Compression Ratio

The following formulas are used to calculate the static compression ratio of an engine.

Compression Ratio = (Swept Volume + TDC Volume) / TDC Volume
Swept Volume = (3.1416 x Bore Size x Bore Size x Stroke) / 4
TDC Volume = Combustion Chamber Volume + Gasket Volume + Deck Volume + Dish or Dome Volume
(**Note:** dome volume is normally a negative number)

Combustion Chamber Volume = Specs from manufacturer or measured volume
Gasket Volume = (3.1416 x Gasket Bore x Gasket Bore x Compressed Gasket Thickness) / 4
Deck Volume = (3.1416 x Bore Size x Bore Size x Deck Clearance)

Combustion chamber and dish or dome volume is normally published in cc's. Convert cc's to cubic inches by multiplying it by 0.061. Calculate all numbers in cubic inches (don't mix cc's and cubic inches in calculations).

Example:
Calculate the compression ratio of a 408-ci stroker small-block with Magnum R/T heads and KB pistons (#KB356). The 340 replacement block is used in this example (deck height of 9.595").

Bore Size:	4.030"
Stroke:	4.000"
Head Gasket:	0.040" compressed thickness with 4.080" gasket bore size
Compression Height:	1.465"
Piston Dish Volume:	23.5cc = (23.5 x 0.061) = 1.434ci
Cylinder Head Volume:	60cc = (60 x 0.061) = 3.660ci
Block Deck Height:	9.595"
Connecting Rod Length:	6.123"
Deck Clearance:	0.007" = 9.595" – (4.000/2) – 6.123" = 1.465"
Deck Volume	= (3.1416 x 4.030" x 4.030" x 0.007") / 4 = .089ci
Gasket Volume	= (3.1416 x 4.080" x 4.080" x 0.040") / 4 = .523ci
Swept Volume	= (3.1416 x 4.030" x 4.030" x 4.000") / 4 = 51.022ci
TDC Volume	= 3.660 + 1.434 + 0.089 + 0.523 = 5.706ci
Compression Ratio	= (51.022 + 5.706) / 5.706 = 9.942

The calculated compression ratio in this example is a little high for a street-driven stroker engine using unleaded pump gas with cast iron heads. The desired compression ratio should be 8.5 to 9.5:1 for use with regular unleaded gasoline and cast iron heads. Premium fuel would be required with this compression ratio when using cast iron heads.

Aluminum heads should use a little more compression ratio – about 9.5 to 10.5:1.

You have several options to reduce the compression ratio without major changes to the engine (i.e., thicker head gasket, larger gasket bore, machining piston notches or dish, or chamber machining on the cylinder head).

bustion chamber volume. Minor compression ratio changes can also be made by using thinner head gaskets with a smaller bore size just big enough to work. Custom head gaskets in different thicknesses and bore sizes are available from Cometic Gasket.

With most stroker engines, a flat-top or dished piston provides a high enough compression ratio. The longer stroke

Most HP pistons with full-floating pins use Spirolocks. These special locks take some practice to install, but they provide the best method to keep the piston pin from coming loose.

Dished Magnum pistons have an oval-shaped dish that sits just under the heart-shaped combustion chamber. This dish shape combined with the chamber on the head allows efficient burning of the air-to-fuel mixture.

allows high-compression ratios without the need for a heavier domed piston. Some dished pistons are designed with a special oval-shaped dish that fits directly under the closed combustion chamber on Magnum cylinder heads. This dish shape

provides efficient fuel burning and a reasonable compression ratio with smaller-volume closed chamber heads.

Valve Clearance

Most pistons need notches for valve clearance so the valves cannot contact the piston. Extra clearance is also needed so that the valve won't hit the piston if it has false motion or bounces off the cam. This false motion can occur when the valvetrain isn't working together correctly or if the engine is over revved.

In most cases, a 0.080" to 0.100" minimum valve-to-piston clearance is needed. Note that the angle of the valve notches must match the valve angle in the cylinder head. Most off-the-shelf Mopar pistons are made with notches that match the stock 18-degree valve angle. Some Mopar cylinder heads have a 15-degree valve angle, so modifications are needed to make the notch flatter. Most pistons probably have enough extra material to handle the 3-degree change with machining.

Most HP pistons have piston pin oilers. The KB piston on the right has an oil passage that leads from the oil scraper piston ring to the piston pin bore.

Thickness and weight of piston pins can vary and is often an easy way to make slight adjustments when balancing a stroker engine.

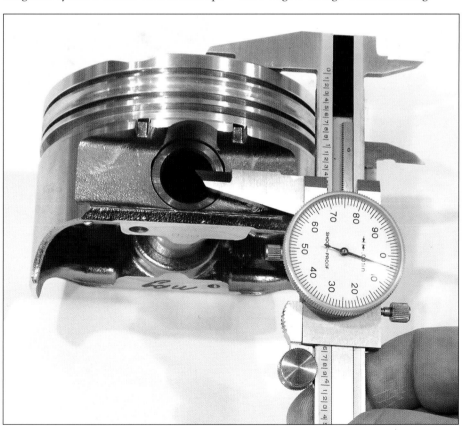

The compression height is the distance from the top outer edge of the piston to the centerline of the piston pin. The shortest recommended compression height is about 1.250", and this keeps the piston pin out of the piston rings.

Compression Height

Engine Block	Deck Height	Conn. Rod Length	Stroke	3.310" (340)	3.580" (360)	3.790"	4.000"	4.250"	4.500"
LA	9.585"	6.123"		1.807"	1.672"	1.567"	1.462"	1.337"	1.212"
Magnum	9.585"	6.123"		1.807"	1.672"	1.567"	1.462"	1.337"	1.212"
340 Replacement	9.595"	6.123"		1.817"	1.682"	1.577"	1.472"	1.347"	1.222"
R3	9.560"	6.123"		1.782"	1.647"	1.542"	1.437"	1.312"	1.187"

These numbers assume that everything has been machined perfectly to 0.001 of an inch. In the real world, machining tolerances on blocks, rods, pistons, and cranks can vary by +/- 0.010", so be conservative on the compression-height numbers. Additionally, used blocks may have been decked. This shortens up the deck height and reduces the compression height. It is best to reduce the compression height by at least 0.005" to 0.010" so that the piston does not stick out the top of the block (due to machining tolerance variations).

Remember that as the compression height gets shorter, the piston pin gets into the bottom (oil scraper) piston ring. At compression heights of about 1.250", the piston will not have much support where the pin goes through the side of the piston. Special support rings can be used to help support the oil scraper piston ring, but these require custom pistons. The special support rings increase the cost and weight of the piston.

Mopar small blocks are blessed with a tall deck height. Most stroker engines using a 4.000" stroke crank can keep the piston pin clear of the piston rings. This piston has a 1.412" compression height.

If the stock-style 18-degree valve notches are used with 15-degree heads and piston-to-valve contact occurs, the likely result is bent valves. The valves won't hit the piston squarely, so it pushes them to the side and bends them.

Compression Height

Compression height is the distance from the top edge of the piston to the centerline of the piston pin (excluding any raised dome). Compression height is reduced in a stroker engine so the piston doesn't come out the top of the bore with the longer stroke. Ideally, the compression height should not be reduced to the point where the piston pin interferes with the bottom piston ring. If the piston pin and ring are trying to use the same space, the rings won't have enough support and won't work very well. The minimum compression height without getting into the rings is about 1.250" on most Mopar pistons.

Piston Speed

Piston speed is the number of feet per minute that the piston travels. On stroker engines, the piston travels farther on each revolution of the crank since the stroke has been increased. As the RPM is increased, the piston also travels farther per minute.

The piston has limits on how far it can travel before it starts to hurt itself or wear out quickly. This is one of the reasons why stroker engines are not well suited for high-RPM operation.

The piston speed is calculated using the following formula:

Piston Speed (in Feet per Minute or FPM) = Stroke / 12 x 2 x RPM

Example:

Stroke =	4.000"
RPM =	6,500
Piston Speed (FPM)	= 4.000" / 12 x 2 x 6,500
	= 4,333 fpm

Listed below is the calculated piston speed for common Mopar small-block engines:

Displacement	340	360	408	476
Stroke	3.310"	3.580"	4.000"	4.250"
RPM	6,500	6,500	6,500	7,500
Piston Speed	3,586 fpm	3,878 fpm	4,333 fpm	5,313 fpm

Cast pistons work fine in most stroker engines with a piston speed up to about 4,400 fpm. Forged pistons should be used for any engine with a piston speed over 4,500 fpm. Very high-quality custom-made (expensive) forged or billet pistons are needed with any engine that has a piston speed over 5,000 fpm. Better material and very close tolerance machining is needed on engines with a high piston speed.

The best way to control the piston speed is by reducing the RPM. Most stroker engines make gobs of torque at a low RPM, so a high speed is not needed.

In order to allow shorter compression heights and decent ring seal, some piston manufacturers use a special support ring that goes into the oil ring groove under the piston ring. This situation should be avoided if possible since this extra steel ring adds weight to the piston and is one more thing that can go wrong.

Pistons with shorter compression heights also weigh less than ones with taller compression heights. Support for the piston pin takes less aluminum when it is closer to the top of the piston.

Weight

Magnum-style pistons, pins, and rings can reduce the reciprocating mass since they are lighter than LA style pistons. The weight of these component parts is shown in the LA vs. Magnum Pistons section of this chapter.

Flat-top pistons are lighter than domed or dished pistons since it takes less material to make them. The shape of the dish or dome also increases surface area and runs slightly hotter than flat-top pistons.

Rings

Most cast stroker pistons use 5/64", 5/64", 3/16" thick rings. These rings are the stock LA size and the same as used in production LA engines. Don't use stock Magnum rings with these pistons since the Magnum rings are about 0.018" thinner and won't seal. I have seen an engine built this way in error – it smoked and had excessive blow-by.

Most forged pistons use 1/16", 1/16", 3/16" thick rings. They are the most common size for use in HP engines. These thinner, lighter rings reduce drag and friction as the piston goes up and down. Since the piston is moving farther in a stroker engine, this reduction in drag can be significant.

Most production engines use cast-iron or ductile rings. These work fine in standard engines, but HP engines should use Moly rings. The Moly ring has a special coating in a groove on the edge where it contacts the cylinder bore. High-performance Moly rings are available from Speed-Pro (Federal Mogul), and Sealed Power (Dana).

These rings are the best choice for most HP stroker engines.

Some engine builders use newer low-tension rings in drag-racing applications. This reduces friction but may lead to detonation if too much oil is left on the cylinder bores. These rings are best suited for frequently serviced racing engines, and when long-term durability is not an issue. Most HP street and endurance stroker engines should not use low-tension rings.

Other racing engine builders use Total Seal piston rings. These rings have special two-piece top rings that reduce blow-by for higher engine output.

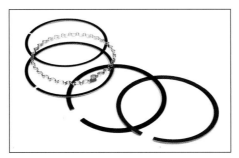

Most HP engines use Moly-coated piston rings. This Moly coating is on the edge of the piston rings where they rub on the bores.

These rings are very expensive and may cause higher than normal cylinder bore wear. Street stroker engines should not use these rings (use HP Moly rings).

The ring end gap is set to its manufacturer's recommendations. The bore honing must be done using the honing stones and process recommended by the manufacturer. They also specify bore-to-piston clearance. Each piston manufacturer has a specific place on the piston where the size is measured (see the instructions with each set of pistons).

Conclusion

Proper piston selection for your stroker engine is pretty involved since it must fit correctly, provide the proper compression ratio, and work with your cylinder heads. The piston must also be reliable and durable for the type of engine you want. This is one area in which buying a quality stroker kit can avoid mistakes, rework, or additional cost to modify the pistons. Make sure the pistons in the stroker kit work correctly with the rest of your engine (i.e., block, heads, and other parts).

The best way to measure piston ring end gap is to push the ring in the bore and square it up with a piston. Once in the bore, the end gap can be measured with a feeler gauge.

KB Pistons

Keith Black (KB) pistons are probably the most commonly used stroker pistons in small-block Mopar engines. KB sells hypereutectic and forged stroker pistons in various sizes and compression ratios. The forged pistons are a brand new offering from KB.

KB now offers stroker-forged pistons in addition to the hypereutectic cast pistons. These two pistons are KB744 (right) and KB745 (left). These pistons are for use with a 4.000" stroker crankshaft and are ideal for most stroker engines.

These three pistons are also new forged offerings from KB. These pistons are for the 360 stroke, and can be used in 340 blocks with a 360 (3.580" with 0.040" or 0.060" oversize) stroke. The only difference between the three is the compression ratio due to design of the dome. A 0.040" oversize 360 piston is the same bore diameter as the 340 (bore size of 4.040").

Some KB pistons like the one shown above have a step-dish design. KB says the step-dish design helps performance in three ways:

Faster flame travel
Forces fuel/air to the center of piston
Less of the piston exposed to heat
Reduced piston weight

This piston has a step-dish design, and in this case it sticks out past the top of the deck. This is OK as long as you have open-chamber cylinder heads since the stepped portion of the dome makes them work like a smaller closed-chamber design. I am not using open-chamber heads, so I need to modify these pistons.

The step-dish design makes an open chamber head work like it is a more modern closed chamber head by filling in a portion of the chamber at TDC. The step-dish pistons also have Attenuator Grooves or shallow pockets on each side of the valve notches. These pockets keep the piston away from the hottest area in the combustion chamber (next to the valves). The advantage of keeping the piston off the hot areas is that this keeps the piston cooler and makes the engine less prone to detonation.

This machining fixture from KB has all the parts necessary to allow modification of its pistons. The separate piece on the lower left corner is for use with KB-forged pistons. See the following photos to see how the fixture is used with hypereutectic pistons.

In some cases, the step-dome interferes with a closed chamber cylinder head, and must be machined for clearance. The best way to machine these pistons is with a special fixture available from KB. This piston fixture is reasonably priced and can be used in a mill or on a lathe.

The angled notches in the bottom part of the fixture are machined for common valve angles and are designed for cutting or modifying valve pockets with a mill. The fixture is installed in a vice and the valve pockets can be machined on a mill. The fixture has common 23-degree, 20-degree, 18-degree, and 15-degree angles that work with most common valve angles. The 15-degree angle is an easy way to modify stock-style 18-degree piston notches for use with 15-degree W2 or W9 heads.

This fixture has angled grooves at the bottom edge that can be used to modify or machine valve notches by mounting the fixture in a vise on a mill. The fixture has all the common valve angles for most engines (i.e., 23-degree, 20-degree, 18-degree, and 15-degree). Most Mopar heads have an 18-degree valve angle, but some like the W8 and W9 have a 15-degree angle. This fixture is an easy way to modify stock pistons for use with the 15-degree W9 valve angle.

Hypereutectic pistons are centered on the fixture using dowel pins. The dowel pin-holes are used in the production fixtures for KB hypereutectic pistons, so they are already there. The smaller hoop-and-cap screw is used to hold the piston in the fixture by the piston pin. KB-forged pistons use a different fixture attachment piece that sits on top of the dowel pins. Once assembled, the piston is firmly attached to the fixture and can be modified with machining.

The fixture is now mounted in a lathe and is ready for machining. In this operation, I reduced the height of the step to allow clearance to my heads. Use a diamond cutter if possible since the hypereutectic material is tough to machine. I used carbide, and the cutting bits got dull quickly.

Hypereutectic pistons are located on the fixture using dowel pins. The piston is held down on the fixture by the piston pin when the cap screw is tightened (mounted inside the fixture).

Here is what the piston looks like attached to the fixture. The upper portion of the fixture can rotate to allow use with splayed valve heads or complex angles. A small setscrew locks the rotation feature in place. This piston is now ready for machining in a lathe or mill.

The piston shown on the left is before any machining was done. The one of the right has the step machined away for clearance with the combustion chamber. This special KB fixture makes it really easy to machine pistons without damaging them.

This piston is machined on a lathe. The step-dome was too tall for use with the R3 block and Magnum R/T cylinder heads. The Magnum R/T heads have a closed combustion chamber and the R3 block has a shorter than stock (9.560") deck height. This combination allowed the piston to stick out of the deck by about 0.085".

The piston on the left is the stock KB356 with the step-dish design. The piston on the right has been modified to remove the stepped portion of the dome for use with Magnum closed chamber heads.

Mopar heads have so many different combustion chamber sizes and shapes that it is often difficult to get the perfect piston. A neat little fixture like this one makes it easy to modify the pistons to suit your stroker engine.

CAMSHAFTS

The camshaft is the brain that provides mechanical logic to control opening and closing of the valves. Minor changes in the cam grind can make or break engine performance since the timing, duration, lift control, and cylinder pressures dictate overall engine performance. When the camshaft does not work in harmony with the cylinder heads and intake manifold, the engine does not perform well. Bigger is not always better, since any camshaft change must be tailored to work with rest of the engine.

Production Cams

Most production engines came with hydraulic camshafts. The only engines that had a mechanical cam are the 1970 340 T/A Six-Pack cars (Trans-Am, Barracuda, and Challengers). In 1987, production cams changed from a flat tappet design to a hydraulic roller camshaft.

Cam Bearings

The two different types of camshaft bearings are Babbitt and roller bearings. Also, two different types of Babbitt cam bearing sets are available.

Most LA engines came with a hydraulic flat tappet camshaft.

1988 and later engines came with a hydraulic roller camshaft. These tappets use a dog bone for each pair of tappets that keeps them from turning.

The 59-degree tappet bore blocks use the stock-style Babbitt bearings. Each of the five bearings is a different diameter with the largest bearing in the front of the block and the smallest bearing in the back. The same cam bearings are also used on 59-degree R3 blocks and 340 replacement blocks.

59-degree tappet bore blocks can be used with almost any stock or aftermarket HP camshaft. These cams are made to the stock size.

All five cam bearings are the same diameter in the 48-degree tappet bore R3 blocks. With more room to fit the lobes through the bearings, the larger size on all five journals allows the use of a larger base circle on the camshaft. A larger base circle allows the tappets to follow the lobe better and also allows more aggressive cam grinds. All 48-degree R3 blocks recommended in this book are machined for use with Babbitt cam bearing set P4876372.

48-degree blocks have the tappets moved forward and back in the block to get them farther away from the intake ports. This allows the use of larger intake ports (and straightens out the pushrods), but also requires the use of special camshafts that have larger journals and lobes in the proper places. Most aftermarket camshafts don't fit the 48-degree blocks. The only supplier that sells camshafts made for the 48-degree blocks

Camshaft Types		
Engine Type	Model Years	Type of Camshaft
LA	1964-'87	Hydraulic Flat Tappet Camshaft
LA	1988-'92	Hydraulic Roller Tappet Camshaft
Magnum	1992-'03	Hydraulic Roller Tappet Camshaft

is COMP Cams. Mopar sells special Un-Ground Lobe (UGL) cam cores that must be custom ground to your specifications. The UGL is semi finished, so it does not have ground lobes. Mopar sells these UGL cam cores under part numbers P4876633 (for roller tappets), and P4876634 (for flat tappets). These two camshaft cores are for use with Babbitt bearing set P4876372.

Some HP engines use roller camshaft bearings. These bearings have a metal housing that keeps all the rollers inside the bearing. Custom-made tools are required to install these bearings without damaging them.

Most used R3 blocks and all-aluminum blocks are machined for use with 50-mm roller camshaft bearings. These roller cam bearings are more expensive and require the use of special UGL cam cores that have the proper size journal for

Some machine shops can coat the cam bearings for extra protection. Automotive Machine in Fraser, Michigan coated this cam bearing.

the roller bearings. These blocks use roller cam bearing set P4876707 and UGL cam cores P5007134 (lightweight) or P5007932. Both cam cores are for use with roller tappets only.

Care must be taken to select the proper cam bearings and camshaft for each engine block. This is pretty confusing since there are so many variables with different cams, cam bearings, and types of blocks. The chart listed below shows which camshaft and cam bearings should be used with each block. Also, be sure you select and use the cylinder heads that are designed for the block (i.e., 59-degree or 48-degree tappet bore).

You are probably wondering why 48-degree R3s and aluminum blocks use larger camshaft bearings. The first reason is that the camshaft can twist

while the engine is running. The second reason is that a larger base circle can be used with more room to get it through the bearings (when installing it in the block). A larger diameter camshaft with larger bearings resists twisting for more stable valve operation and ignition timing.

Cam Drive

Mopar small-block engines have a relatively long timing chain. The spacing between the centerline of the camshaft and crankshaft is 6.125". The chain is long because the camshaft is mounted high in the block, and this leaves much more room for connecting rod clearance on stroker engines. The connecting rods do not even come close to the cam on most Mopar stroker small blocks. Most other (GM & Ford) small-block stroker engines have major problems in this area and may require the use of special blocks that have the camshaft moved upward.

Most stroker engines use a high-quality timing set. Gear-drive and belt-drive setups are also available, but they are normally only used in racing applications. Gear-drive systems are available from Mopar, Milodon, and other sources. Belt-drive systems are available from Jesel and require a special timing cover to keep the belt dry (out of the oil).

Cam Bearing and Camshaft Selection

Block Part Number	Description	Tappet Angle	Roller Cam Bearing Set	Babbitt Cam Bearing Set	Roller Tappet Camshaft UGL	Flat Tappet Camshaft UGL
Production	Prod. LA 273/318/340/360	59 degree	N/A	Std LA	Std LA	Std LA
Production	Magnum 5.2L/5.9L	59 degree	N/A	Std LA	Std Magnum	Std LA or Magnum
P5007552	340 Block Replacement	59 degree	N/A	Std LA	Not Recom.	Std LA
P4876791AC	R3 Block	59 degree	N/A	Std LA	Not Recom.	Std LA
P4876792AC	R3 Block	59 degree	N/A	Std LA	Not Recom.	Std LA
P4876793AC	R3 Block	59 degree	N/A	Std LA	Not Recom.	Std LA
P4876671AC	R3 Block	48 degree	N/A	P4876372	P4876633	P4876634
P4876672AC	R3 Block	48 degree	N/A	P4876372	P4876633	P4876634
P4876673AC	R3 Block	48 degree	N/A	P4876372	P4876633	P4876634
P4876674AC	R3 Block	48 degree	N/A	P4876372	P4876633	P4876634
P5007580	Alum. A Block	48 degree	P4876707	N/A	P5007134	N/A
P5007581	Alum. A Block	48 degree	P4876707	N/A	P5007134	N/A
P5007582	Alum. A Block	48 degree	P4876707	N/A	P5007134	N/A

All small-block Mopar engines have a relatively long timing chain since the camshaft is located high in the block. The high camshaft location provides more room for longer strokes without the rods hitting the camshaft.

Timing Chain Tensioner

The extra length of the timing chain presents more opportunity for problems. I have seen a large number of used engines with timing chain problems (i.e., broken chain, loose chain, and timing gears that have slipped a tooth). The best insurance to prevent these problems is to install a high-quality timing set and use a timing chain tensioner. The tensioner keeps slack out of the timing chain as it wears. Even if the chain fits well when the engine is new, it often becomes loose as the timing chain is subjected to normal wear.

A timing chain tensioner is recommended for all stroker engines. It is used instead of the camshaft thrust plate (right). A fourth mounting hole can be drilled in the tensioner if desired (use the stock thrust plate as a template to mark and drill the extra hole). This tensioner takes up the extra slack as the timing chain wears.

Don't remove the wire-retaining pin until the timing chain is installed. If the wire-retaining pin is removed, it is difficult to get the timing chain installed.

Timing chain tensioner P5007709 is used instead of the thrust plate. This tensioner was originally developed for Magnum V-6 engines (used in production), but it fits all small-block LA and Magnum engines (1964-'03).

HP Thrust Plate

Diamond Racing makes a special thrust plate with needle roller bearings to cushion the thrust forces. The part number is Diamond #03-6160 – it includes the thrust plate and two sets of needle-thrust bearings and fasteners. This special thrust plate requires some machining and modifications to the timing set gear.

Fuel Pump Eccentric

The fuel pump eccentric bolts onto the front of the camshaft over the top of the timing gear. The same bolt that holds the timing gear holds the eccentric. All LA camshafts have enough room on the front snout to install the fuel pump eccentric. The hydraulic roller tappet camshafts used on production engines have a shorter snout that does not allow use of a fuel pump eccentric.

Some HP hydraulic roller camshafts are made with the longer snout that allows the use of a mechanical fuel pump. These camshafts must be used with an LA timing cover that has provisions for the fuel pump. Mopar camshafts P5249663, P4876348, and P5007547 are hydraulic roller camshafts made with the longer snout. These hydraulic roller camshafts are used with the fuel pump

Stock LA camshafts have a snout that is about 1.100" long from the edge of the first journal to the front end of the camshaft. This style camshaft is designed for use with a fuel pump eccentric.

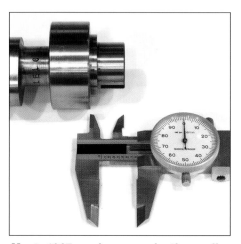

Most 1987 and up production roller cams are designed for fuel injection and have a shorter snout (about 0.800" long). These cams are designed for use without the fuel pump eccentric.

eccentric. See a Mopar Performance catalog or look on the web for detailed specifications on these camshafts.

If you have a camshaft made with the shorter snout, but you want to run a mechanical fuel pump, you can add a special extension that allows use of the fuel pump eccentric. This part is available from Hughes Engines, part number 7013.

The recommended fuel pump eccentric is P4120484. This eccentric is Moly coated for improved wear and should be used in all HP engines. An oil-squirter hole should be drilled in one of the front oil galley plugs to provide additional oiling. See Chapter 5 for more details on this oiling modification.

If you want to use a mechanical fuel pump and short-snout camshaft, you can use a special extension available from Hughes Engines #7013. This extension and special key allow the use of an LA fuel pump eccentric. The LA front cover must also be used so that you have a place to mount the fuel pump.

Problems with Flat Tappet Camshafts

Many problems with camshafts in LA and other engines have popped up over the past several years. Most problems result in lobes being worn away shortly after installation of a new camshaft. This occurs due to three common problems.

First, flat tappet camshafts for the small-block Mopar went out of production in 1987. Most people who sell cams use the same cast camshaft blanks from the same sources. These camshaft blanks are then ground to the their specifications. Material hardness on the camshaft cores is often too soft, and this causes accelerated wear on one or more lobes at initial start-up of an engine with a new camshaft. The hardness specification for cams is pretty tough to achieve. The tooling used to make and heat treat these

Here is another view of what the extension looks like when added to the front of the cam. The special key interlocks into the timing gear and mounting washer.

camshafts is out of date and worn out. Most people who knew how to make and harden these cam cores have retired.

The second major problem is that many used blocks are worn and don't have good lifter bores anymore. Used 340 blocks are now over 30 years old and pretty worn out. Used 360 blocks that came with flat tappet camshafts are at least 17 years old, with the oldest ones being 33 years old. These older blocks may not have straight tappet bores that are the proper size anymore. In instances with lifter bore (i.e., taper or excessive wear) or camshaft machining problems, the tappets don't rotate as the camshaft turns. When the tappet doesn't rotate, it wears away the lobe on the camshaft.

The third major problem is that many camshaft lubes have an oil-like consistency and may drip off the camshaft prior to initial startup. This is usually a problem when the engine is stored for too long before it is started for the first time. The best camshaft lubes have a grease-like consistency so they don't drip off the cam, even after an extended time.

Stroker Cams

As the stroker engine gets larger, it requires a slight increase in cam duration due to the larger displacement. For each increase in engine size of 25 to 30 cubic inches, the cam should increase duration by about four to six degrees. For example, if the desired small-block 360 Mopar cam with 220 degrees duration has the desired idle quality and performance, you can step up to a 224 or 228 degree cam in a 402- to 418-inch engine (and get about the same performance quality).

Stroker Cam Duration

Stroker Engine Size	Recommended Extra Duration
402 to 418ci	6-8 degrees
419 to 440ci	8-12 degrees
441 to 476ci	12-16 degrees

The lift is more a factor of cylinder head airflow and camshaft type. Most hydraulic flat tappet cams are used for lift up to 0.550". Mechanical flat tappet cams

are used for lift from 0.500" to 0.625". Roller mechanical cams are normally used for lifts from 0.575" to 0.750".

The lift numbers must be in a usable range with the cylinder head airflow. For example, Magnum heads flow pretty well up to about 0.500" to 0.550" before airflow stalls, so it makes no sense to run any more lift than this unless the heads are ported to flow more air at higher valve lift. W9 heads flow very well up to 0.650" to 0.700", so these heads could use a camshaft that has more lift.

Roller Tappets on R3 Blocks

Roller camshafts are <u>not</u> recommended for use on 59-degree tappet R3 and 340 replacement blocks. The problem is that the tie bar on most roller tappet cams hits the outer wall of the block, leaving no room to grind for clearance. The tie bar cannot be turned around the other way or it gets in the way of the pushrods. If you grind in this area, you hit the water jacket and ruin the block. See Chapter 10 for more details. Clearance is not a problem with 48-degree tappet R3 blocks since the tie bar is located farther away from the wall of the block (in the valley).

Aluminum Blocks

The aluminum A block must use a special gear-drive set and aluminum timing cover. The stock timing set won't fit since there is not enough room inside the timing-cover area.

The aluminum block must also be used with 50-mm roller camshaft bearings. These roller bearings are larger than the stock size, so Babbitt bearings won't fit. These special parts make the aluminum-block stroker engine more expensive to build. These parts are designed for use in high-dollar racing engines.

Used R3 Blocks

Most used R3 race blocks are machined for use with 50-mm roller cam bearings. Once the cam bores are opened up for use with the larger 50-mm bearings, the stock Babbitt bearings

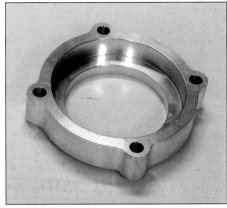

This special seal retainer is needed on the aluminum block to install the damper oil seal. This retainer bolts to the front timing cover.

Aluminum blocks have a different shape for the front cover, and cannot be used with a timing chain/gear set. The front cover does not have enough room on the inside to install a standard timing gear/chain set.

The only option for driving the cam on the aluminum block is a gear drive set. This special gear drive set is expensive and quite noisy. This gear drive set has provisions to drive a dry sump pump off the camshaft and a water pump off the crank.

The aluminum block front timing cover comes with the gear drive set, and is made from billet aluminum.

Cam Recommendations

Magnum Heads

The exhaust port flow on the Magnum heads is not as good as on LA heads. Engines with Magnum heads need slightly more lift and duration on the exhaust for best performance. The exhaust grind on the camshaft should have an extra 4-8 degrees duration and 0.010" to 0.030" extra lift than the intake to help performance with the reduced exhaust port flow.

Some examples of camshafts that work well with the Magnum heads are listed below.

Magnum heads also respond to larger headers since this helps scavenge the exhaust ports. Engines with Magnum heads should use 1-7/8" headers whenever possible.

W9 Heads

W9 heads have great exhaust ports, and they usually pick up HP and torque by reducing the duration and lift on the exhaust (use slightly less than the intake). Most engine builders have picked up about 10 hp and 15 ft-lbs of torque by using four to eight degrees less duration on the exhaust cam grind. These heads don't need as much overlap, and too much reduces the cylinder pressures.

W9 heads work well with any size headers since the exhaust port is so efficient. Even small 1-5/8" headers don't hurt performance and increase the port velocity. In testing, I have found a slight increase in performance by going from 1-7/8" to 1-5/8" headers (without any porting on the heads).

Most camshafts have oiling holes that allow oil flow to the heads only when the holes are lined up (with standard LA oiling). These holes restrict the amount of oil that gets to the heads.

Some camshafts have a groove around the cam bearing journals that provide a constant flow of oil to the heads (with standard LA oiling). This is the best way to ensure proper lubrication of the valvetrain in the heads.

Part Number	Source	Duration	Lift	Cam Type
P4876348	Mopar	230/234 degrees @ .050"	0.501"/0.513"	Hyd. Roller
693801	Crane	222/234 degrees @ .050"	0.467"/0.494"	Hyd. Flat Tappet

won't fit anymore (the holes are too large).

Conclusion

The camshaft must be selected to operate in harmony with the cylinder heads and intake manifold within the RPM that provides usable power for your stroker engine. Get advice from a camshaft expert to make sure the desired cam works with your engine package and vehicle. Most cam suppliers have a tech department that can make recommendations based on your input.

Some racing engines use a billet camshaft rear plug when using the larger 50- or 60-mm roller cam bearings. The stock rear cam plug won't fit when the larger cam bearings are used.

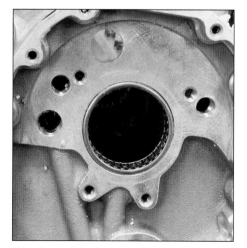

Aluminum blocks must be used with 50-mm roller cam bearings. Babbitt bearings won't fit in these blocks since the roller bearing size is larger than the Babbitt size (thicker bearings).

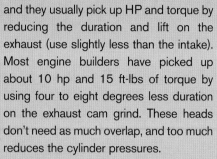

Most camshafts come with a camshaft card that provides the specifications for the cam. This card has recommended spring pressures and other information needed to install the camshaft.

CYLINDER HEADS

Cylinder heads are one of the keys to great performance on any stroker engine. The large-displacement stroker engine demands very good cylinder head airflow to make big power. But great-flowing heads only work when they are used with the other components designed to work together (i.e., camshaft, intake manifold, and headers).

Iron vs. Aluminum

The choice between cast-iron and aluminum heads is based on cost and weight. High-performance iron and aluminum heads are readily available and they both offer great performance in stroker engines.

Aluminum heads reduce the weight of the engine by about 50 lbs. Most aluminum heads are more expensive than iron heads. Aluminum heads are also easier to fix if they ever become cracked and need to be welded.

Cast-iron heads don't transfer as much heat from combustion to the coolant, making them slightly more efficient. This is the reason why engines with aluminum heads generally use a slightly higher compression ratio than a similar engine with iron heads. For example, an engine with iron heads should use a 9:1 compression ratio on pump gas, where the same engine can run 10:1 compression with aluminum heads. Combustion and heat are the way fuel is transferred into mechanical power.

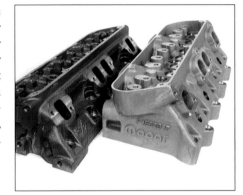

Wide varieties of heads are available today, including aluminum and cast-iron.

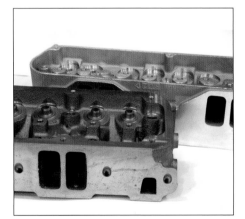

Note the difference in the size of the intake ports on these two heads. The R/T in the front has ports much lower than the raised ports in the W9 (back). No bump in the port for the W9 exists since the pushrods have been moved away from the port.

Valve Angle

All production LA and Magnum heads have an 18-degree valve angle. This valve angle is lower than most other cylinder heads for small-block engines (i.e., most GM heads are 23 degree). In general, when the valve is stood up or made closer to a zero angle, airflow is improved. The fuel and air mixture does not have to turn as sharply when entering the engine through the intake port, and this helps flow.

Most high-performance cylinder heads for Mopar engines also use the 18-degree valve angle. The only ones that have a slightly better valve angle are some versions of the W2 and all W7, W8, and W9 cylinder heads. These heads use a 15-degree valve angle for better airflow. The 15-degree heads are also designed for use with 48-degree tappet bore blocks. One version of the standard W9 and the W9-RP (raised port heads) use a 13-degree valve angle. See Chapter 3 for more information on 48-degree tappet bore blocks.

When the valve angle is changed from the stock 18-degree, the notches in the pistons must be machined to match that valve angle. If the piston machining is not changed, any valve contact with the piston bends the valves since they won't hit square in the notch. Granted, the valves should never touch the piston, but it can happen if the engine is over revved and valve float occurs.

LA Heads vs. Magnum Heads

What are the major differences and similarities between LA and Magnum cylinder heads?

Similarities:

- Same cylinder head bolt pattern (4-bolt)
- Same valve spacing and valve window
- Same 18-degree valve angle
- Same intake port location (very minor differences in port size & shape)
- Same exhaust flange bolt pattern
- Same type of spark plugs
- Same water outlets - on each end of the cylinder head

Differences:

Engine:	LA	Magnum
Model Years:	1971-1992	1993-2002
Engine Size:	360/340	5.2L/5.9L
Valve Cover Shape	Curved at Ends	Square at Ends
Valve Cover Bolt Pattern	5-bolt	10-bolt
Valve Stem Size	3/8"	8mm
Intake Screw Angle	Standard	Vertical
Rocker Arm / Valvespring Oiling	Through Block/Heads	Hollow Pushrods
Rocker Arm Type	Shaft Mounted	Stud Mounted
Intake Valve Sizes	1.880"/2.020"	1.920"
Exhaust Valve Sizes	1.600"	1.625"
Combustion Chamber	Open	Closed
Combustion Chamber Size	70cc	60cc
Approximate Intake Airflow	160 cfm	190 cfm
Exhaust Heat Crossover	Center of Head	None
Coolant Heat Crossover	Center of Head	None
Accessory Mounting Holes – end of head	3-bolt	5-bolt

The Magnum head (right) has the same three holes as the LA head (left), and has two extra holes for mounting accessories. The only difference is that the holes in the LA head (far left side of photo) are spaced about 5/8" farther back. When changing to Magnum heads, spacers, and bolts for mounting, accessories need minor adjustments to handle this change.

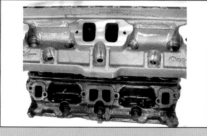

The Magnum R/T head (top) has less restrictive exhaust ports than the LA head (bottom). The exhaust bolt pattern is the same. Cast-iron manifolds may require port matching to allow better flow when Magnum heads are used with LA manifolds.

Magnum heads (left) use individual rocker arms mounted by one bolt per rocker arm. LA heads (right) use rocker arms mounted on a rocker shaft.

The Magnum head (left) has a smaller 60cc closed chamber than the LA head (right) with its 70cc open chamber.

The Magnum head (left) has intake ports and water passages in about the same place as LA heads (right).

Valve Spacing

Most Mopar cylinder heads have 1.870" between the centerline of the valves in each cylinder. This spacing allows maximum valve sizes of up to about 2.080" on the intake valve with 1.600" exhaust valves. Any valves larger than this require offset valve guides or the reduction in size of either the intake or exhaust valve.

W7, W8, and W9 heads have spacing of 1.936" between the valves. This extra room allows much more room for larger valves. It also allows up to 2.200" intake and 1.600" exhaust valves. These larger valves allow the extra airflow to feed a very large stroker engine. Most engines over 420 cubes need large valves to flow enough air to make good power. Think of it this way: if your stroker engine has big-block sized cubic inches, then you need big-block sized valves (i.e., 2.100" to 2.200" intake valves).

Ports & Chambers

The most important area on any cylinder head is the intake and exhaust ports and chamber. The shape and design of the ports control how the air/fuel mixture and combustion performs as it goes into and exits the cylinder.

Most manufacturers publish port volumes to give an idea of the size of the ports on a cylinder head. This data provides some information, but the cross-sectional area (width of the port) is also an important factor. Don't compare Mopar heads with GM or other heads by port volume, since the length of the ports are not the same. For example, a longer port has more volume, but it isn't really any larger. Also, remember that different Mopar heads have different port lengths, and they don't have the intake surface in the same place relative to the bore on all heads. Due to these changes, you cannot directly compare Mopar heads with port volume since the port length is not always the same.

Flow

Most stock production heads flow about 160 to 190 cfm on the intake port. High-performance heads offer intake flow from about 200 to 300 cfm "as cast," or more with porting.

LA vs. Magnum Valve Spacing

Most Mopar cylinder heads have 1.870" between the centerline of the valves for each cylinder. This works well for most heads but limits valve sizes to about 2.080" on the intake and 1.600" on the exhaust. To use larger valves, the valves must be spaced farther apart.

Sometimes the valves can be used with offset valve guides to allow more room for a larger intake valve. Often the exhaust valve is reduced in size to allow a larger intake valve. These changes may help, but they may cause other problems since the valve is no longer located in the center of the port. Reduction in the size of the exhaust valve may cause an imbalance in flow since the exhaust valve may get too small for balanced intake to exhaust flow.

Large-displacement stroker engines should use large valves that flow enough air to make optimum performance. Any engine with over 420ci should use 2.100", 2.150", 2.180", or 2.200" intake valves, and cylinder heads with large ports that flow enough air to support the large engine. The best choices for big-inch stroker engines are W9, Indy, and Brodix heads.

The valve spacing in the W9 cylinder heads allows the use of large valves. This head has 2.150" intake and 1.600" exhaust valve. The valves are spaced 0.066" farther apart than in most Mopar heads, and this allows more room for larger valves.

Valve Spacing by Cylinder Head:

Cylinder Head	Valve Spacing	Largest Valve Size (intake/exhaust)	Space Between Valves
Prod. LA Heads	1.870"	2.080" / 1.600"	0.030"
Prod. Magnum Heads	1.870"	2.020" / 1.625"	0.048"
Aluminum Magnum Heads	1.870"	2.020" / 1.625"	0.048"
R/T Heads	1.870"	2.020" / 1.625"	0.048"
W2 Heads	1.870"	2.080" / 1.600"	0.030"
W7 Heads	1.936"	2.200" / 1.600"	0.046"
W8 Heads	1.936"	2.200" / 1.600"	0.046"
W9 Heads	1.936"	2.200" / 1.600"	0.046"
Edelbrock Heads	1.870"	2.020" / 1.600"	0.060"
Brodix B1BA & SP MO	1.870"	2.080" / 1.600"	0.030"
Indy Heads	1.870"	2.100" / 1.650"	offset guides

Cylinder Heads

LA Cylinder Heads (use w/ 59-degree tappet bore blocks only)

Cylinder Head Part Number	Material	Chamber Size (approx)	Intake Volume/ Shape	Tappet Angle	Valve Size	Valve Angle	Valve Stem	Intake Screws	Valve Cover	Rocker Arm	Casting Number	4/6 Head Bolts
Production LA												
LA 273/318	Cast Iron	70cc	NA/Rect.	59 deg	1.780"/1.500"	18 deg	3/8"	Std	5-bolt	Std-Shaft	Various	4-bolt
LA 340	Cast Iron	70cc	NA/Rect.	59 deg	2.020"/1.600"	18 deg	3/8"	Std	5-bolt	Std-Shaft	Various	4-bolt
LA 360	Cast Iron	70cc	166cc/Rect.	59 deg	1.880"/1.600"	18 deg	3/8"	Std	5-bolt	Std-Shaft	Various	4-bolt
Commando												
P4876785	Aluminum	54cc	177cc/Rect.	59 deg	2.020"/1.600"	18 deg	3/8"	Std	5-bolt	Std-Shaft	P4532900	4-bolt
P4876310	Aluminum	50cc	188cc/Lg. Rect.	59 deg	2.020"/1.600"	18 deg	3/8"	Std	5-bolt	W2	P4532795	4-bolt
LA Replacement												
R/T P5007950	Cast Iron	60cc	180cc/Rect.	59 deg	2.020"/1.625"	18 deg	8mm	Std	10-bolt	Stud	P4532140	4-bolt
W2												
P4529994/995	Cast Iron	70cc	185cc/Oval W2	59 deg	2.020"/1.600"	18 deg	3/8"	W2	5-bolt	Econo-W2	P4532693	4-bolt
P5007355	Cast Iron	68cc	189cc/Oval W2	59 deg	2.020"/1.600"	18 deg	3/8"	W2	5-bolt	T&D-W2	P4532693	4-bolt
P5007769	Cast Iron	65cc	180cc/Oval W2	59 deg	2.020"/1.600"	18 deg	3/8"	W2	5-bolt	T&D-W2	P4532693	4-bolt
W9												
P4510324	Aluminum	60cc	200cc/Rect. W9	59 deg	2.150"/1.600"	15 deg	3/8"	W9	5-bolt	T&D-W9	P4532847	4-bolt
Edelbrock												
60769/60779	Aluminum	63cc	171cc/Rect.	59 deg	2.020"/1.600"	18 deg	11/32"	Std	5-bolt	Std-Shaft	NA	4-bolt
60199/60179	Aluminum	65cc	171cc/Rect.	59 deg	2.020"/1.600"	18 deg	11/32"	Std	5-bolt	Std-Shaft	NA	4-bolt
Brodix												
B1 BA	Aluminum	65cc	195cc/Lg. Rect.	59 deg	2.080"/1.600"	18 deg	11/32"	Std	5-bolt	Std-Shaft	B1 BA	4-bolt
B1 BA MC	Aluminum	67cc	239cc/Lg. Rect.	59 deg	2.150"/1.600"	18 deg	11/32"	W5/W7	5-bolt	T&D-Shaft	B1 BA MC	4-bolt
SP MO	Aluminum	67cc	192cc/Lg. Rect.	59 deg	2.080"/1.600"	18 deg	11/32"	Std	5-bolt	T&D-Shaft	NA	4-bolt
Indy												
360-1	Aluminum	63cc	210cc/Lg. Rect.	59 deg	2.100"/1.650"	18 deg	11/32"	Indy	5-bolt	Indy	NA	6-bolt
360-2	Aluminum	63cc	180cc/Oval W2	59 deg	2.100"/1.650"	18 deg	11/32"	W2	5-bolt	Jesel	NA	6-bolt

Magnum Cylinder Heads (use w/ 59-degree tappet bore blocks only)

Cylinder Head Part Number	Material	Chamber Size (approx)	Intake Volume/ Shape	Tappet Angle	Valve Size	Valve Angle	Valve Stem	Intake Screws	Valve Cover	Rocker Arm	Casting Number	4/6 Head Bolts
Production Magnum												
5.2L/5.9L	Cast Iron	60cc	153cc/Rect.	59 deg	1.920"/1.625"	18 deg	8mm	Vertical	10-bolt	Stud	Various	4-bolt
Magnum R/T												
P5007140/145	Cast Iron	60cc	180cc/Rect.	59 deg	1.920"/1.625"	18 deg	8mm	Vertical	10-bolt	Stud	P4532140	4-bolt
P5007141	Cast Iron	60cc	180cc/Rect.	59 deg	2.020"/1.625"	18 deg	8mm	Vertical	10-bolt	Stud	P4532140	4-bolt
P5007950	Cast Iron	60cc	180cc/Rect.	59 deg	2.020"/1.625"	18 deg	8mm	Std	10-bolt	Stud	P4532140	4-bolt
Aluminum Magnum												
P4876624	Aluminum	53cc	177cc/Rect.	59 deg	1.920"/1.625"	18 deg	8mm	Vertical	10-bolt	Stud	P4532900	4-bolt
Pro Topline												
Pro-Topline	Cast Iron	60cc	NA/Rect.	59 deg	1.920"/1.625"	18 deg	8mm	Vertical	10-bolt	Stud	NA	4-bolt
Edelbrock Magnum												
61769/61779	Aluminum	58cc	176cc/Rect.	59 deg.	2.020"/1.600"	18 deg	11/32"	Vertical	10-bolt	Stud	NA	4-bolt

LA Cylinder Heads (use w/ 48-degree tappet bore blocks only)

Cylinder Head Part Number	Material	Chamber Size (approx)	Intake Volume/ Shape	Tappet Angle	Valve Size	Valve Angle	Valve Stem	Intake Screws	Valve Cover	Rocker Arms	Casting Number	4/6 Head Bolts
W2												
P5007445AB	Cast Iron	65cc	191cc/Oval W2	48 deg	2.020"/1.600"	15 deg	3/8"	W2	5-bolt	T&D-W2	P4532693	4-bolt
P5007708AB	Cast Iron	47cc	185cc/Oval W2	48 deg	2.020"/1.600"	15 deg	3/8"	W2	5-bolt	T&D-W2	P4532693	4-bolt
W8												
P4876281	Aluminum	(req. mach)	(req. mach)	48 deg	(not mach)	15 deg	11/32"	W7/W9	W8	T&D-W8	P4876281	6-bolt
W9												
P5007065AB	Aluminum	62cc	200cc/Rect. W9	48 deg	(not mach)	15 deg	11/32"	W7/W9	5-bolt	T&D-W9	P4532847	6-bolt

The general rule of the thumb regarding airflow is that the engine has the potential to make about 2 hp for each CFM of intake airflow. The other component parts of the engine must be working in harmony to get this output, but it gives a good idea of what the potential output could be. So a cylinder head that flows 200 cfm may make about 400 hp, and one with 300 cfm may make about 600 hp.

The camshaft must be designed to complement the airflow performance of the cylinder heads. For example, most Magnum heads flow pretty good up to about 0.550" valve lift. The desired valve lift to work with these heads should probably be in the range of 0.475" to 0.525" to perform properly with these heads. A camshaft with valves opened to 0.600" or more would not work well since the heads cannot flow in this lift range.

Study the manufacturer's flow data and consider getting additional data from a second independent source if possible. Remember, not all flow benches work the same way or provide consistent data. Many flow benches are homemade and don't correlate with other benches. Sometimes the test procedures are also different, and some give higher numbers based on the procedure changes.

Cylinder Head Selection

Mopar LA Cylinder Heads

The specifications for these heads are shown in the chart listed above. Notes on the special features and comments are shown for each head below. Be sure to select a cylinder head that works with the tappet angle of your block. The tappet angle is shown below in parentheses after each cylinder head (in the heading).

LA Production Heads – Cast Iron (59 degree blocks): 273 and 318 heads have very small ports and small valves. These heads don't offer much performance potential and should not be used on a stroker engine.

340 and 360 LA heads have larger intake ports and are the only production LA heads worth using on a stroker engine. 340 heads have a larger intake valve with a 2.020" size. 360 heads use a 1.880" intake valve, but they can be remachined for use with 2.020" valves.

LA heads cannot be used on Magnum blocks since there is no oil passage to feed up through the block to the heads. This oil passage can be drilled in a Magnum block, but this must be done by an experienced machinist.

With some porting work, LA heads work well on most stroker engines up to about 418ci. LA heads are probably the least expensive heads out there, but they are only available used at this time. Mopar previously sold these heads, but they have now sold out of them and can't get any more.

W2 – Cast Iron (different versions for 48 and 59 degree blocks): W2 cylinder heads flow the most air of any iron Mopar cylinder head (about 260-265 cfm on the intake port). The most unique feature of the W2 heads is the oval-shaped intake port. The intake ports are raised and must be used with special W2 intake manifolds that have the oval ports. The bolt pattern on the W2 is also spaced out farther from the ports, and is not the same as standard LA intakes.

These heads are best suited for oval-track racing and drag racing. The valve gear is pretty expensive, since T&D rocker arms are required for most W2 heads made since 1/10/02. Early heads are prone to cracking when milled too thin, but changes made in about 1998 added ribs that made the heads stronger.

Commando – Aluminum (59 degree blocks): Commando heads are offered with two different intake ports sizes. The standard port heads (P4876785) are a direct replacement for the iron LA

The W2 cylinder head was originally introduced in 1974. It has been updated several times since then, and it offers the highest performance with a cast-iron head.

The most unusual feature of the W2 head is the oval-shaped intake ports. These heads use special intakes that have the oval-shaped ports and a wider spacing for the intake bolts. Note that this head has slots machined in the bottom edge of the intake surface. This is the easiest way to identify the W2 for use on 48-degree tappet bore blocks. W2s for 59-degree blocks don't have these pushrod slots.

heads. They use the same valves, intake, rocker arms, valve covers, and all other parts. The only special change is that larger oil passages must be drilled in the underside of the rocker shafts. The holes should be drilled around two of the rocker shaft screws for oil flow (drill to 7/16" diameter). These heads use 3/8" rocker shaft bolts, and this requires modification to the rocker shaft.

The large port Commando heads (P4876310) have a significantly larger intake port. Because the ports are so large, you must use W2 style rocker arms with more offset to clear the intake ports. All other components are the same as a standard LA head (i.e., valves, springs, LA intake manifold, etc.). The ports are large enough to see the pushrods in the intake screw holes. Use a little RTV on the intake screw thread near the intake ports to prevent leakage at the intake screws.

Commando heads are made using the same casting as the aluminum Magnum. The only difference between these heads is in the machining. This common casting has a bump or boss inside the top of the intake ports. This boss allows enough material for the rocker arm screws on the aluminum Magnum, but it is not needed on the Commando heads. This extra bump can be ground out of the port on Commando heads (not needed and this helps airflow slightly).

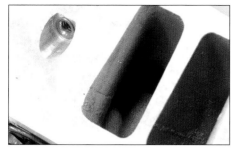

Aluminum Magnum and Commando heads use the same casting, but they are machined differently. The bump in the top of the intake port (port on the left – lower left corner) is not needed on the Commando head and can be ground out for better airflow. Aluminum Magnum heads need this bump to allow enough material for the rocker arm bolts.

W9 – *Aluminum (48 degree blocks)*: W9 heads have the most performance potential for very large stroker engines (over 420ci). These heads have huge intake ports that flow over 300 cfm "as cast." The wide valve spacing allows the use of large intake valves up to 2.200". The exhaust port is very efficient and doesn't need to be larger than 1.600" or 1.625" even on the largest displacement engines.

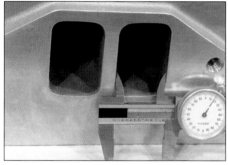

W9 cylinder heads have very large intake ports to supply enough airflow for the largest stroker engine. This intake port flows about 290 to 309 cfm "as cast" without any porting. These ports don't have the bump in the side that makes the ports narrower for pushrod clearance. This is one of the advantages of using a 48-degree tappet bore block (tappets and pushrods moved away from the intake ports).

P5007065AB is for use with 48-degree blocks only. To allow flexibility in selecting the valve sizes, this head does not have the valve job done. The guides are designed for 11/32" valve stems. Most

engine builders use Manley +0.600" long GM valves (i.e., Manley #11766-8 2.150" intake and #11767-8 1.600" exhaust). The +0.600 long" indicates generic racing (small-block Chevy) valves that are 0.600" longer than stock. The actual length of these valves is 5.540" on the intake and 5.560" on the exhaust.

P5007065AB has a CNC-machined chamber designed for use with gasoline. The chamber machining un-shrouds the spark plug, and the spark plug machining allows the use of common 3/4" reach spark plugs.

W9 heads must be used with T&D rocker arms. Though expensive, these rocker arms are very high-quality parts designed for racing and HP applications. The rocker-arm's screw holes go right into the intake ports. This looks funny but doesn't hurt anything, and you should use Loctite or another fuel-resistant sealant on the threads of the rocker stand screws.

The valvesprings are very close to the valve cover on the W9. This means trimming must be done on the valve cover gasket for spring clearance. The valve covers must also be wider than stock for valvespring clearance. Valve cover set P4876124 uses sand-cast covers that have the rail rolled inward for extra clearance. Some grinding may still be necessary on the valve covers for spring clearance. Custom fabricated W9 aluminum valve covers are also available from Moroso. Carbon fiber valve covers are available from Crawford & Crawford Composites.

This is the W9 cylinder head.

W9s need a wide valve cover since the valvespring is so close. This valve cover has the rail rolled over from the outer edge. This provides a little more room for the valvespring. Some grinding may still be required with this valve cover. This cover is sand-cast aluminum and is extra tall for rocker arm clearance (part number P4876124).

The tapped holes for the rocker stand on the W9 go right into the intake port. It looks funny, but it doesn't cause problems since the screw fills up the hole when assembled. You should use sealant on the intake screw to make sure oil cannot leak into the port (I use Loctite).

This is a photo of the underside of the same valve cover. Note the clearancing done to the cover for pushrod and valvespring clearance.

W9 – Aluminum (59 degree block): The version of the W9 that works on 59-degree blocks is P4510324. This head has been modified for pushrod clearance on a 59-degree block. This modification removes material from the outside of the intake ports, and this limits the amount of porting than can be done. This head is

P4510324 has large notches machined into the outer edge of the intake ports for pushrod clearance. This is done to provide enough clearance on 59-degree blocks where the tappets are closer to the intake ports. This modification limits the porting that can be done since the port is thinner at these points.

delivered with the valve job machined and is recommended for use with 3/8" stem valves P4876580 (2.15" intake) and P5249886 (1.600" exhaust).

The combustion chamber on this head is CNC machined to unshroud the spark plugs for better performance. Use extended-tip spark plugs with W9 heads for best performance (i.e., Champion racing plug C59YC or C61YC to add 5 to 10 hp).

The outer edge of the extra head bolts has been machined away since the bolts cannot be used on 59-degree blocks. This makes the heads look better since the extra holes look funny without any studs or bolts there.

Most versions of the W9 heads use a 15-degree valve angle. Be sure to use pistons that have valve notches with the 15-degree angle to match the valves. You could machine pistons to change the valve angle from the standard 18 degrees to 15 degrees. This machining may reduce the compression ratio of the piston/combination.

Aftermarket LA Cylinder Heads

Several other sources for LA cylinder heads can be found in the aftermarket.

Edelbrock – Aluminum (59 degree blocks): Edelbrock offers two versions of its Chrysler heads with slightly different combustion chamber sizes. The Performer RPM 340 has a slightly larger chamber size. It is designed for use on higher-compression 340 engines that need more clearance from the piston to the chamber. The Performer RPM Chrysler version works on all other engines with dished or flat-top pistons.

These heads use special Edelbrock 11/32" stem valves (2.020" intake and 1.600" exhaust valves), and they require special head bolts. All other stock parts can be used (i.e., rocker arms, valve covers, and intake manifolds). Edelbrock heads cannot be used on Magnum short blocks since they use the stock LA oiling system that requires oil passages through the block to the head.

Brodix – Aluminum (59 degree blocks): Brodix heads are designed primarily for oval track and drag racing. Two different versions are available with different intake port sizes and different valve spacing.

The B1 BA heads use standard intakes, headers, and valve covers. Standard LA rocker arms may be used, but they require the use of special B1 rocker stands. GM rocker arms may also be used when the heads are oiled through the tappets and hollow pushrods. Custom guide plates must be fabricated for use with the GM rocker arms.

The B1 BA MC has a larger intake port and must be used with a W5 or W7 intake manifold. The exhaust header bolts are not machined – this is to leave flexibility in what can be used. An aftermarket shaft-mount racing rocker arm set is required (i.e., T&D). Machining may be required for pushrod clearance. The valve spacing is wider than stock and can be used with 2.140" intake and 1.600" exhaust valves.

Indy – Aluminum (59 degree blocks): Indy offers two different versions of its 360 aluminum heads. These heads have the six-head bolt pattern with two extra head bolts per cylinder. The problem is they are designed for a 59-degree block with an 18-degree valve angle. 59-degree blocks don't have two extra head bolts per cylinder, so the

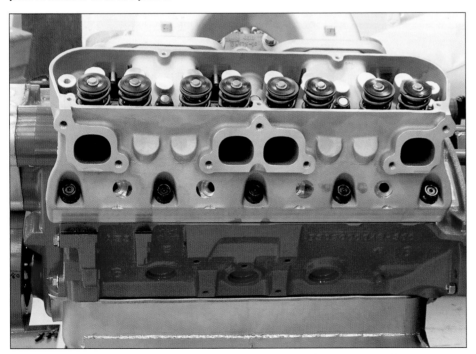

One version of W9 cylinder heads is specially modified for use on 59-degree tappet bore blocks. The extra head material for the head bolts on the outer edge is machined away since the 59-degree blocks don't have these bolts. This head comes fully machined with the valve job for 2.150" / 1.600" (3/8" stem) valves.

extra head bolts are not used. These heads come with two exhaust bolt patterns, one for the LA and one for the W2 header bolt pattern.

The 360-1 has rectangular intake ports and is usually sold in kit form including all parts between the block and carburetor. The recommended intake manifold for this head is Indy #360-R3, and it is designed for use with 0.800" offset Indy rocker arms. Indy recommends this head for 360- to 426-ci engines.

360-2 is similar but has oval-shaped intake ports. This head is also sold in kit form, but it can be used with an Indy or W2 intake manifold. Indy recommends this head for 318- to 370-ci engines.

Magnum Heads

Magnum heads are designed for use on 1992-'98 5.2L and 1993-'03 5.9L engines. These heads can also be installed on any LA and offer an inexpensive way to build good power. See the special section of this chapter that explains how to install Magnum heads on an LA short block.

Magnum heads use stud-mounted rocker arms and must be oiled through the tappets and pushrods. Magnum heads use the 10-bolt valve cover. All Magnum heads except P5007950 use vertical intake screws that are different from the LA side-mounted intake screws.

Magnum Production (59 degree blocks): The intake port of the production cast-iron Magnum heads flow more air through the "as cast" ports than any other production Mopar small-block head. The intake port flows about 30

Magnum valve covers (left) have a 10-bolt pattern, and LA covers use only five bolts (right). The 10-bolt setup provides a much better seal.

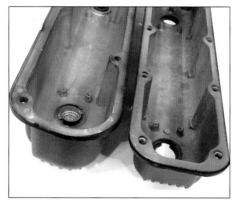

Note how the Magnum valve cover (right) has a more squared-off shape on the ends as compared to the LA cover (left).

cfm more than any LA cylinder head. The exhaust port is not quite as good as the best LA heads.

Since the Magnum exhaust port does not flow as well as some LA heads, the camshaft should add more lift and duration to the exhaust for optimal performance. Increase the exhaust lift by about 0.010" to 0.030" and about four degrees duration (more than on the intake).

Production Magnum heads are prone to crack on the exhaust seats between the valves. Check used heads carefully for any cracks. Stock production Magnum heads are no longer available new from Mopar or your Dodge/Jeep/Chrysler car dealer. Most cracked heads are now replaced with the Magnum R/T cylinder head P5007140.

5.2L and 5.9L production heads are about the same. Both use the same valve sizes and all other component parts. The 5.2L and 5.9L castings were made in two different foundries, so the casting itself has some very minor differences, but nothing significant. Mopar sold both of the Magnum castings as service parts for both 5.2L and 5.9L engines (based on availability).

Magnum R/T (59 degree blocks): The Magnum R/T was developed as a heavy-duty HP cylinder head for Mag-

Magnum rocker arms bolt onto special cast-in rocker stands. LA heads have a unique rocker shaft.

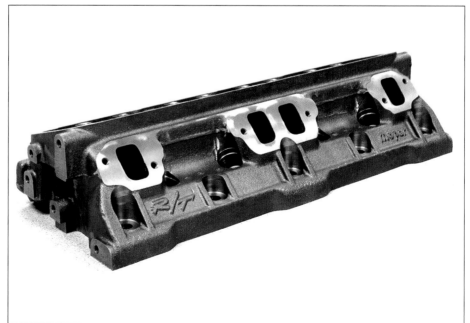

Magnum R/T cylinder heads are high-performance heavy-duty cast-iron heads that increase output of Magnum engines by about 20 hp. This head is a direct replacement head for Magnum engines, but it can also be used on LA engines.

Magnum R/T heads have larger intake ports than the production heads. The bigger port leaves less room for the intake screw and it can bottom out when installed. The best way to overcome this problem is to use 5/16"-18 x 1.5" long grade-8 bolts with a lock washer instead of the stock bolt (bolt on left).

The intake bolts on the Magnum heads go in at a different angle than in LA heads. These bolts go down vertically when the heads are installed on the engine.

num engines. The R/T heads have better ports, and this gives a stock engine an extra 20 hp and 9 ft-lbs torque by installing these heads (as compared to stock Magnum heads). The performance gains are even higher when compared to LA heads.

P5007140 is fully interchangeable with all stock Magnum components (i.e., valves, springs, retainers, keepers, valve covers, etc.). P5007141 is the same except that it uses a larger 2.020" intake valve. The large-valve version of this head is a better choice for most stroker engines. P5007145 is the same as P5007140 (smaller valve), but it comes as a complete assembly with valves, HP valvesprings, and all component parts.

R/T heads have larger than stock ports, and this leaves less room for the intake screws since they mount on the top of the head above the ports. The stock rocker-arm screws are too long and bottom-out in the intake screw holes. A shorter 5/16"x 1.5" long grade 8 bolt with a lock washer should be used for the rocker arms (16 pieces needed). The stock bolt can also be used if a 1/16"-thick washer is also installed, but these screws are not as strong as the grade 8 bolts.

LA Replacement Head (59 degree blocks): LA replacement heads are the same as the big-valve Magnum R/T P5007141, except they have been machined for use with an LA intake manifold. The intake screws are drilled and tapped at the standard LA angle so that more intakes fit. All other components such as the valves, springs, retainers, and other parts are stock Magnum. The intake valve is a large 2.020" size, use Mopar valve #P5249878.

These heads can be used on Magnum blocks where another intake is desired (i.e., Edelbrock, Six-Pack, stock LA, or other manifold). Because of the limited selection of Magnum intakes, this head allows the option of more choices using LA intakes.

The Magnum intake port is slightly taller and narrower than an LA intake, but they are both very close in size. Minor grinding can be done to match these ports. Use an intake manifold gasket as a template for the port matching.

These can also be used on LA blocks by using tappets and pushrods that oil the heads. See the instructions in this chapter for installing Magnum heads on an LA engine.

Aluminum Magnum (59 degree blocks): The aluminum Magnum is a HP aluminum version of the Magnum head. The aluminum heads reduce the engine weight by about 50 lbs. These heads have improved intake and exhaust ports, and they provide a 15- to 20-hp gain over stock production Magnum heads.

Most all-stock Magnum component parts fit these heads. The only difference is the rocker-arms screws, which are a larger 3/8" size (use 3/8"x 1.75" grade 8

The LA replacement head (part #P5007950) is the same as the Magnum R/T except that it has the LA-style intake screws. This head allows the use of any LA intake manifold, and still has all the other benefits of the Magnum R/T heads.

Magnum Heads with an LA Intake Manifold

You can use an LA intake manifold with Magnum cylinder heads two different ways.

The first way is to have the heads re-machined to add a second set of tapped intake screw holes on the Magnum cylinder heads. This can be done using a mill at an experienced machine shop.

These extra tapped holes must be machined using a mill since they are being started inside the hole for the existing vertical screw holes. Hughes Engines, Inc. can drill and tap your Magnum heads for the LA intake manifold bolt pattern. The cost to machine these extra holes is $64.00 for each pair of cylinder heads. After this machining, the heads can be used with both the Magnum and LA intake manifolds. See Appendix B for the address and phone number for Hughes Engines.

Another solution to this problem is to use the new LA replacement head from Mopar Performance Parts (P5007950). This head is a Magnum R/T head, but it is machined for use with LA intake manifolds (standard LA intake screw holes only).

This cylinder head allows the use of any LA intake manifold and provides the performance features of the R/T (i.e., more airflow, lighter valves, inexpensive rocker arms, increased compression ratio, big valves, and better valve cover seal).

This head requires the use of hollow pushrods and tappets that have oil passages to oil the top of the engine. See the section in this chapter that shows the detail on installing Magnum heads on LA engines.

This head can also be used on Magnum engines without any changes, except for the LA intake. This allows intake options that were never available before (i.e., Six-Pack, Edelbrock, or other special intakes not available for Magnum heads).

These methods can be used in racing classes that require cast-iron heads and intakes. The Magnum heads offer good performance potential, but no cast-iron intakes will fit Magnum heads. Cast-iron intakes were never made for Magnum engines, so only LA iron intakes are available. A used stock cast-iron intake is easy to install on Magnum heads using the two methods shown above.

The intake ports on Magnum heads are slightly narrower than LA heads, but they still flow more air. Note the bump-out area on the outer edge of the intake ports for pushrod clearance. The intake screw holes on this head have a steel threaded insert for improved strength.

bolts). The larger size is needed to provide strength in the aluminum casting. The larger screws require rocker arm pivots with the larger 3/8" hole in the center (package of 16 pieces – P4876514). The guide plates must also be drilled out to work with the larger 3/8" rocker bolts.

Aftermarket Magnum Heads

ProTopline Magnum (59 degree blocks): ProTopline produces the only aftermarket iron Magnum head. Based in New Zealand, the company was in receivership due to financial problems and not operating at the time this book was written.

Currently, bankers controlling the company are selling some of ProTopline's heads. The heads are stock-replacement cast-iron. These heads use all the stock component parts.

Edelbrock Magnum (59 degree blocks): Edelbrock also offers an aluminum head to fit Magnum engines. These heads use 2.020"/1.600" valves with an 11/32" valve stem. These heads feature 3/8" rocker studs with guide plates. The larger-diameter rocker studs require modification to the rocker arms since Magnum heads normally use 5/16" studs/bolts.

Other Used Heads

The following heads are no longer available new, but they may be available used. Be sure to thoroughly check any used heads for signs of damage before

Aluminum Magnum heads are similar to other Magnum heads, but they are cast in aluminum. The intake and exhaust ports flow more air than stock and make about 15 to 20 more HP than stock Magnum heads. These heads take about 50 lbs. off the weight of the engine.

Installing Magnum Heads on an LA Short Block

Many people want to know how they can install the later-style Magnum heads (1992-2003) on an earlier LA short block (1967-1992). The increased airflow of the Magnum heads leads to performance gains of 20 to 50 hp without any porting, depending on the head selected and the heads previously used. The increase in intake airflow is from 20 to 60 cfm, and this is the reason for the substantial performance gains.

Some of the common reasons are listed below:

- Magnum heads flow more air and this creates more HP.
- LA cast iron heads are getting difficult to find in good condition.
Inexpensive valvetrain options.
- Improved cylinder-head oiling.
- Better valve cover seal using 10-bolt Magnum valve covers.
- Slight increase in compression ratio.
- Larger and lighter valves.

These instructions apply to all Magnum cylinder heads when installing them on an LA short block. Magnum head choices include: 1992-'03 production Magnum heads, aluminum Magnum heads (P4876624), Magnum R/T cylinder heads (P5007140, P5007141, P5007145), and LA replacement heads (P5007950).

The Magnum heads use the same cylinder head-bolt pattern as LA heads, so they bolt on pretty easily. The exhaust header bolt pattern is also the same, so headers and exhaust manifolds bolt on without any problems. The rocker arms, valve covers, valves, pushrods, valvesprings, retainers, keepers, and valve seals are different, so Magnum parts must be used for these components.

Most Magnum cylinder heads use vertically mounted intake manifold screws instead of the traditional

Magnum R/T heads are installed on this 59-degree tappet bore R3 engine block. This engine combination uses the high-flow R/T heads with a flat-tappet LA camshaft that oils the heads using AMC tappets and hollow pushrods.

screws that go directly into the side of the head. This requires a change to the Magnum intake manifold that is set up for use with the vertical screws. The one exception to this change for the LA replacement head P5007950 is that the head is specially machined for use with the LA-style intake screws (not vertical screws). If you want to use an LA manifold that you already have or a manifold that does not fit the Magnum heads, use P5007950.

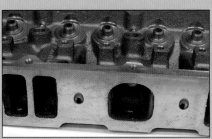

Magnum heads do not have a heat or exhaust crossover like LA heads. Magnum R/T heads have a hollowed-out area, but it doesn't do anything. Some intake manifolds don't completely cover these holes. It looks funny, but it does not cause any problems. Magnum intake gaskets work best to seal up this area of the head since there are no holes in the gasket.

The LA replacement is the same as the Magnum R/T, but it works with LA intake manifolds.

The trick to installing the Magnum heads on an LA block is to use tappets that have oil passages and hollow pushrods to provide oil to the heads. AMC (American Motors 360-401 V-8, or Jeep 4.0L I-6) flat tappets are the same diameter as LA tappets and have the needed oil passages. These hydraulic tappets are available from Mopar, part number P4529220AB, and are also available from most mail-order and cam suppliers. COMP Cams also sells mechanical (solid) tappets with these oil passages (part number 801-16).

The pushrod and tappet on the left have oiling passages that allow oil to flow up to the heads. These are the parts required when using this oiling method. The tappet and pushrod on the right look similar, but they don't have these oil passages (standard LA parts).

Stock Magnum rocker arms and special tappets and pushrods are required to install Magnum heads on an LA short block. Note the grade-eight rocker-arm bolts. These bolts should be 5/16"-18 x 1.5" long. Be sure to use a lock washer with these bolts.

ARP now offers head studs for Magnum cylinder heads. These studs fit all Magnum and Commando cylinder heads.

The pushrods must be 5/16" diameter to fit through the heads, and hollow to allow oil flow to the heads. The pushrods must be 7.625" long when using hydraulic tappets P4529220AB, and the stock production Magnum rocker arms (where the heads and block have not been milled). This length works with most HP hydraulic flat tappet camshafts. These pushrods are available from Mopar, part number P5007477 (set of 16).

The head gasket and Magnum heads block off the unused oil passages that come up through the deck on the block. You can tap and install allen-head style plugs to cover these unused oil passages, but the engine must be completely disassembled to get the block clean after drilling and tapping the oil passages at the deck (see Chapter 5 for more information on plugging these holes). I have built several engines without plugging these holes and have not had any problems with oil leaks at the deck.

The Magnum cylinder heads have a smaller combustion chamber (60cc with iron heads, and 53cc on the aluminum Magnum) than LA heads, and this increases the compression ratio by about one point. With most stock engines this is a plus from a performance standpoint, as long as the compression ratio doesn't get too high for use with pump gas. If you don't want the increase in compression ratio, consider using thicker head gaskets. Thicker head gaskets (up to 0.120" thick) are available from Cometic Gasket. You should use flat-top or dished pistons to avoid any interference with the closed combustion chamber on the Magnum heads.

The recommended parts when installing Magnum heads on an LA block are listed below:

The stock Magnum production valvesprings and retainers also work, but the springs are a beehive design, and this makes the retainer too small for use with HP springs. The best bet is to use P5249464 and P4452032 in high-performance applications (listed above).

Another way to save some money is to get a set of used production Magnum cylinder heads (i.e., 1992-'98 5.2L or 1993-'03 5.9L heads). Be sure to get the valve covers, rocker arms, and all other hardware that can be reused. Thoroughly inspect any used production Magnum heads, since they are prone to crack. The cracks are normally between the valve seats. You may have to remove the valves to inspect for cracks. If the heads are cracked they are probably junk, as they are expensive to repair.

The cylinder heads oiling method shown above can also be used with other heads that oil through the tappets and pushrods (i.e., W8, W9, and some versions of the W2). These heads use different rocker arms and valve-gear, so it would be best to mock-up the engine and measure the exact pushrod length and custom order the pushrods for the application.

Part Number	Quantity	Description
Your Choice	1	Hydraulic flat tappet camshaft for LA engine
P4529220AB	16	AMC Hydraulic tappet
P4876050	8	Production Magnum Rocker Arm (or Prod. Magnum)
P5007477	1	Hollow Pushrod Set – 7.625" long
P4452032	16	HP Chrome Moly Retainer
P5249464	16	HP Valvespring – up to 0.525" lift
P4529218	2	Valve Locks (or Prod. Magnum)
P5249661	1	Valve Seals (or Prod. Magnum)
P5249876	8	Exhaust Valve – 1.625" (or Prod. Magnum)
P5249875	8	Intake Valve – 1.92" (or Prod. Magnum)
or P5249878		Intake Valve – 2.02" with heads P5007141 or P5007950
P5007617	1	Die Cast Valve Cover Set (or Prod. Magnum)
P5249660	1	HP Valve Cover Gasket set (or Prod. Magnum)
P4876759	1	Head Bolt Set (or Prod. Magnum)
P4876049	1	Intake Manifold gasket set (or Prod. Magnum)

buying them. The casting numbers shown in this chapter can help when identifying used heads. Mopar doesn't sell heads by the casting number in most cases, so the cross-reference chart is needed.

W5: A W5 head is basically a W2 made in aluminum with rectangular intake ports (instead of oval shaped W2 ports). These are designed for use on 59-degree blocks, and they use all the same component parts as the W2 (i.e., rocker arms, valves, and springs). W2 intake ports also fit the W5, except for the port shape. The W2 intakes may be ported to match the shape of the W5 with some extra work.

W7: The W7 was phased out when the W9 was launched. The two heads are interchangeable and have pretty much the same dimensions. Three versions of the W7 were made for different applications (drag racing, sprint cars, and NASCAR Craftsman Truck). The drag-racing heads have raised intake ports and may require custom fabricated intake manifolds. The sprint car heads had extra machining for the methanol injector between the exhaust side of the head and the intake ports.

Most component parts are common with the W9 heads (i.e., valves, springs, etc.).

W8: Two versions of the W8 heads were made for NHRA drag racing, and for NASCAR Craftsman Truck. The drag-racing heads have special raised intake ports. These heads are made from

High-Performance Cylinder Head Casting Numbers

The chart listed below helps to identify most HP cylinder heads by the casting number. Most Mopar Performance cylinder heads are not sold by the casting number, so it is difficult to identify the heads when they are sold used.

Cylinder Head	Casting Number
W2	P4532693 or 3870810
W5 – std chamber	P4452926
W5 – small chamber	P4532724
W7	P4532442
W7 – Sprint Car	P4532755 or P4532766
W8	P4876281
W9 – std port	P4532847
W9RP – raised port	P5007904
Magnum R/T	P5007140
LA Replacement	P5007140
Aluminum Magnum	P4532900
Aluminum Commando - std port	P4532900
Aluminum Commando - large port	P4532795
Mopar / Brodix B1 BA MC	P5007928

heavy-duty castings and feature thick wall construction for improved durability.

W8 heads are cast without much of a chamber and must be CNC machined before use. The same is true for the ports, since they are cast small and must be ported before they flow.

W8 heads require a special W8 valve cover with a wider rail and gasket than all other LA heads. These covers are pretty expensive since they are specially made for these heads. Some valve covers were cast in aluminum and some in magnesium.

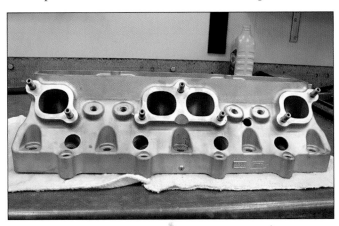

The intake and exhaust ports on the W9RP have been raised about 5/8" higher than the standard W9. These heads were designed for sprint cars and midgets, and no intake manifold is available for these heads at this time.

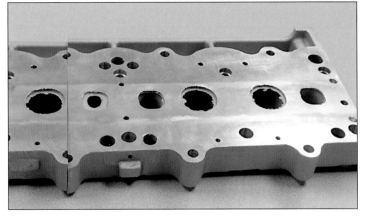

W9RP heads are cast with no chamber and must be CNC machined to make the chamber. This is done for flexibility and to allow almost any chamber size (machined), but makes the heads expensive to prepare/complete. The ports are also cast small and must be CNC machined for the desired flow. These heads are not recommended for most stroker applications due to high cost and complexity.

Other Non-Recommended Heads

W9RP: The "RP" in the W9RP heads stands for "Raised Port" heads. These heads use a completely different casting from the standard W9. The intake and exhaust ports are raised about 5/8" more than the standard W9 heads. The raised ports improve flow, but the heads are designed for sprint cars using individual runner intake manifolds. No carburetor intake manifolds for these heads are available at this time. A fabricated intake manifold is the only way to build an engine with these heads.

The W9RP heads are sold semi finished and require extensive CNC machining on the chamber and intake ports. The ports and chamber are cast very small and don't flow without the porting. The intake screws and rocker arms are not machined for flexibility in high-dollar racing applications. The extra work makes these heads expensive for use in most stroker engines.

P5 and P5 Hemi: The P5 and P5 Hemi® heads are for use on small-block Mopar engines but are not a wedge head. These heads are called poly-sphere heads and use a different bolt pattern on the deck. They use a different version of the R3 block that was not available in a tall deck height. These heads are also very expensive to use since a custom-fabricated intake manifold is needed, and the heads require extensive (expensive) machining and porting. The valve-gear and other component parts are also very expensive.

P7: The P7 cylinder head is another poly-sphere head that does not fit on the production or R3 blocks. These heads are currently used in NASCAR Nextel Cup, Busch, and Craftsman Truck. These heads have a unique bolt pattern and can only be used on the R5 engine block. This block is a short deck height (9.000"), so it would be difficult to build a large stroker engine with the short deck height. All component parts in the P7/R5 engine are unique and can be expensive to buy.

General Recommendations

Recommended cylinder heads for stroker engines:

Stroker Engines from 371 to 418ci: Stroker engines from 371 to 418 inches

Six-Bolt Heads and MLS Head Gaskets

Small-block Mopar engines have had problems with head-gasket sealing at high compression ratios ever since they were originally introduced. With only four bolts around each cylinder, this is fewer bolts than are used in most other V-8 engines. When the compression ratios get above 11:1 or higher, the head gasket is prone to leak.

In severe cases, the compression leaks into the water jacket or oil passages in the block. Sometimes this causes water to get blown out of the radiator and/or overflow bottle.

The best way to resolve this problem is to use a 48-degree R3 block and heads that have six bolts around each cylinder. The only two types of blocks with the six-bolt pattern are the R3 (48-degree versions only) and the aluminum A block. The cylinder heads that have the six-bolt pattern are the W7, W8, and W9 heads.

The 59-degree tappet bore R3 blocks don't have the six-bolt pattern since the extra inner bolts get in the way of the pushrods. These blocks are made from the same casting, but they do not have enough material left to hold the extra bolt and fit the pushrods in at the same time.

The 59-degree R3 blocks don't have the six-bolt pattern (only four head bolts around each cylinder). The material that would be used for the extra bolt is partially machined away for pushrod clearance. The 59-degree blocks have the tappets closer to the intake ports. This makes for less room for the extra bolts.

On 59-degree blocks where the compression is lower than 11:1, standard-style composite gaskets work well. In higher-compression applications, use Cometic MLS (Multi-Layer-Steel) head gaskets.

This is a Multi-Layer-Steel (MLS) head gasket. This gasket provides a very good seal, particularly on four-bolt blocks. The outer layers of this gasket are made from spring steel with a special coating, and the inner layer is galvanized steel. The raised areas in the spring steel are the parts of the gasket that provides a good seal.

These gaskets are multi-layer steel and have raised areas providing a good seal at high compression ratios. The outer layers are spring steel and the inner layer is galvanized steel. These gaskets work well on cast-iron or aluminum blocks and heads.

The gaskets are available in several different thicknesses, from 0.030" to 0.120". Changing the gasket thickness is an easy way to make small changes in the compression ratio. For example, if you calculate the compression ratio at 11:1 and you want to use pump gas, you could install a thicker gasket and reduce the compression ratio by about one point or slightly more.

The deck surfaces must be clean and dry and in good condition without any nicks or scratches that could allow a leak. Don't use oil on the threads of the head studs when using these MLS gaskets since the oil leaks down and gets the gasket wet before it can seal. Moly paste on the head studs can avoid this problem since it has a consistency like grease and won't drip down onto the gasket-sealing surface. ARP sells a Moly-based lubricant that works well in this application.

can use stock or high-performance cylinder heads. Some port work may be needed to allow good performance as the engine gets larger. The larger 2.020" intake valves should be used in these heads. The best choices for cylinder heads with this size engine are listed below (all 18-degree heads for use with 59-degree tappet bore blocks):

Engine Size
371 to 418ci
Cast Iron
340 or 360
Production Magnum
Magnum R/T P5007141
LA Replacement P5007950
W2
Aluminum
Commando
Large Port Commando
Edelbrock
Indy 360-1
Brodix B1 BA

The best choice with cast-iron heads is the Magnum R/T P5007141 or the LA replacement heads P5007950. These heads flow more air out of the box and come with the valve job already done for the 2.020" intake valves. Choose the head that works best with your desired intake manifold. P5007141 uses the Magnum-style intake manifold with the vertical intake screws, and P5007950 works with LA-style intake manifolds.

Stroker Engines from 420 to 475ci: Larger stroker engines need larger intake valves and enough airflow to feed a stroker with big-block sized cubes. The heads listed below are the best choices for large stroker engines:

Engine Size	
420 to 475ci	
Cast Iron	**Aluminum**
W2	Brodix B1 BA MC
	W9

If you want to use cast-iron heads and plan on using a 59-degree tappet bore block, use the W2 heads P4529994, P4529995, P5007355, or P5249769. With aluminum heads and the 59-degree tappet bore block, use Brodix heads or W9 P4510324. With W2 and Brodix heads,

use 2.080" intake valves. The W9 P4510324 already has the valve job done for 2.150"/1.600" valves.

Use W2 P5007445AB, P5007708AB, or W9 P5007065AB with 48-degree tappet bore blocks. Modify the W2 heads to use a larger valve size when available (i.e., 2.080"/1.600"). The recommended valve sizes for the W9 is 2.150"/1.600". You can also use 2.180" or 2.200" intake valves, but porting is needed on the heads to use the larger valve sizes.

CNC Porting

W2/W7/W8/W9 cylinder heads have been used extensively in racing programs. Many cylinder head porters have developed CNC programs to port these heads. The heads are ported on a computer-controlled mill that duplicates the port the same way each time.

Some of the CNC porters that have experience with Mopar heads are listed below (and in Appendix B):

- Chapman Racing Heads, Woods Cross, Utah
- Ultra Pro Machining, Charlotte, N.C.
- Weld Tech, Brownsburg, Ind.

- Indy Cylinder Heads, Indianapolis, Ind.
- Brzezinski Racing Products, Pewaukee, Wisc.
- Hughes Engines, Washington, Ill.

The typical cost of CNC ported heads is about $1,000 per head (not counting the cost of the base un-ported head). This is expensive, but it can significantly improve the output of the engine.

If you don't want to spend the extra money on porting heads, then select a head that flows well "as cast." Some good choices are the Magnum R/T (229 cfm), LA replacement head (229 cfm), W2 (260 cfm), and W9 heads (300 cfm). These produce very good airflow numbers right out of the box without any porting.

Conclusion

Be sure to select cylinder heads that fit the block you want to use (48- or 59-degree tappet bore). The heads must work in concert with the camshaft, intake manifold, and headers to provide optimal performance. Be sure to select these parts together so that they all perform well in the same RPM range (i.e., 2,500 to 6,500 rpm for most stroker engines).

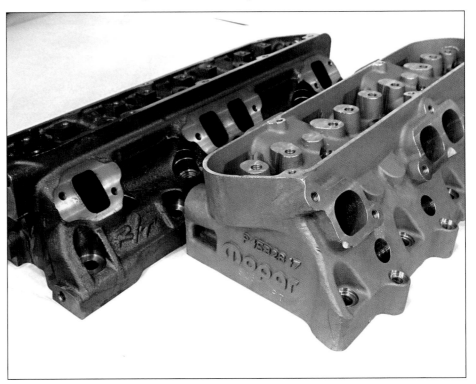

The best cylinder head choice for most stroker engines is the Magnum R/T or W9. These heads offer good flow "as cast" and are reasonably priced.

VALVETRAINS

For many years in racing, the valvetrain was the "Achilles heel" of the small-block Mopar. It wasn't reliable enough for extended operation at high RPM. When the RPM was over 7,000 for an extended period of time, the end result was many broken or worn-out valvetrain parts. The angle of the pushrods and tappets in production engines is not a straight path from the camshaft to the rocker arms.

This all changed in the mid 1990s when Dodge and Mopar went NASCAR Craftsman Truck and NHRA Pro Stock truck racing. The problems were fixed by a complete redesign of the valvetrain by changing the tappet and pushrod angles.

48-Degree Valvetrain

The tappet angle was changed to 48 degrees from vertical on some versions of R3 blocks. The reason for making this change was to straighten out the tappet and pushrod angles and make the valvetrain reliable for high RPM in racing applications. The camshaft lobes and tappets are also moved forward or backward in the block to position them farther away from the intake ports.

These improvements required changes to the block, heads, cams, and cam bearings. When the tappet angle on the block was changed to 48 degrees (instead of 59

degrees), it straightened out the pushrod angle. The valve angle in the heads was changed to 15 degrees (instead of 18 degrees). The camshafts lobes were moved away from the intake ports and larger journals were used for a stronger cam with a larger base circle. The oiling system was changed to provide a constant supply of oil to the heads through the tappets and pushrods, and to work with modern T&D and Jesel rocker arms.

By 1998 or 1999, the improved racing valvetrain could turn 9,000+ rpm in races that were several hours long. High RPM like this is not really feasible with a stroker engine since the piston speed is too high. The longer stroke forces the piston to travel farther in the same amount of time and this causes extra wear on the piston, rings, and bore. The RPM should probably be limited to 6,000 to 7,000 rpm for a limited amount of time on most stroker engines.

Changes to location of the tappets on the 48-degree block (moving them away from the intake ports) are a big plus for stroker engines. This allows very large intake ports and makes the valvetrain more reliable at the same time. For example, stock unported W9 heads flow over 300 cfm. When ported, they can flow 340 to 400 cfm to feed a very large stroker engine. These larger intake ports (with porting) need the tappets and pushrods moved away from the

ports since they are much wider ports than is possible with a stock 59-degree tappet bore block. With the stock setup, the pushrod would need a hole or slot in the side of the port for clearance, and this limits the amount of porting that can be done to the heads.

The change to the tappet angle and straightening out of the pushrods (on 48-degree engines) does not create any additional power, but it does make the valvetrain much more reliable. In most cases, the valves may open a little farther with the same camshaft lift since the tap-

1992 to 2003 Magnum engines use hydraulic roller tappets with special dog bones that keep the tappets from turning. A spider-shaped retainer presses down on and holds the dog bones in place. The oil is fed through the tappets and pushrods to lubricate the heads.

LA vs. Magnum Valvetrain

Engine	1967-'92 LA	1992-'03 Magnum
Rocker Arm Type	Shaft Mounted	Stud Mounted
R/A Offset	Intake – Yes	Intake – No
	Exhaust – No	Exhaust – No
Oiling Method	Through block/head/rocker shaft	Through tappets & pushrods
Pushrod	Std w/o oil passage	Hollow w/ oil passage
Tappet Type	Hyd. Flat Tappet (up to '87)	Hyd. Roller Tappet w/ oil passage
	Hyd. Roller Tappet (1988-'92)	–
Valve Sizes (318)	1.780"/1.500"	1.920"/1.625"
Valve Sizes (360)	1.880"/1.600"	1.920"/1.625"
Valve Sizes (340)	2.020"/1.600"	–
Valve Stem Size	3/8"	8mm
Valve Length	4.980"/4.970"	4.910"/4.930"
Valvespring Diameter	1.500"	1.420"
Valvespring Installed Height	1.650"	1.640"
Number of Valve Cover Bolts	5-bolt	10-bolt

This photo shows the LA valvetrain on the right-hand side and Magnum valvetrain on the left-hand side of the photo. The tappets shown in this photo are for use with a hydraulic flat-tappet camshaft. Note that the Magnum valvetrain includes hollow tappets and pushrods.

Magnum roller tappets are about 2.5" tall and must be used in blocks that have tall tappet bosses (i.e., 1988 and up blocks). You won't have enough support if these tappets are used in other blocks.

pet and pushrod angle is straighter. Some engine builders have made the change to 48 degrees and have experienced a power gain using the same camshaft grind. The real reason for the power gain is the additional lift at the valve, not any other factor.

Valvetrain Oiling

Valvetrain oiling is discussed in detail in Chapter 5. The oiling system must be the proper type to work with the block, heads, tappets, pushrods, and rocker arms that you want to use in your stroker engine.

For example, if stock LA-style rocker shafts are used, then the oiling system must have the oil passages up through the block and heads to feed oil through the oil passages in the block, heads, and rocker shafts.

to the rocker shaft. If Magnum rocker arms or T&D rocker arms are used, then the tappets and pushrods must have oil passages to lubricate the top of the engine. Some HP racing aftermarket rocker shaft systems are designed for use with oil passages in the tappets and pushrods (i.e., Jesel and T&D shaft rocker systems).

Tappets

Most production engines use hydraulic flat tappets. On LA engines these tappets don't have oil passages that feed oil up through the pushrod to the heads. Stock LA tappets can only be used on engines that oil the heads through the oil passages in the block, heads, and rocker shafts.

Some of the rocker-stand screws in W9 heads go right into the ports. This doesn't hurt anything, but looks funny before assembly. I recommend the use of Locktite on these screws to help seal the threads on these bolts.

T&D rocker arms use a special steel stand that bolts to the head. Each pair of rocker arms is bolted to the rocker stand using small studs and nuts. These rocker arms are installed on a W9 cylinder head, and the valvetrain oiling is through the tappets and pushrods.

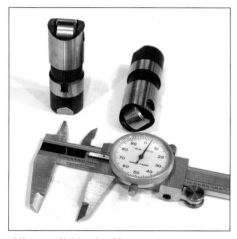

All small-block Mopar tappets are 0.904" diameter. This size is larger than in most other small blocks (i.e., GM and Ford) and allows more aggressive camshaft profiles. This size is the same as mushroom-style tappets on GM engines. The tappets shown here are Magnum hydraulic rollers.

If you want to use flat tappets and oil through the tappets and pushrods, use AMC (American Motors 290/304/343/360/390/401 engine sizes) V-8 tappets (P4529220AB). AMC tappets are the same diameter as Mopar tappets, but they have the needed oil passages to oil the heads. These AMC tappets are available from most camshaft suppliers. I have used part number SUM-HT2011 from Summit Racing Engines (hydraulic), or COMP Cams #801-16 (mechanical). If you are going this route, purchase the camshaft and

tappets separately to get the correct ones that have the oil passages you need. All camshaft packages that include tappets have the stock-style tappets, and this costs extra money for tappets that won't work in your engine (without tappet oiling to the heads).

AMC V-8 tappets have the same diameter as Mopar tappets, but they also have oil passages that allow valvetrain oiling through the tappets and pushrods. The tappets must be used with hollow pushrods when converting an LA block for use with Magnum or other heads that oil through the pushrods (using a flat tappet camshaft).

Magnum hydraulic roller tappets (#P5249862) are the same diameter but taller and must be used in a Magnum block. The extra height makes them too tall for use in LA blocks. LA blocks don't have enough material to support these tappets.

Mopar, COMP Cams, and Crane offer Magnum roller camshafts designed for use in Magnum blocks with these tappets.

The paint dot on the Magnum hydraulic roller tappets must be facing toward the center of the block when installing these tappets. If the paint dot is facing outward, the tappets can trap air bubbles that reduce lift and are tough to bleed out. These tappets can only be used on newer-stock blocks that have the taller tappet bores and bolt bosses for installing the tappet retainer.

Mechanical roller tappets are available from many sources for use in LA blocks (i.e., P4452919 w/o oil passages). These tappets use a guide bar that keeps them from turning. Sometimes the block needs minor grinding to allow enough clearance for the tie bar.

Don't use tie-bar type roller tappets on 59-degree R3 blocks or 340-replacement blocks. The tie bar must be placed on the outer wall of the block or it gets in the way of the pushrods. These blocks require too much grinding for tie-bar clearance on the outside, and the grinding gets into the water jacket. The only mechanical roller tappets recommended for use with 59-degree R3 bocks and 340 replacement blocks are Jesel keyway tappets (must be used with special tappet bushings) and Isky special-order tappets that have the tie bar below the pushrod mounting point (tie bar can be turned toward the inside of the block for more clearance).

48-degree R3 blocks have more room for tie-bar clearance and can use Crane tie-bar mechanical roller tappets #69552-16. These tappets have the needed oil passages for cylinder head oiling since all the heads that fit the 48-degree blocks use tappet/pushrod oiling.

Tie-bar style roller tappets are not recommended on R3 and 340 replacement blocks (w/ 59-degree tappet bores). The tie bar must be facing outward to clear the pushrod, but it interferes with the block casting on 59-degree tappet bore blocks. If the block is ground for clearance, the grinding gets into the water jacket and destroys the block.

Pushrods

The pushrods must be hollow if used with tappet/pushrod oiling for the heads. You should use the larger diameter 3/8" pushrods if possible. Magnum heads must be used with 5/16" diameter pushrods since that is all that fits through the heads. The pushrod is too close to the intake ports to allow a larger diameter on the Magnum heads.

The best way to determine pushrod length is to measure it after the engine is assembled. Many variables can change the pushrod length, so it is best to meas-

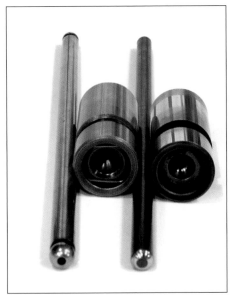

This photo shows the AMC tappet and hollow pushrod (left side) compared to the stock LA parts. The suggested parts when using Magnum heads on an LA block are pushrod set P5007477 (hollow with a length of 7.625"), and tappet set Summit #SUM-HT2001 (AMC V-8 tappets).

The suggested pushrod length when using W9 59-degree heads (P4510324) on a stock Magnum block with the Magnum hydraulic roller tappets is 7.575" to 7.600" long. This pushrod is made by Trend Performance Products.

ure and order the proper size and type of pushrods. I use custom-order pushrods from Trend Performance Products. This company stocks just about any size needed and allows exchanges if you order the wrong length pushrods (if the engine has not be run with the pushrods). Trend has pushrods available in every length in 0.025" increments (very good selection).

The best way to measure the pushrod length is to use an adjustable pushrod to determine the correct length and then order the pushrods to fit. After the correct length is determined, the pushrods can be custom ordered from any supplier.

I suggest the use of an adjustable pushrod in determining the proper length (when the engine is mocked up). With so many variables and stack-up issues in machining tolerances, it is best just to measure the length. This allows some adjustment to get the length correct, and then it can be measured to order the proper size.

Magnum heads are the only small-block Mopar heads that use guide plates. The stock guide plates work fine with the stock rocker arms.

Rocker Arms – LA Heads

The rocker arms on LA heads use a rocker-shaft system that mounts to five stands cast into the heads. This type of rocker-arm system is very stable and allows more offset than other systems. The offset is needed to clear large intake ports.

Stock LA rocker systems work fine on a low-budget stroker engine using production LA heads with a hydraulic

camshaft. The camshaft specifications must be conservative (i.e., 0.500" lift). A slight improvement can be made to the stock system by upgrading to stock-style rocker arms made from a thicker stamping – P4529742. The stock LA rocker arms must be used with the stock oiling system in which the oil comes up through the block and heads and into the rocker shaft through one of the rocker stands.

On Mopar small-block engines, just about every type of head uses a different rocker-arm system. Stock LA rocker arms fit Edelbrock and Commando (standard port) heads, but do not fit most other heads. Brodix heads use GM-style T&D rocker arms. Indy heads are designed for use with the rocker

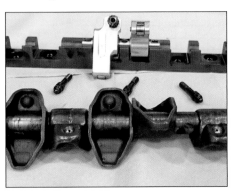

Stock LA rocker arms are made from stamped steel and work fine on mild performance applications. Most high-output stroker engines use roller shaft/roller tip rocker arms like the T&D system (top).

Magnum rocker arm pivots are available in two sizes. The one on the left is designed for use with 3/8" rocker bolts (pivot set P4876514), and the one on the right is the stock pivot for 5/16" bolts. The larger bolt size makes the rocker arms more stable, but it requires drilling and re-tapping of the heads. The larger pivots are standard on the aluminum Magnum heads P4876624. Grade-8 bolts are recommended on all Magnum rocker arms.

The valvesprings and pushrods are very close to the edge of the valve cover on W9 heads. In most cases the valve covers need to be trimmed for extra clearance.

The machining was changed on the W2 heads on 1/10/02 (rocker stand height changed and rocker stand bolt holes relocated). All heads made after this date must be used with T&D rocker arms and must lubricate the valvetrain through the tappets and pushrods. Prior to this machining change, most engine builders had to plug the rocker stand screw holes and re-machine them for use with modern racing rocker arms. The machining date is stamped on the end of the W2 heads.

changes were made to W2 cylinder heads part numbers P5249769, P5007355, P5007708AB, and P5007445AB. The rocker stands are now machined to work with T&D rocker arms without any special machining. Prior to these changes, most racers had to plug and re-machine the rocker stand holes and change the height of the rocker stands. All other older-style rocker arms don't work on the W2 heads machined this way.

If you have older W2 heads, you need to use shaft-style rocker arms like the ones available from Harland Sharp. Some older versions of the W2 heads use

The valve cover gasket also needs to be trimmed when using W9 heads. The valvesprings are so close that they rub on the gasket and may get gasket material into the engine oil.

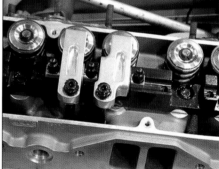

Use Mopar or T&D rocker arms with W9 cylinder heads. This rocker arm set is Mopar P5007470, and features 1.6:1 ratio double roller rocker arms.

arms available from Indy (similar to Indy big-block rocker arms). Most other heads use a special rocker arm set designed specifically for that head. W2, W7, W8, and W9 rocker arms are not interchangeable.

For high-output stroker engines, the best choice is roller rocker arms.

Minor machining changes were made to all race W2 heads machined on or after January 10, 2002. The changes included the machining of the rocker stands to fit T&D rocker arms, and elimination of the oil passages up through the heads (not required with T&D rocker arms). These

a rocker shaft that has the mounting holes on-center. These heads are called Econo W2s. Crane and Mopar sell special rocker-arm systems for the Econo W2 heads. The older racing W2 heads have the rocker shaft holes offset to one side and require different rocker shafts. These older heads have oil passages through the head, allowing oil to flow through the rocker shafts and to the valvetrain.

Mopar or T&D rocker arms are recommended for W7, W8, and W9 cylinder heads. Mopar part number P5007470 is for the W9 cylinder head (two sets required for a V-8 engine).

All stock-style LA rocker arms are designed for oiling through the block and heads (standard LA oiling system). Most of the T&D rocker arms are designed for use with head oiling through the tappets and pushrods. Make sure you understand the type of oiling required with each rocker arm system.

Rocker Arms – Magnum Heads

Magnum heads use rocker arms that each individually bolt to the head without a rocker shaft. The stock rocker

Rocker Arms

Cylinder Heads	Part Numbers	Rocker Arms	Oiling System
LA Heads:			
Production LA	All	Stock LA Crane #69790-1	Through Block & Heads
W2 (after 1/10/02)	P5007355, P5007445AB P5007708AB, P5249769	T&D #8001	Through Tappets & Pushrods
W2 Econo	P4529994, P4529995	Mopar #P4876343 or P4876344 Harland Sharp #S70025EW2K T&D # 8100	Through Block & Heads
W2 Race (prior to 1/10/02)	P5007089, P5249769, P5249770, P4529446, P4876336, P5007355	Harland Sharp # S70025W2K T&D #8001	Through Block & Heads Through Tappets & Pushrods
W5	P5249002, P5249435	Harland Sharp #S70025W2K T&D #8005	Through Block & Heads Through Tappets & Pushrods
W7	All	T&D #8085	Through Tappets & Pushrods
W8	All	T&D #8090	Through Tappets & Pushrods
W9 - Std Port	All	T&D #8095 Mopar P5007470 (2)	Through Tappets & Pushrods
Brodix	B1 BA B1 BA MC	Stock with stand B1 BA RS T&D #8018 or 8019 Jesel or T&D #8013	Through Block & Heads Through Tappets & Pushrods Through tappets & Pushrods
Edelbrock	All	Stock LA	Through Block & Heads
Indy	All	Indy	Through Block & Heads
Magnum Heads:			
Production Magnum, ProTopline	All	Stock Magnum, Mopar #P5249800AB, P5007404 T&D #8009	Through Tappets & Pushrods
Magnum R/T	P5007140, P5007141 P5007145, P5007950	Stock Magnum Mopar #P5249800AB, P5007404 (requires grinding for pushrod clearance) T&D #8009	Through Tappets & Pushrods
Aluminum Magnum	P4876624	Stock Magnum w/ P4876514 pivots Mopar #P5249800AB w/ stud kit P5007645	Through Tappets & Pushrods
Edelbrock Magnum	61679/61779	Stock Magnum	Through Tappets & Pushrods

arms bolt on a pivot and guide plate with 5/16" bolts. All Magnum rocker arms are designed for oiling through the tappets and pushrods. The stock Magnum rocker arms work on mild performance hydraulic camshafts (lift up to about 0.525").

Roller rocker arms are also available for Magnum heads in 1.6:1 (P5249800AB) and 1.7:1 (P5007404) ratios. These rocker arms are available from both Mopar and Crane. These roller rocker arms require special-length pushrods and taller (than stock) valve covers for rocker clearance. The recommended valve cover with the extra clearance is P5007617. The Mopar Magnum roller rocker arm sets include the special-length pushrods.

Aluminum Magnum heads use 3/8" bolts for the rocker arms (cast-iron heads use 5/16" bolts). When stock Magnum rockers are used on aluminum Magnum heads, pivots with a larger 3/8" center hole must be used (part number P4876514 – set of 16 pivots). The stock Magnum pivot is very hard and cannot be easily drilled out for use with the larger 3/8" bolts. These larger pivots can also be used on cast-iron heads if the tappet screw holes are drilled and tapped to the larger 3/8" size. This larger bolt size makes the Magnum rocker arms a little more stable.

Valvesprings

The valvesprings must be designed to close and control the valve. As the lifter moves past the top of the lobe (highest lift), the spring must have enough force to keep the lifter in contact with the lobe as lift goes down. If the

Magnum R/T heads have larger-than-stock intake ports and this leaves less room for the rocker arm bolts. The stock bolt (right) has an extended tip that may bottom-out on the bottom of the screw hole (bolt looks tight, but may break off when the engine is run). The best way to avoid this problem is to use 1.5" long 5/16" grade 8 bolts with a lock washer instead of the stock bolt.

Stock Magnum rocker arms use special pivots that press into the guide plate and are bolted on in pairs. Grade-8 bolts are recommended on all Magnum rocker arms.

lifter does not stay in contact with the lobe, the result is called "valve float."

The valvesprings must be selected to work with the type of camshaft used in the engine. The cam grinder or cam manufacturer supplies or specifies what springs should be used with the camshaft. Be sure to follow all the break-in procedures supplied by the manufacturer. Most manufacturers also supply an RPM limit for the valvetrain and camshaft.

Most heads have a recommended installed height for the valvesprings. It is measured from the bottom of the valvespring seat to the top of the retainer. This height can be measured with a special tool or a caliper. If adjustments are needed to change the installed height, the valvespring seat can be cut deeper or shims can be installed under the valvespring. Another way to make a change is to use special keepers that move the top height of the retainer up or down relative to the valve lock. Some retainers are available with a +0.050" taller or shorter installed height.

Allow 0.080" to 0.100" clearance from the bottom of the retainer to the valve seal at maximum lift. Without enough clearance, the retainer hits the

Valve Spring Pressures

Most cam suppliers have recommended valvespring pressures for use with their camshafts. The general recommendations may vary somewhat by engine and manufacturer, but they should be close to the following recommendations:

Camshaft Type	Seat Pressure (lbs.)	Open Pressure (lbs.) @ Max Lift
Flat Tappet (hydraulic or mechanical)	100-130	250-280
Roller (hydraulic)	130-150	300-325
Roller (mechanical)	160-225	340-400

Some engine builders also prefer to start near the top of these ranges for the seat pressure. This is because the valvespring pressure may reduce or drop off 10 or 20 lbs. after the valvesprings have been in service for some time. Check with the cam grinder or manufacturer for the exact valvespring recommendations since they have springs that are tested to work with the cam.

Installing shims that change the installed height can make minor changes in the valve-spring pressures. Another option is to cut the valve-spring seat deeper in the cylinder head. A third option is to use a retainer that increases or decreases the installed height by moving the keeper up or down relative to the retainer. These adjustments only change the seat pressure by 10 to 20 lbs.

Stock Magnum retainers (right) are too small to work with most HP valvesprings since the stock Magnum valvesprings are a beehive-style spring (tapered). The HP Magnum springs (P5249464) like the ones shown are not tapered like the beehive springs.

The stock Magnum retainer won't cover enough of the spring to fit correctly (right). The recommended retainer for most Magnum springs is P4452032 (left), which is made from a chrome-Moly material.

seal and destroys it. When mocking-up the valve gear, also check the valvespring to make sure it has enough clearance between the coils in the spring. You should have at least 0.060" clearance between the coils at maximum lift, or the valvespring binds and ruins the camshaft and other valvetrain parts. Be sure to check the inner and outer valvesprings (if equipped with dual springs).

Retainers

Most HP stroker engines use chrome-Moly or titanium retainers. Stock-style retainers are not as strong and don't normally work well with the desired valvespring. The retainers are normally specified by the manufacturer of the valvesprings. Use the recommended retainers so they fit well on the valvespring and control its motion. If the retainers don't fit the valvespring properly, they may allow the valvespring to dance around (more than normal) while the engine is running.

Most HP engines should also use a valvespring seat with steps that keep the valvespring in the proper location. Some cast-iron heads have steps in the

The stock Magnum intake valve (left) is not as smooth on the backside as a HP stainless racing valve P5249875 (right).

valvespring seats to help locate the spring. Aluminum heads must use a steel valvespring seat or the spring ruins the head when it moves around.

Most HP valvespring retainers have a 7- or 10-degree surface where the locks fit into the retainers. The 7-degree retainers work in most mild performance engines, and the 10-degree retainers are normally used on higher-output engines with a more aggressive camshaft.

Stock Magnum retainers are too small to work with most HP valvesprings. The stock Magnum

The HP valve (right) is also polished smooth on the head to resist carbon deposits. Minor differences in the shape of the valve on the chamber side of the head can make small changes in the combustion chamber volumes.

valvesprings are a beehive shape that is smaller at the top than at the bottom edge of the spring. The retainer is so small it doesn't have a large enough diameter to work with the HP valvesprings (no beehive shape). The beehive shape of the spring and small diameter retainer are designed to make them lightweight on a production engine, but most HP valvesprings have standard-shaped springs and larger (heavier) retainers. COMP Cams has started to experiment with the beehive-style springs, but most aftermarket HP springs and retainers are not made this way yet.

High Performance Valves & Springs

Cylinder Head	Valve Sizes	Intake Valve	Exhaust Valve	Valvespring Installed Height	Valvespring Seat
LA Heads:					
LA 360	1.880"/1.600"	P4876397	P5249187	1.65"-1.70"	N/A
LA 340	2.020"/1.600"	P5249185	P5249187	1.65"-1.70"	N/A
Commando P4876785	2.020"/1.600"	P5249185	P5249187	1.65"-1.70"	0.100" thick
Commando P4876310	2.020"/1.600"	P5249185	P5249187	1.65"-1.70"	0.060" thick
W2-Race	2.020"/1.600"	Manley #11702-8	Manley #11703-8	1.95"	N/A
	(Use with K-Line Liners to reduce valve guide from 3/8" to 11/32")				
W9-P4510324	2.150"/1.600"	P4876580	P5249886	1.95"-2.00"	0.060" thick
W9-P5007065AB	2.150"/1.600"	Manley #11766-8	Manley #11767-8	1.95"-2.00"	0.060" thick
Brodix B1 BA	2.080"/1.600"	Brodix #600299	Brodix #60030	1.95"	-
Brodix B1 BA MC	2.140"/1.600"	Brodix # 81050	Brodix #81051	1.95"	-
Edelbrock 60779, 60179	2.020"/1.600"	Edelbrock #9366	Edelbrock #9368	1.80"	-
Indy 360-1, 360-2	2.100"/1.650"	Indy # 360-12	Indy # 360-13	2.00"	-
Magnum Heads:					
Magnum 5.2/5.9L	1.920"/1.625"	P5249875	P5249876	1.64"	N/A
R/T P5007140	1.920"/1.625"	P5249875	P5249876	1.64"	N/A
R/T P5007141	2.020"/1.625"	P5249878	P5249876	1.64"	N/A
R/T P5007950	2.020"/1.625"	P5249878	P5249876	1.64"	N/A
P4876624	1.920"/1.625"	P5249875	P5249876	1.64"	0.060" thick - VSI-507
Edelbrock 61769,61779	2.020"/1.600"	Edelbrock	Edelbrock	1.80"	0.060" thick
Pro Topline	1.920"/1.625"	P5249875	P5249876	1.64"	N/A

Valves

Most stroker engines should use HP stainless valves. These valves have an improved shape on the valve head that increases airflow slightly. The HP valves are normally polished, and the stainless material doesn't allow as much carbon buildup as on standard valves.

The recommended HP valves are shown in the chart above.

Some high-dollar stroker engines use titanium valves, but these engines are only for the owner who has lots of money and wants to service the engine often. Titanium valves are much lighter and substantially more expensive. Some engine builders also have trouble with titanium exhaust valves in high-heat applications (exhaust valves are subject to more heat than intake valves).

Valve to Guide Clearance

The valve-to-guide clearance is the difference in the diameter of the guide as compared to the valves. With most HP engines the suggested valve-to-guide clearance should be:

Intake Valves:	0.0018" to 0.0021"
Exhaust Valves:	0.0020" to 0.0024"

The exhaust normally needs more clearance since these valves are subjected to higher heat than the intake valves. Higher intake and exhaust clearance is needed on engines that sustain higher-than-normal heat. Custom-built engines with carefully fit and machined valves and guides can run a little tighter clearance.

The major problem is that low-cost HP stainless valves don't have very good machining tolerances, and this can cause problems. Minor changes in the stem size of these low-cost valves make the clearance too tight or too loose on some of the valves. The only way to correct the problem is by select fitting the valves and reaming out some of the guides.

All stainless valves should be polished to a very smooth finish on the valve stem. This can be done with very fine steel wool and some elbow grease.

Conclusion

The valvetrain is one area where it may be best to purchase the whole system from one supplier so that you get a reliable and complete package that works together. Be sure to spend your money on high-quality parts that operate trouble-free for years.

Mild-performance stroker engines can use the 59-degree tappet angle parts and save some money. Higher output and larger displacement engines should use the 48-degree tappet angle valvetrain for better performance and reliability. The 48-degree engine is more expensive since the block, heads, and valvetrain are special parts (HP racing parts) made in lower volumes.

INDUCTION SYSTEMS

The intake manifold must be selected to complement the other engine components. The critical components are the intake, cylinder heads, and camshaft. For optimal performance, these three components must be selected to operate and work together in the same RPM range. For most high-performance street-stroker engines, the usable RPM range is about 2,500 to 6,500 rpm.

Manifold Types

The three basic types of intake manifolds are individual runner, dual plane, and single plane intakes.

Dual-plane intake manifolds have two levels, and half the engine is fed from each level. Most are used on stock

The second basic type of intake manifold is a dual-plane unit. Half the engine is fed from each side of the plenum of the manifold. Dual-plane manifolds provide good torque and drivability at lower RPM, and they are normally used on heavy vehicles or for towing.

The intake manifold on this sprint car engine is an individual runner (IR) design. It has one stack and intake passage for each cylinder. An IR manifold is normally only used in racing applications, and it performs best at high RPM.

or mild-performance engines. Dual-plane intakes provide more torque and drivability than other types of intake manifolds and work best on heavy vehicles in the 1,500- to 5,500-rpm range.

Single-plane intakes have a common plenum that feeds all eight cylinders. Most work with a 4-barrel carburetor and provide more power with a slight reduction in torque. The RPM range varies, but most single-plane intakes work best in the 2,500- to 6,500-rpm range.

Individual runner (IR) intake manifolds are for racing and provide a very high output. They work best at very high RPM in light vehicles. The most common IR intake manifolds are used on V-8 sprint cars and midgets (4-cylinder sprint cars). These manifolds work best for high RPM from 4,500 and up.

Mild-performance stroker engines used in trucks or heavy vehicles should use a dual-plane intake manifold. Most other stroker engines should use a single-plane intake manifold.

Each type of Mopar cylinder head uses different port shapes, port alignment, and intake mounting bolt patterns. The following section discusses the intakes available by type of cylinder head.

LA 340/360 Heads

The stock LA intake pattern also fits Mopar Commando heads, Brodix B1 BA

The third type of manifold is the single-plane unit. This type of manifold uses a common plenum that feeds all the cylinders. Single-plane intakes are normally used in high-performance applications with a single 4-barrel carburetor.

Intake Manifold Selection

Cylinder Heads	Deck Height	4-Barrel Single Plane	4-Barrel Dual Plane	6-Barrel Dual Plane	MPI Single Plane
Production LA,	Standard	P4876334	P4876335	P4529054	Edelbrock #3526
& LA Repl.		Edelbrock #5076	Prof. Prod #55025		
& Edelbrock		Edelbrock #2915	Edelbrock #2176/3776		
& Brodix B1 BA		Weiand #7445	Edelbrock #7576/7176		
& Commando		Holley #300-8	Weiand #8007/8022		
W2, Indy 360-2	Standard	P4529408	P5249572	N/A	N/A
		Indy #360-3			
		Edelbrock #2920			
		Holley #300-17			
W2	9.200"	P4876829AB	P5249572AB	N/A	N/A
W5, Brodix B1 BA MC	Standard	P5249460	N/A	N/A	N/A
		P5249614			
W8/W9	Standard	P4876162	N/A	N/A	N/A
W8/W9	9.000"	P4532598	N/A	N/A	N/A
Magnum	Standard	P5007380	P5007381	N/A	P5007398AB
Magnum R/T,			Prof. Prod #55025		P5007852
Alum. Magnum			Edelbrock #7577		P5007790
					P5007791
Indy 360-1	Standard	Indy #360-3R	N/A	N/A	N/A

Note: The part numbers shown above on the Mopar intakes may not be the same as the casting number (see the casting numbers elsewhere in this chapter).

Modifying Magnum MPI Intake for LA Heads

An easy way to build a Multi-Point Injection (MPI) engine is to use the Magnum intakes already machined for use with injectors. Four MPI intake manifolds are available to fit Magnum heads. Magnum intakes use the vertical mounting screws that do not fit on LA heads.

You will have no problems if you are using Magnum heads, since the MPI intakes bolt right on. If you are using LA heads you can modify the manifold for use on LA heads.

The vertical bosses, where the intake screws go, are machined away and the manifold is re-drilled for the standard intake screws. This modification leaves the extra vertical holes through the intake flange that can be welded up or plugged.

Manifolds P5007790 and P5007791 work best for these modifications. Manifolds P5007398AB and P5007852 are lighter and don't have as much material in the flanges and ports, and they don't work as well with this modification.

Note how the Magnum intake uses vertical intake screws. This is a different angle than is used on the LA heads.

The vertical bosses on the Magnum intake manifold can be ground away and the intake screw holes can be re-drilled to work with LA heads. This is an easy way to add an MPI system to an engine with LA heads (since LA MPI intakes are not available). The screw hole on the left is for the LA heads, and the second angled hole on the right was previously used for Magnum heads.

Mopar HP Intake Manifold Casting Chart

Manifold Kit #	Casting #	Manifold Type	Deck Height	Cyl. Heads
P4876335	P4532852	4-barrel Dual Plane	Standard	LA
P4529116	P4532058	4-barrel Dual Plane	Standard	LA
P4876334	P4532851	4-barrel Single Plane	Standard	LA
P4452891	P4452892	4-barrel Single Plane	Standard	LA
P4529054	3418682	6-barrel Dual Plane	Standard	LA
P5249464	P4532175	8-barrel Tunnel Ram	Standard	LA
P5249572	P4532646	4-barrel Dual Plane	Standard	W2
P5249572AB	P5249572AB	4-barrel Dual Plane	9.200"	W2
P4529408	P4532155	4-barrel Single Plane	Standard	W2
P4876829	P4532966	4-barrel Single Plane	9.200"	W2
P4876829AB	P4532966AB	4-barrel Single Plane	9.200"	W2
P4529874	P4532330	8-barrel Tunnel Ram	Standard	W2
P4529295	8015	4-barrel Dual Plane	Standard	W5
P4529460	P4532172	4-barrel Single Plane	Standard	W5
P5249614	P4532658	4-barrel Single Plane	Standard	W5
P5249357	P4532597	4-barrel Single Plane	Standard	W5
P4529875	P4532331	8-barrel Tunnel Ram	Standard	W5
P5249375	P4532590	4-barrel Single Plane	Standard	W7
P4532598	P4532598	4-barrel Single Plane	9.000"	W7/W8/W9
P4876162	P4532772	4-barrel Single Plane	9.560"	W7/W8/W9
P5249500	P4532588	4-barrel Dual Plane	Standard	Magnum
P5007381	P4510018	4-barrel Dual Plane	Standard	Magnum
P5249501	P4532587	4-barrel Single Plane	Standard	Magnum
P5007380	P4510017	4-barrel Single Plane	Standard	Magnum
P5007398	P4510016	2-barrel MPI	Standard	Magnum
P5007398AB	P4510016	2-barrel MPI	Standard	Magnum
P5007852	P4510852	2-barrel MPI	Standard	Magnum
P5249816	P4532731	2- or 4-barrel MPI	Standard	Magnum
P4876615	P4532731	2- or 4-barrel MPI	Standard	Magnum
P5007790	P4510046	2- or 4-barrel MPI	Standard	Magnum
P5007791	P4510046	2- or 4-barrel MPI	Standard	Magnum

heads, R/T P5007950, and Edelbrock heads. A wide variety of intake manifolds fit the stock-style LA bolt pattern.

Dual Plane

Some of the more popular dual-plane intakes are listed below:

Manufacturer	Part Number	Model	RPM Range	Deck Height
Mopar	P4876335	Std	Idle-5,800	Standard
Professional Products	55025	Crosswind	1,500-6,500	Standard
Edelbrock	2176	Performer	Idle-5,500	Standard
Edelbrock	7576	Air-Gap	1,500-6,500	Standard
Edelbrock	7176	Performer RPM	1,500-6,500	Standard
Weiand	8007	Action+Plus	Idle-6,000	Standard
Weiand	8022	Stealth	Idle-6,800	Standard

Single Plane

Some of the more popular single-plane intakes are listed below:

Manufacturer	Part Number	Model	RPM Range	Deck Height
Mopar	P4876334	M-1	2,600-6,600	Standard
Edelbrock	5076	Torker II	2,500-6,500	Standard
Edelbrock	2915	Victor	3,500-8,000	Standard
Weiand	7545	X-CELerator	1,500-7,000	Standard
Holley	300-8	Strip Dominator	4,500-8,500	Standard

W2 Heads

W2 intake manifolds also fit Indy 360 2-cylinder heads since they have a similar oval-shaped intake port and the same bolt pattern. The bolt pattern on W2 heads is wider than the stock LA pattern.

Dual Plane

Mopar P5249572 is the best choice for a W2 dual-plane intake manifold. P5249572AB is not recommended for stroker engines since it is for the shorter 9.200" deck height. Both manifolds are 4-barrel dual-plane intakes that have the oval shaped intake ports.

Some of the more popular dual-plane intakes are listed below:

Manufacturer	Part Number	Model	RPM Range	Deck Height
Mopar	P5249572	Std	Idle-6,000	Standard
Mopar	P5249572AB	Std	Idle-6,000	9.200"

Single Plane

There are several choices for single-plane W2 intakes.
Some of the more popular single-plane intakes are listed below:

Manufacturer	Part Number	Model	RPM Range	Deck Height
Mopar	P4529408	W2	2,600-7,000	Standard
Mopar	P4876829AB	W2	2,800-7,200	9.200"
Indy	360-3	W2	N/A	Standard
Edelbrock	2920	Victor	3,500-8,000	Standard
Holley	300-17	Strip Dominator	4,500-8,500	Standard

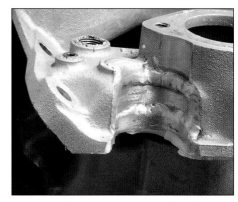

This manifold has been modified for use with front oiling on an R3 engine block. R3 blocks have an oil-feed hole in the front china wall, and this gets in the way of some manifolds that have a cast valley tray as part of the manifold.

This W9 intake manifold P4876162 has dividers in the plenum to minimize the difference in port length and equalize fuel distribution.

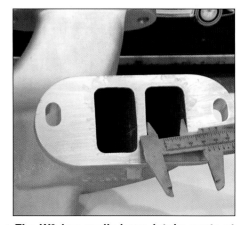

The W9 has really large intake ports at about 1.25" wide. This port size matches the as-cast ports on the W9 cylinder head P5007065AB.

W9 intakes don't have a valley tray cast as part of the manifold. The open area between the bottom of the runners and the engine keeps the air/fuel mixture cooler. The best way to cover the open area in the valley is with a sheet metal valley tray.

This is what the valley tray looks like on the rear of the engine. The tray must be shaped to fit around the distributor pocket. No bolts are needed to hold the valley tray in place, since it can be siliconed in before the heads are installed (it fits under the heads on Mopar blocks).

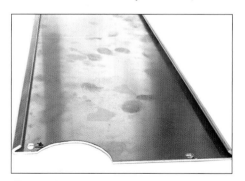

This valley tray is available from Mopar (part number P4510327), or it can be custom fabricated from sheet metal. The edges are formed on a sheet metal brake. Use a cardboard template to determine the best shape before cutting the sheet metal.

W8, W9 Heads

Single Plane

The best choice for W8 and W9 heads is the single-plane intake P4876162. This manifold is a single-plane intake for use on stock deck-height blocks, and it is set up for the square bore carb flange. This manifold has a large plenum and matches up very well with stock unported W9 heads.

W8 heads need extensive porting to match the manifold since the head ports are cast small and don't flow well without porting.

The only other intake currently available is part number P4532598. This manifold is not the best choice since it is designed to work with a 9.000" deck height and the short deck height doesn't allow enough room for long rods and a long stroke.

All W8 and W9 intakes require a separate piece for the valley tray since it is not cast into the manifold. This keeps the heat off the air/fuel charge and helps performance. The least expensive way to cover the top of the block is with a custom-fabricated sheet metal valley cover. Make a cardboard template to determine the proper shape and test fit before cutting it out in metal. With stock deck height blocks, the edges near the heads need to be bent upward to seal (use a sheet-metal brake if possible). Cast-aluminum valley trays are also available from Arrow Racing Engines. Carbon fiber valley trays (short 9.000" and 9.100" deck height only) are available from Crawford & Crawford Composites.

The W8 and W9 intakes don't have any provisions for a thermostat or water passages in the intake. The water lines must be custom AN lines and use a remote water manifold. See Chapter 13 (Cooling Systems) for more information on plumbing the cooling with these heads.

Manufacturer	Part Number	Model	RPM Range	Deck Height
Mopar	P4876162	W8/W9	3,600-8,500	Standard
Mopar	P4532598	W8/W9	3,600-8,500	9.000"

Indy 360-2 Heads

The only intake manifold that fits the rectangular-port 360 heads is 360-3R. This is a single-plane intake made by Indy specifically for these heads.

Magnum Heads

Dual Plane

The intakes for Magnum heads must have the special bosses for the vertical-intake screws. Only three manufacturers currently sell Magnum intakes. Each of these manufacturers sells one dual-plane carburetor intake manifold.

Mopar manifold P5007381 is very similar to the LA dual-plane intake except it is set up for vertical intake screws. This manifold works well with late-model Magnum air conditioning systems, but it may interfere with the A/C pump on early 1970s muscle cars. The thermostat housing is moved over to the side, and this gets in the way of early A/C pumps.

Professional Products manifold #55026 is made with a dual-intake screw setup, allowing it to fit on both LA and Magnum heads. This manifold comes with special plugs that cover up the unused set of intake screw holes. This manifold has an air space under the plenum to keep the fuel/air mixture cool. The thermostat housing on this manifold is in the center and may interfere with the A/C pump on late-model Magnum engines (1992 & up production vehicles).

Manufacturer	Part Number	Model	RPM Range	Deck Height
Mopar	P4007381	Magnum	idle-5,800	Standard
Professional Products	55025	Crosswind	1,500-6,500	Standard
Edelbrock	7577	Air-Gap	1,500-6,500	Standard

Edelbrock air-gap manifold #7577 is another new manifold for use with Magnum heads. This manifold is similar to the other air-gap manifolds offered by Edelbrock. The air space under the runners keeps the engine heat and hot oil off the intake system for a cooler fuel/air mixture. The thermostat housing is located on the passenger side and this may interfere with the A/C compressor on early 1970s muscle cars.

Single Plane

Currently, there is only one single-plane carburetor intake manifold on the market for Magnum heads P5007380. This manifold works well with late-model Magnum air conditioning systems, but it may interfere with the A/C pump on early 1970s muscle cars. The thermostat housing is moved over to the side and this gets in the way of early A/C pumps.

If you use a different intake with Magnum heads, consider using R/T cylinder heads P5007950. This head

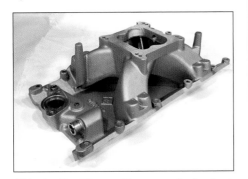

This is the Mopar Magnum single-plane intake manifold part number P5007380. This manifold is for use with all Magnum cylinder heads (with vertical intake screws).

This is what the vertical intake screw holes look like on a Magnum head. This particular head is an aluminum Magnum head and it has steel threaded inserts to make the threads more durable on the aluminum casting.

Carburetor Selection

Carburetor selection is a pretty complex subject and many books have been written on this topic, so just the basics are discussed in the limited amount of space available in this book. Most stroker engines use one four-barrel carburetor or Six-Pack (three two-barrel carburetors), so that is what is discussed here.

Selecting Carburetor Size (CFM)

The maximum airflow requirements should be calculated using the following formula:

$$\frac{\text{Engine CID} \times \text{Maximum RPM}}{3,456} = \text{Carburetor CFM}$$

This formula doesn't take into account that most engines don't operate at 100% volumetric efficiency. Most engines range from 75% to 95% in volumetric efficiency. Most stock street engines are in the 75% to 80% range, and HP and racing engines are in the 85% to 95% range for volumetric efficiency.

The chart listed below calculates the carburetor CFM for common sizes of Mopar stroker engines and shows the CFM requirements at various levels of volumetric efficiency.

(*Note:* Most high-performance stroker engines should operate in the 80% to 90% volumetric efficiency range.)

As you can see, most stroker engines require a 750- or 850-cfm four-barrel carburetor.

Mechanical or Vacuum Secondary

A mechanical linkage connected to the throttle pedal always operates the primary portion of the carburetor. The secondary portion of the carburetor can be mechanically or vacuum operated.

Vacuum secondary carburetors work best on the following types of vehicles:

- Heavy cars or trucks
- Standard-production final drive gears (i.e., 3.00:1 through 3.90:1)
- Automatic transmissions
- Engines with more low-end torque

Mechanical secondary carburetors work best in the following vehicles:

- Race cars with high HP
- Light cars / trucks
- HP final drive gears (4.11 or lower – numerically higher)
- Standard transmissions

Stroker Engine Size (CID)	372	408	416	447	476
Maximum RPM	7,000	7,000	7,000	7,500	7,500
% Volumetric Efficiency	CFM	CFM	CFM	CFM	CFM
75%	565	620	632	728	775
80%	603	661	674	776	826
85%	640	702	716	825	878
90%	678	744	758	873	930
95%	716	785	800	922	981
Reference 100%	753	826	843	970	1,033
Recommended CFM	600-700	750	750	750-850	850-950

Stroker engines by design are built for more low-end torque than top-end power. This is a good reason to consider vacuum secondary carbs for many street driven stroker engines.

Choke

The Holley HP series 4150s and Dominators don't have a choke and are designed for racing applications. These carburetors are not well suited for high-performance street use in colder climates like Michigan where I live. I often like to drive my toys (vehicles) on nice days when the temperature is cold, and I need a choke for easy start-up.

The choke on most carburetors can be cable operated or electronically controlled. Either type of choke works fine and is up to the owner's preference.

Kick Down Linkage

Kick-down linkage is needed with automatic transmissions. Some carburetors come with the brackets for this linkage, and some have optional bolt-on pieces to make the linkage fit. Some aftermarket companies like Lokar Performance Products offer cable-operated linkage systems that work on most custom hot rods.

Four-Barrel Carburetors

The most common high-performance four-barrel carburetors are available from Holley, Demon, and Edelbrock.

Holley

The most popular Holley carbs are the model 4150 and 4160. The 4150 has a mechanical secondary, and the 4160 has a vacuum-operated secondary. Some versions of these carbs have a polished silver finish or more traditional light brown "classic" color.

This carburetor is the 750-cfm Holley 0-3310 model 4160 carburetor with vacuum secondary and a mechanical cable-operated choke.

Popular Holley Four-Barrel Carburetors:

Part Number	Model Number	CFM	Choke	Finish
0-3310S	4160	750	Manual	Shiny
0-3310C	4160	750	Manual	Classic
0-4779C	4150	750	Manual	Classic
0-4780S	4150	800	Manual	Shiny
0-4781C	4150	850	Manual	Classic

These carburetors come with a manual choke but can be upgraded to an electric choke with a Holley conversion kit.

HP Series 4150 and Dominator carburetors don't have a choke and can be used in racing applications or where a choke is not needed. Dominator carbs require a larger mounting pattern not available on most Mopar small-block intakes. The 4150 and 4160 carburetors use a square-mounting flange that is more common on most small-block intakes.

Demon (Barry Grant)

Demon carburetors are similar in design to the Holley carbs, but some models have more features for improved off-idle performance. The Idle-Eze adjustable idle tuning allows idle adjustment without changing position of the throttle blade. This can be a big advantage on high-performance stroker engines that may not get enough air and fuel at idle and require modifications with a standard carburetor.

The best choices for street engines are listed below:

Continued on next page.

Carburetor Selection *continued*

Part Number	Model	Secondary	CFM	Choke	Finish
6402020VFE	Road Demon Jr.	Vacuum	725	Electric	Shiny
1402010VE	Speed Demon	Mechanical	750	Electric	Shiny
1563010VE	Speed Demon	Mechanical	850	Electric	Shiny

the Mighty Demon and Race Demon carburetors don't have a choke and may be used in racing applications or where a choke is not needed. Demon carburetors use a square-mounting flange that is common on most small-block intake manifolds.

Edelbrock

Edelbrock carburetors are based on the design of Carter carburetors but have many updates. They have a silver shiny finish and look great on hot rods and show cars. These carbs are dyno tuned to work with many of the intakes sold by Edelbrock. This testing and tun-

ing can make these carbs easier to tune in some applications.

The most popular Edelbrock carburetors are shown below:

Adapter Plate

Many small-block Mopar intake manifolds are designed for a spread-bore Carter carburetor. This is because most production Mopar muscle cars used Carter carburetors. Virtually all high-performance aftermarket carburetors (shown above) use a square-bore bolt pattern.

Intake manifolds P5007380 and P4876335 need an adapter that allows

Some Mopar intakes are designed for use with a spread-bore Carter carburetor (stock Mopar carb). Most aftermarket high-performance carburetors use a square-bore bolt pattern. In this situation, the carb doesn't fully cover the mounting surface on the intake. This adapter fixes the problem without adding much height to the carb since it is only about 1/16" thick.

Part Number	Model	Secondary	CFM	Choke	Finish
1407	Performer	Vacuum	750	Manual	Shiny
1411	Performer	Vacuum	750	Electric	Shiny
1412	Perf. EPS	Vacuum	800	Manual	Shiny
1413	Perf. EPS	Vacuum	800	Electric	Shiny
1812	Thunder AVS	Vacuum	800	Manual	Shiny
1813	Thunder AVS	Vacuum	800	Electric	Shiny

Edelbrock carbs use a square bore-mounting pattern.

Here is what the adapter looks like on intake manifold P5007380.

uses the stock LA intake bolt pattern. This opens up more choices for intakes since any LA intake fits (see the intakes listed above for stock style LA 340/360 heads).

All Magnum intake manifolds use special 5/16" screws that should not be re-used. The screws are called torque-to-yield screws. Mopar intake manifold gasket set P4876049 includes these special screws with the gaskets. Be sure to follow the recommended torque sequence in which the bolts are torqued in five steps up to the final 12 ft-lb for Magnum intakes.

Fuel Pump

Most high-performance fuel pumps offered for Mopar small-blocks are based on the design of a GM pump. A common problem with these pumps is that they don't have enough clearance to install the fuel lines on the pump. The inlet and outlet on these pumps are on the opposite sides of the pump body, and these fittings normally get in the way of the front cover or block. An easy way to fix this problem is to buy a new bottom plate for the pump (Edelbrock #1797). This special bottom plate relo-

cates the fittings to the bottom of the pump for more clearance. This plate comes with two pipe plugs installed in the old fitting outlets to block them off. This bottom plate works well with most HP fuel pumps such as P4529368.

A mechanical fuel pump can be added to a Magnum engine if the front cover and water pump are replaced with LA parts. In most cases, a special adapter is needed to allow installation of the LA fuel pump eccentric on a Magnum camshaft. This special adapter is available from Hughes Engines #7013. The LA water pump must be turned in

The Six-Pack induction system is available with all new parts from Mopar:

Part Number	Quantity	Description
P4529054	1	Aluminum Intake Manifold – Small-Block
P4349235 (1969-'70)	1	Center Carb 440
P4349236 (1969-'70)	2	Outboard Carb 440 (or)
P4349237 (1971)	1	Center Carb 440 (Manual Transmission)
P4349238 (1971)	2	Outboard Carb 440
P4529058	1	Installation Kit – Small--Block
P4529057	1	Air Cleaner Assembly with Filter

the use of a square-bore carburetor. The best adapter is Edelbrock part number 2732. I like this adapter since it is very thin (about 1/16" thick plus gasket thickness), and this leaves more room for hood clearance on high-rise intake manifolds. Most other adapters are much thicker and take up too much room to get the hood closed without modifications or changes to the air cleaner (and hood).

Six-Pack

The Six-Pack (three two-barrel Holley Model 2300 carbs) can be used on stroker engines with intake manifold P4529054. This intake works with all heads that use the stock LA intake manifold bolt pattern. This manifold and carb setup was stock in some HP versions of the LA 340 in 1970.

The Six-Pack can provide good drivability since the center carb has mechanical linkage, and the two end carbs are vacuum operated. The center carb has the choke, power enrichment, and accelerator pump. The end carbs (front and rear) don't have these components.

When the Six-Pack is used on most stroker engines, the big-block (Mopar 440) carburetors should be used instead of the 340 carbs. The reason for the change is that the displacement of most stroker engines is closer to 440 than 340 cubic inches.

In back-to-back tests, the 440 carbs provided more power than the stock 340 carbs.

The installation kit comes with the fuel lines, throttle cable, choke hardware, throttle return spring and bracket, kick-down bracket, coil bracket, and all linkage hardware to install the Six-Pack.

The Six-Pack can provide an exotic look and great performance, but may require extensive tuning. For tuning, think of these carbs as one larger carb with a mechanical primary with two vacuum-operated secondary throttle blades.

This section on carburetors is by no means complete and has covered only the very basics of carburetor selection. For more information on Holley carburetors see the SA Design book written by Dave Emanuel: Super Tuning and Modifying Holley Carburetors.

An LA fuel pump can be used on a Magnum engine when a carburetor is used. The trick is to use this special adapter that adds enough extra length to the camshaft so that the fuel pump eccentric can be bolted on.

The LA timing cover and water pump must be used with the special adapter so you have a place to bolt on the fuel pump. This timing cover/water pump must be used with standard V-belts so that the water pump turns the same way as the crankshaft. This engine also features the W9 heads P4510324 and P4876162 intake manifold.

Fuel Pump Clearance

The fuel pump is located on the side of the timing cover and is very close to the block and water pump. Most HP fuel pumps do not allow enough room to install the fuel fittings on the sides of the pump.

One solution to this problem is to use a HP fuel pump like P4529368 with a special bottom pump cover from Edelbrock #1797. This special bottom cover relocates the pump fittings to the bottom cover instead of out the side of the pump. In most cases this leaves more room for the fittings and allows flexibility. This special kit comes with

The fuel pump is located between the front of the block and water pump, and this doesn't leave much room for the fuel line fittings on most high-performance fuel pumps. The water pump inlet fitting is also too close to the fuel pump.

two plugs used to plug the standard fittings in the pump body.

This bottom cover also works with other fuel pumps, but I have only tested it with P4529368.

The water pump can also be modified to change the angle of the water inlet tube. The tube is normally cut at a slight angle, rotated, and then welded back on for more fuel-pump clearance. If you don't feel comfortable welding the pump, it is available from Mopar #P4510325.

This special fuel pump bottom plate and gasket can be added to pump P4529368 to provide more clearance for the fuel line fitting. The fuel line fittings can be moved to the bottom of the pump instead of on the sides. The bottom plate also fits other HP fuel pumps.

This is what the fuel pump looks like with the new bottom plate installed on it. Plugs are installed in the original side fittings, and the fuel lines are moved to the bottom of the pump. The old fuel pump bottom plate is shown for reference at the bottom of the photo.

The water pump shown in this photo has been modified to change the angle of the inlet tube. The tube is cut off at a slight angle and then rotated and welded back on. You can also buy a pump with this modification from Mopar – part number P4510325.

the same direction as the crankshaft. This requires changing pulleys/drive systems over to LA components with a V-belt setup. The Magnum serpentine belt system turns the water pump in the wrong direction for use with the LA front cover and water pump.

Magnum Fuel Injection (MPI) Intakes

Two types of high-performance Magnum MPI intake manifolds are available from Mopar.

The first choice is a 2-barrel Mopar manifold for Magnum MPI engines. Manifolds P5007398AB and P5007852 are basically the same manifold except P5007852 does not have provisions for the EGR system. These two manifolds are a direct replacement for the stock

barrel-style manifold. Simply remove the stock manifold on Magnum engines and replace it with one of these manifolds. The special installation kit P5007638 allows reuse of the stock fuel rails, A/C, and cruise control (and all other factory options). P5007852 is recommended for 1997 and up Magnum vehicles since they don't have an EGR system. P5007398AB works on all model years since the EGR system can be blocked off when it is not needed, but it is a little more expensive than intake P5007852.

The second choice is manifold P5007790 or P5007791. These two manifolds are the same as the single-plane Magnum carburetor intake, but they are machined for use with MPI (fuel injector bosses machined and extra boltholes on the carb-mounting surface). These

A special installation kit is required for intake manifolds P5007398AB and P5007852. This kit allows re-use of the stock fuel rails and A/C brackets and provides the necessary hardware for an easy installation.

manifolds can be used with a 4-barrel carburetor replacement throttle body or with the stock 2-barrel Magnum throttle body. The stock 2-barrel throttle body is

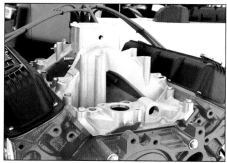

This intake manifold is for use with Magnum heads in MPI applications. The design of this manifold allows use of all-stock fuel injection components (i.e., fuel rails, 2-barrel Magnum throttle body, cruise control, and air conditioning). This manifold provides improved performance at 3,500 rpm and up.

P5007380, P5007790, and P500791 are Magnum intakes made from the same intake manifold casting (shown above). P5007380 is the carburetor version without machining for fuel injectors. The MPI versions: P5007790 has driver's-side throttle linkage (used in most cars), and P5007791 has passenger-side throttle linkage (used in most trucks). The MPI manifolds come with the special adapter that allows use of the stock Magnum 2-barrel throttle body.

used with a special adaptor that comes with the manifold. This adapter bolts on between the carb surface and throttle body. P5007790 is for most trucks with the throttle linkage mounted on the passenger side of the engine. P5007791 is for use on most cars with driver's side throttle linkage.

Magnum Intake – Oil Leaks

Mopar Magnum intake manifolds have three small dowel holes in the end of the intakes (underside of the valley cover – on the ends). Normally, not all of these

dowel holes are used, and the extra ones must be filled with RTV so that they don't leak. Some of the holes are used on Magnum blocks and some are used on LA blocks (when Magnum heads are used on an LA block). Intake gasket set P4876049 is prone to leak from this area since the narrow rib on the end-seals is in the same area as the unused dowel hole.

These unused dowel holes can cause a leak from the back of the engine. Many

customers think the leak is from the distributor. This is because the leak is close to the distributor at the sealing surface between the back of the intake and block. Add a little RTV to fill the unused dowel hole to solve this problem.

Distributor Clearance

Interference between the back of the intake manifold and the distributor can be a problem on some intake manifolds. Either the distributor housing or manifold requires minor grinding to provide enough clearance. Check the fit of the distributor when mocking up the engine to make sure you have enough clearance.

Always check for distributor clearance when mocking up a new engine. Sometimes the manifold is too close to the distributor. When this happens the distributor cannot be installed or is too tight to turn. Minor grinding on the manifold or distributor can cure this problem.

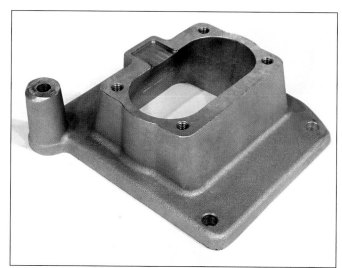

This special casting allows the use of a stock Magnum throttle body on just about any 4-barrel intake manifold. This adapter is available separately under part number P5007865, and is also included with Magnum MPI intakes P5007790 and P5007791.

The thermostat is located on the passenger side of the Magnum intake manifolds. This works well with the Magnum accessory drives (serpentine belt setup), but can be in the way when using most LA air conditioning. The A/C compressor won't fit with the thermostat on the passenger side (LA V-belt setup).

Recommendations for MPI Engines

Magnum engines are the only production small-block Mopars that came with Multi-Point Injection (MPI). Magnum engines have the same port layout and port location as LA engines, so many of the production Magnum parts can be used on an MPI engine. The Magnum intake ports are slightly taller and narrower than the LA, but the difference is so small that minor port matching can fix the difference. The fuel rails, injectors, wiring, throttle body, and other component parts may be re-used on LA MPI engines.

Fuel Rails

Some of the LA intake manifolds have bosses that can be machined for use with fuel injectors. After machining for the injectors, these intakes work with the Magnum production fuel rails. This saves money since aftermarket fuel rails can be expensive. Special brackets must be fabricated to hold the fuel rails on.

Magnum fuel rails can be used on any small-block Mopar engine. The port spacing is the same on all small-blocks, so production rails are an inexpensive alternative to billet fabricated units. Any LA intake with injector bosses can be drilled for use with these fuel rails. Custom fabrication is needed to mount the fuel rails.

Throttle Body

The production 2-barrel throttle body on the 5.2L/5.9L Magnum engines flows about 600 to 650 cfm and may be used on smaller stroker engines. This throttle body has two 50-mm throttle blades and can be modified for improved flow. Holley sells a billet 52-mm throttle body that improves flow

over the stock unit. In testing, the Holley throttle body increases engine output by 6 hp and 2 ft-lbs torque. The Magnum intakes have two 52.5-mm openings, so you cannot go much larger than 52-mm without modifications to the manifold.

Mopar sells a special adapter (P5007865) that can be used to install these throttle bodies on most 4-barrel intake manifolds. This adapter has two cast-in stands that can be used to mount the fuel rails. This adapter takes some modifications and custom fitting when used on most intake manifolds.

Intake Manifold

The easiest intake manifold to use is one of the Magnum MPI intake manifolds (P5007398AB, P5007852, P5007790, or P5007791). P5007790 and P5007791 include the special throttle-body adapter shown above.

If you are not using Magnum heads, you could modify one of these manifolds to fit LA heads (see another sidebar in this chapter). Many intake manifolds come with unfinished injector bosses that can be machined for use with MPI. This machining is pretty difficult and should be done by an experienced machinist.

ECU

Mopar production Electronic Control Units (ECU) are not programmable. The chips in these systems cannot be removed and replaced since they are enclosed in the ECU and are filled with plastic that seals everything up and keeps it weatherproof. The only way to reprogram the ECU is to replace it with a HP unit or send it to an expert that has specialized equipment to reprogram (re-flash) it.

A new fuel map is needed since the engine is much larger and requires more fuel than the production ECU can

The Magnum throttle body and adapter can be used on any 4-barrel intake (even GM and Ford products). This is an inexpensive way to add all fuel injection using used fuel rails, throttle body, and injectors.

The stock Magnum throttle body flows about 600 to 650 cfm. This is not bad for a 2-barrel unit, and it can be used on many stroker engines up to about 408ci.

The stock Magnum 5.2/5.9L throttle body has two 50-mm bores. Some HP throttle bodies have 52-mm bores (i.e., billet unit from Holley). The manifolds have a 52.5-mm hole, so no modifications are needed to use the larger unit.

Many intake manifolds come with injector bosses that can be machined for use with multi-point fuel injectors. An experienced machinist should do this modification. This photo compares two intakes made from the same casting.

provide. The best ECUs are programmable units that allow custom fuel maps and are programmed with a laptop com-

Calculating Injector Size

Injector Flow Rate (lbs./hour) = (Engine HP x BSFC) / (# of Injectors x Duty Cycle)

Engine HP = HP of Engine
BSFC = Brake Specific Fuel Consumption – Approx. 0.50 (good estimate)
Duty Cycle = 0.80 (designed duty cycle of injector)
# of Injectors = 8 on MPI V-8 engines

Example: 450 HP engine with 8 injectors: (450 x .50) / (8 x 0.80)
Injector Flow Rate = 35.16 lbs./hour

Cross-Over Pocket

Magnum R/T and W2 heads don't have an exhaust or heat crossover in the center of the head. An unused pocket exists where the heat and exhaust crossover would be, and sometimes it appears above the intake manifold-mounting flange.

Some intakes don't cover up the pocket in the head where the heat crossover used to be. The heads with this pocket but no crossover are the Magnum R/T (shown) and W2 heads. This looks funny but does not cause any problems if the Magnum or W2 intake gasket is used. Don't use the stock LA gasket in this situation or you could have an oil leak in this area.

puter. Programmable ECUs and wiring harnesses are available from Holley, FAST, Accel, and other companies.

Some of these ECUs feed fuel to the cylinders all at once (batch fire), or individually at the proper time, just as the intake valve is opening (sequential fire). Sequential systems are preferred since they provide more precise fuel control, but they are more expensive and complex.

Injectors

Fuel injectors flow a specified amount of fuel in pounds per hour. The ECU switches them on and off for a specified amount of time to change the amount of fuel injected into the intake port.

The proper-size injectors are needed for the engine and must be carefully selected to have the correct duty cycle. The proper injector size can be calculated using the formula shown above.

Keep in mind that injector flow rate varies with fuel pressure. Most Mopar

Mopar sells these injectors in packs of four pieces. The pricing is very good since the price includes four injectors and is probably half the price charged by most other suppliers. These HP injectors were originally designed for a 2.2L turbo, but they also fit early Magnum engines.

fuel injection systems operate at 3.0 bar (about 44 PSI fuel pressure). Some systems operate at 3.8 bar (about 56 PSI). For example, a 26-lbs./hr injector (at 3.0 bar) really flows 30 lbs./hr (at 3.8 bar).

Complete MPI System

The best way to add MPI to an engine is to buy a complete system. Edelbrock is the only manufacturer that currently offers a complete system for small-block Mopar engines (Edelbrock #3526). The Edelbrock system includes the intake manifold, injectors, fuel rails, throttle body, distributor, fuel pressure regulator, fuel pump, wiring harness, ECU, and all needed hardware. This system is rated for up to 450 hp on small-block Mopar engines. This system is set up to work with 318/340/360 engines with the stock deck height with LA heads.

MPI systems are pretty complex and may require assistance from a specialist for tuning or solving problems. Kinsler Fuel Injection is a good source for custom systems and technical assistance. Don't expect a supplier to provide you with technical assistance unless you bought the system from them. Many suppliers may charge for services if you don't buy the stuff from them. MPI systems are complex and often require substantial support after the sale (consider customer support when purchasing the system).

In most cases this pocket looks funny, but it doesn't cause any problems. Intake gaskets that don't have any holes in this area are the best way to seal up any potential oil leaks. Magnum (P4876049) and W2 gaskets don't have any holes in this area and are recommended with these heads.

Conclusion

With so many different port shapes, sizes, and bolt patterns on various heads, manifold selection can be confusing. The intake must be selected after the cylinder head in order to get parts that fit together. Select an intake that works on your stroker engine's RPM range (i.e., about 2,500-6,500 with 59-degree blocks, or slightly more on 48-degree blocks).

EXHAUST SYSTEMS

Most stroker engines use headers instead of cast-iron manifolds on the exhaust system. Headers allow a smoother flow and more efficient scavenging of the exhaust from the engine. This is particularly important on larger engines since the extra cubes require an efficient exhaust system.

Header Basics

Most Mopar headers should be 1-5/8" to 1-7/8" diameter on the primary tubes, and the primary tube length should be 35 to 40 inches long. The rest of the exhaust system should be 2.50"- or 3.00"-diameter tube. The collectors between the primary and secondary tubes should provide a very smooth transition from the smaller tubes to the larger exhaust tubes.

Types of Headers

Most applications use "4-into-1" headers with equal-length primary tubes. The design of the header tries to make all primary tubes the same length (if possible). Sometimes the tubes are bent into funny shapes to make them about the same length. Most general-purpose and racing headers are a 4-into-1 design.

Some racing headers use a "Tri-Y" design in which two of the primary

This header fits tightly to the block, but the sharp bends restrict airflow somewhat. In some applications in which space is limited, this is the way to go.

Most headers are a "4-into-1" style where each primary tube is approximately the same length. Mopar small-block headers should use 1-5/8" to 1-7/8" primary tubes with a length of about 35"-40".

Schoenfeld Header Flanges

Schoenfeld offers a good selection of Mopar header flanges. In many cases, it may be difficult to get the proper headers for some cylinder heads. Sometimes the easiest way is to buy the correct flange and weld it on an existing set of headers. The Schoenfeld part numbers are listed below.

Header flange plates are available from many sources. This W9 flange is made by Schoenfeld (#0407) and is designed for use with 1-7/8" primary tubes.

Cylinder Head	Part #	Tube Diam.	Port Shape
LA	0410	1 5/8"	Std
LA	0411	1 3/4"	Std
LA or W2 (dual Pattern)	0417	1 5/8"	Oval
LA or W2 (dual Pattern)	0418	1 3/4"	Oval
W2	0414	1 3/4"	Oval
W5	0420	1 3/4"	Std
W7	0423	1 7/8"	Std
W9	0407	1 7/8"	Std
W9	0408	2"	Std
W9 Raised Port	0404	1 7/8"	Std

tubes are merged into one larger tube midway between the exhaust flange and collector. The other two pipes on each header are also merged in two steps the same way so that the two larger pipes are joined at the collector. This Tri-Y design generally produces a little more torque than 4-into-1 headers.

Some 4-into-1 racing headers use more than one sized tube for the primary tubes. These headers have steps in the size of the tube and are called "stepped" headers. Sometimes a reversed step is needed where the primary tube side is reduced a few inches from the head. It stays that size until it reaches the collector. Sometimes the primary tube is increased in size partway to the collector. This type of header is often used in sprint cars using W9 heads.

Some sizes and types of headers perform best with certain cylinder heads and combinations. Some specific recommendations are listed below for each type of cylinder heads.

LA Heads

LA heads have good exhaust ports for a stock head. The center two exhaust ports are compromised a little for clearance to the center head bolt.

LA heads should be used with 1-5/8" or 1-3/4" headers. The primary

"Tri-Y" headers like this one from SPD (Specialty Products Design, Inc.) have three collectors on each header. Two pair of primary tubes merge together and then these two merged tubes meet at the collector. This type of header usually makes a little more torque than a typical 4-into-1 header.

LA cylinder heads have an angled inner edge on the two exhaust ports that are in the center of the head (bottom). This angled edge hurts flow, but it's made that way to allow stock around the head bolt and for socket-wrench clearance. The Magnum R/T heads (top) have a full rectangular port without the funny edge that limits flow.

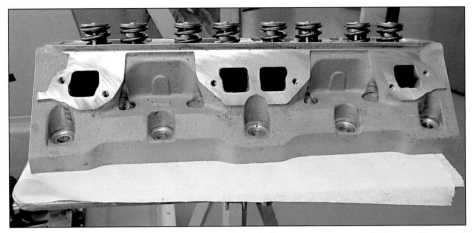

The exhaust port on aluminum Magnum heads has a very unusual shape. The port has a bump that goes around the bolt holes to allow a larger port without changing the bolt pattern. In most cases, some grinding is required to match these ports to your headers. Use an exhaust header gasket as a template and duplicate the shape on the header flange with a die grinder.

tube length for most HP street cars should be about 35 to 40 inches long. The rest of the exhaust system should be 2.50"- or 3.00"-diameter tube.

Magnum Heads

Magnum heads have a great intake port that flows more air than any stock LA head. The same is not true for the exhaust port. The Magnum exhaust port does not flow as well as most LA heads, and it needs larger headers for the best performance.

This is why Mopar crate engines recommend 1-7/8" headers. The larger headers help to scavenge the exhaust port and minimize this problem. Headers smaller than 1-7/8" restrict output on Magnum engines.

This is also why the best Magnum cams have slightly more lift and duration on the exhaust (compared to the intake). The extra duration and lift also help to overcome the lower flow of the exhaust on Magnum heads.

Aluminum Magnum heads have a slightly different port shape with a bump around the bolt holes – this helps flow. The ports are also a little wider than stock Magnum heads. The center two-intake ports close to the center head bolt are not restricted in flow. Most LA and stock Magnum heads have an unusual shape on the center exhaust ports to clear the center head bolt.

The Magnum R/T has better exhaust ports than the stock Magnum heads. The two center ports are moved farther apart and don't have the funny angled edge of the port for clearance to the center head bolt.

W2 Heads

The most unique feature of the W2 heads is the "D"-shaped exhaust ports. The floor on the W2 exhaust ports is the flat part of the D – this helps the flow.

Most early W2 heads came with a dual-exhaust header bolt pattern. The W2 bolt pattern is wider and allows more room for porting the heads. The narrower LA bolt pattern allowed use of LA headers or exhaust manifolds when required. The narrower bolt pattern was often plugged when not used since it was very close to the edge of the ports.

In early 2002, the machining on the W2 was changed to eliminate the second LA header bolt pattern. Most racers were not using the second bolt pattern anyway, and most LA headers didn't have large enough holes in the header plates to match the W2 exhaust ports.

W9 Heads

W9 heads have great exhaust ports and flow really well relative to any other Mopar heads. In racing applications, flow rates of 80% to 85% of intake port flow are common on the W9. The W9 exhaust port is so efficient that header size is not as critical as with other heads. When smaller headers like 1-5/8" are used, the flow velocity is increased and it really doesn't hurt power or torque much. The best primary tube size for un-ported heads is 1-3/4" (use 1-7/8" with ported heads).

The bolt pattern used on the W9 heads is called a reverse-Stahl pattern.

W2 heads have a D-shaped exhaust port with the flat part of the "D" on the floor of the port. This head is a later version of the W2 since it does not have the dual exhaust flange bolt pattern (machined after January 10, 2002).

Cast-Iron Exhaust Manifolds

In some cases you may want to use cast-iron exhaust manifolds to make your stroker engine a "sleeper" and look completely stock. In other cases, some racing classes require the use of manifolds instead of headers. The two choices for the best cast-iron exhaust manifolds are described below.

1968-'70 HP 340 Exhaust Manifolds

Up until 1992, the best cast-iron exhaust manifolds were made for the 1968-'70 high-performance 340 engines. These manifolds fit on all LA and Magnum heads since they all have the same bolt pattern. These manifolds are pretty tough to find today since they are now almost 35 years old. Additionally, the manifolds tend to rust and may crack due to heat cycling (getting hot each time the engine is run).

1992-'93 5.2L/5.9L Exhaust Manifolds

The 1992-'93 5.2L/5.9L exhaust manifolds are better on the left side than the older 340 HP manifolds, and not quite as good on the right side. These manifolds are still available new from Mopar under part number #53006620 (right side – casting #53006618), and number #53006621 (left side – casting #53006619).

Mopar has a limited supply of these parts available now, but they are in stock at this time. The casting numbers are provided (shown above) so that you can identify used parts. In 1994 and later, the Magnum exhaust manifolds were changed and are not as good as the early units.

The best possible setup would be the left-side Magnum unit #53006621 and the older used HP 340 right-side manifold. Unless these manifolds came stock in your vehicle, you need to custom fabricate the exhaust system to use these parts. The best way to do this is to install the manifolds and take the car to a muffler shop that can custom bend the rest of the exhaust system. The vehicle should be towed there since it doesn't have an exhaust system.

Remember that the LA and Magnum heads have the same bolt pattern and the port shape is very close, so you can use early or late manifolds on either engine.

This pattern is used on many racing cylinder heads in which the center-two exhaust ports are spread farther apart.

Exhaust System

Most stroker engines should use a dual exhaust system with 2.50" or 3.00" tube. The best systems use an "H-Pipe" and high-flow performance mufflers. The H-Pipe connects the two exhaust pipes together just behind the collectors. In most cases the H-Pipe increases torque and equalizes the exhaust pressure on both banks of the engine.

Be sure to check the entire system so it fits correctly and doesn't rub on the chassis or any components. Remember, the engine moves slightly in the motor mounts, so an inch or more clearance is needed to avoid rattles and scrapes underneath the car.

Make sure you can get the spark plugs in and out without removing the headers. Sometimes just a few very minor changes make all the difference in the world and can avoid future hassle. Be sure the mufflers are quiet enough for street use so you aren't hassled by the law for excessive noise.

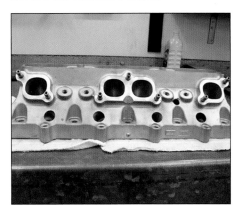

Header studs are recommended with all-aluminum cylinder heads to minimize the risk of stripping the threads. These studs are from ARP and have an allen head for easy removal.

W9 heads use a reverse Stahl bolt pattern on the flange. Note that the notches in the edges of the exhaust ports are for socket wrench clearance. These heads have a very efficient exhaust port that works well with almost any size headers.

COOLING SYSTEMS

Building a stroker small-block with big-block sized cubic inches and keeping it cool is a challenge. Special care and modifications are needed to prepare a system that stays cool in even the hottest temperatures.

This chapter discusses cooling theory, potential problems with the cooling system, and concludes with recommendations to provide a bullet-proof cooling system for your stroker engine.

Cooling Theory

Stock Mopar Cooling System

On the stock Mopar cooling system, coolant is pushed from the water pump into the two passages in the timing cover and into the front of the engine block. The coolant enters the front on the inner wall of each bank of cylinders in the block, and then circulates through the block and up into the heads. Coolant exits the block and moves into the heads through the water passages in the deck that feed the cylinder heads. Through passages on the intake surface, coolant exits the heads into the intake manifold at the front of each head. The coolant exits the intake manifold when the temperature allows the thermostat to open, and then returns to the radiator through the upper radiator hose. The coolant flows through the radiator and back to the water pump through the lower radiator hose.

Some coolant bypasses the thermostat through the bypass hose that connects the intake to the water pump. The bypass keeps the coolant moving and prevents the water pump from cavitating.

The stock-style cooling system works fine on a stock engine or a stroker engine without the Siamese bore block. On large-displacement stroker engines that use the Siamese bore block, several things can contribute to cooling problems on racing and stroker engines. A few basic problems can occur with the stock-style cooling system.

Problems with the Stock Cooling System

Sometimes the impeller in the water pump is located too far away from the front face of the timing cover. This makes the water pump less efficient. The timing cover can be machined to make the impeller closer, but then shims must be added to the water pump pulley to make it in line with the other pulleys.

A substantial amount of water may bypass the high-heat areas of the engine and exit the system without transferring much heat. The areas with the highest heat are in the cylinder head around the combustion chamber, exhaust valves, and spark plugs. The coolant in these areas often boils and steams away very quickly. Much of the coolant enters the block along the inner wall of the block and exits up into

the head and intake manifold without picking up much heat from high-heat areas. Coolant that exits quickly doesn't do much to cool the engine. The cylinders in the back of the engine don't get as much coolant flow, so they may run hotter.

Much of the coolant enters the block and exits quickly out the large core print through the deck and into the head (large core print at the front of the block on the intake side of the head). From there, the coolant can go out into the intake manifold and back to the radiator without picking up much heat. This is a bigger problem on LA and R3 blocks since the Magnum 5.9L production block does not have core prints in the front in this area.

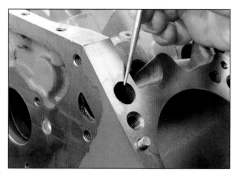

LA, R3, and 340 blocks have a water passage through the front of the block on the intake side of each deck. Coolant enters the block from the water pump and exits into the cylinder head without picking up much heat.

Differences in LA and Magnum Cooling Systems

LA Cooling System

The water pump on the 1967-'92 LA engine turns the same way as the crankshaft and is driven by a standard V-belt setup. The timing cover for this cooling system is also the back portion of the water pump.

The standard water pump has six blades on the impeller and works well in most applications. A heavy-duty eight-blade pump is available from Mopar – part number P5249559.

Magnum Cooling System

The water pump on the 1992-'03 Magnum engine turns the opposite way and is driven by a serpentine belt system. The front cover is also the back portion of the water pump, but it has a different shape to work with the reverse-direction water pump.

The reverse rotation Magnum water pump should not be used with V-belts since the water pump flow drops off by at least 50% when it is turned the wrong way.

Either Magnum or LA cooling systems can be used on your engine if the entire system is used. Don't mix and match LA and Magnum compo-

This is the stock front cover for the LA engine (1967-'92). Note that the back of the water pump is a flat surface.

This is the stock LA water pump. This pump is designed for use with V-belts and turns in the same direction as the crankshaft.

This is the Magnum timing cover. The front of the timing cover is not flat and has raised areas to work with a reverse-direction water pump.

nents or they will not work properly. The entire system must include the front cover, water pump, pulley drive system, tensioner, and accessories that run off the pulleys.

If you want to run a mechanical fuel pump on an engine with a carburetor, you must use the LA system since the Magnum front cover does not have provisions for the fuel pump. If you are installing the engine in a newer truck that came with a Magnum engine, you should stick with the Magnum system.

Magnum blocks do not have a coolant passage in this same area, and this forces the water to circulate more before it can exit into the cylinder heads.

On most cylinder heads, the coolant exits the heads from the front only. This situation causes extra heat in the back and center of the heads. The cooling system is not as efficient in the back and center since the hot coolant cannot exit easily from these areas. These cylinders are more likely to overheat or detonate sooner since the cooling system doesn't work as well there.

The heat from combustion is generated in the chamber and heats the exhaust valves, valve seats, spark plugs, and the cylinder head casting in those areas. The layout of Mopar wedge-style heads have the intake and exhaust valves situated in the following locations E-I-I-

E-E-I-I-E. About 25% of the heat is generated at the end of each head near the exhaust valves, with the remaining 50% in the center of the head since two exhaust valves are right next to each other. Not enough water flows in each of these three high-heat areas of the cylinder head with the stock cooling system.

Improved Cooling (Especially for Siamese Bore Blocks)

The ideal cooling system for a racing or stroker engine (using a Siamese bore block) should have coolant fed into the sides of the block using external water lines from the water pump. AN-16 lines

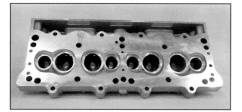

This semi-machined cylinder head has the valves arranged in a pattern E-I-I-E-E-I-I-E. This layout causes extra heat to build up in the head near the exhaust valves, especially in the center of the head where two exhaust valves are next to each other.

are run from the water pump to the sides of the block. Custom-made plugs are pressed into the center freeze plug and AN fittings are installed. The center on each side of the block is the best location to feed coolant to the system since the hottest part of the engine (two exhaust valves right next to each other) is just above in the head, and the water can separate here and cool each cylinder with about the same force and pressure (along the hot exhaust side of the engine).

This block has a special fitting pressed into the center freeze plug. This fitting is used to feed water directly into the side of the block with external cooling lines for better cooling in the hottest area on the engine (center of the head).

This is the special AN-16 90-degree bulkhead fitting used to feed coolant into the side of the block. This fitting screws into the custom-made freeze plug shown in the previous photo.

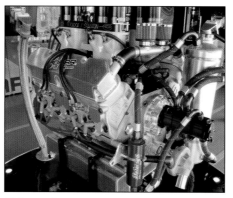

This sprint car engine shows how the external cooling lines attach between the water pump and the side of the block. This engine uses a crankshaft-driven water pump specially designed for sprint car use only.

The water pump must also be modified to allow external plumbing of the coolant. AN fittings are welded on the water pump to attach the external lines. The two normal coolant passages through the front cover into the block are plugged when the external lines are used. An easy way to plug these passages is to use a motor plate without the holes that normally allow coolant flow into the block.

This high-performance water-pump housing has been modified to add AN-16 fittings used for the external water lines. Care must be taken when welding the pump so the seals are not melted.

After coolant enters the side of the block, most of it goes upward and into the cylinder head along the exhaust side of the head. Here it can pick up heat from the hottest areas of the engine. Once the coolant is in the head, it should flow across the top side of the combustion chambers and exit the head. There are three exits for the coolant from the head – one at each end, and one larger

outlet in the center of the head. About 25% of the coolant should exit the head at each end, and 50% of the coolant should exit the center of the head. These numbers are based on the heat generated from each cylinder with the most flow in the center since the two exhaust valves are right next to each other. I recommend a 3/8" (AN-6 lines) diameter hose at the ends and a 1/2" hose (AN-8 lines) in the center for the coolant exits.

The best way to get the water to flow in the desired manner is to restrict water flow on the cooler intake side of the head. The easiest way to do this is to install plugs in the two large core prints

This is a photo of a W9 cylinder head that has been sectioned (sawed in half) just above the deck surface. Most of the coolant should enter the cylinder head on the exhaust side of the head (top). The coolant should pick up heat around the spark plugs, combustion chamber, valves seats, and then flow out the intake side of the head (bottom of photo) and back to the radiator.

W9 cylinder heads have three coolant lines that allow coolant to exit the cylinder head. These three lines carry coolant away from the hottest areas of the heads. AN-8 lines should be used in the center of the heads, and AN-6 lines should be used at the end of each head.

Special AN-8 size O-ring fittings are used to attach the lines to the cylinder heads. These fittings are available from Earls and other distributors of quality AN lines. The thread size is AN-8 in W9 cylinder heads. The part numbers are Earls #985008 (for center of heads w/ AN-8 thread for AN-8 hose), and #985068 (both ends of heads w/ AN-8 thread and AN-6 hose).

at the ends of the block on the intake side. Two plugs that restrict flow should be installed on each bank of the engine. These plugs should have a 1/8"-hole drilled in them so that the water still circulates around the block and does not become stagnant. These plugs force most coolant to go through the head on the exhaust side and pick up heat from the high-heat areas (exhaust area on the chamber, and spark plugs).

The best way to restrict flow in the two large coolant passages at the front and rear of the block (intake side of the block at the ends) is to install a plug with a small hole drilled in it. A 0.125"-diameter hole is normally drilled in these plugs.

The six coolant lines exiting the heads must be run to the radiator or to a fabricated water manifold with a single line leading to the radiator. This common line, if used, must be large enough to handle the flow of all six lines. A 1.5" radiator hose allows enough flow for all six lines. If a thermostat is used in this system, allow a bypass for coolant flow from each head at all times.

Cross Drilling Block

Siamese bore R3 blocks don't allow any water to pass between the cylinders, so they tend to run hotter than a stock-style block. Since we want to build

large-displacement engines, we need to use the Siamese bore block when the bore size is over 4.080".

Siamese bore blocks should have extra water passages drilled at two angles between the bores. Each hole is

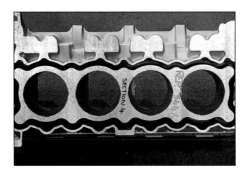

Siamese bore blocks allow larger bore sizes, but they don't allow any coolant to flow between the bores. These blocks run hotter than a standard block since the coolant does not go all the way around each bore.

Vertical holes should also be drilled in the head to allow coolant to flow from the block up to the head. Use the gasket as a template and drill these vertical holes with a drill press or hand drill.

The holes are drilled at a 55-degree angle from the centerline of the bores. These two holes intersect in the middle and allow some coolant flow between the bores on a Siamese bore block. These holes should be drilled on a mill by an experienced machinist (hand drill shown for illustration purposes only).

Use an HP gasket like this Cometic gasket to locate and drill the passages that go between the bores. These extra holes are only needed on Siamese bore blocks.

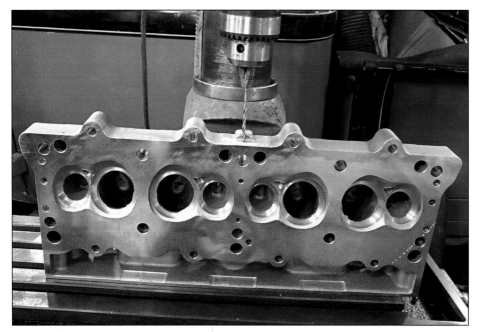

A hole is drilled in the deck of the head 0.300" up from the deck (aluminum heads only). It is drilled from the exhaust side of the head to connect the two small vertical holes on each side of the combustion chamber. This water passage allows some water flow to keep the aluminum from becoming soft and losing its heat treat. The outer edge of the hole is tapped and a small setscrew is installed on each side of the head-bolt hole to prevent coolant leakage.

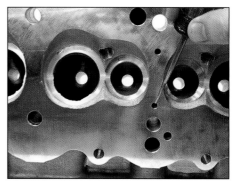

The small hole is drilled from the exhaust side of the head up to the second small hole shown by the pointer in this photo.

The outer edge of this passage must be tapped and plugged with an Allen-head screw. The tapped portion of the hole must go beyond the head bolt hole, and the plug is installed behind the head stud before the head is installed on the engine.

drilled from the deck to the water jacket at an angle. They intersect in the middle and continue on into the water jacket on the other side of the cylinders. Most high-performance head gaskets (like Cometic) have two extra water passages between each pair of cylinders to show where these holes should be drilled. Using a Cometic head gasket as a template to mark the location of these holes on the head deck, drill 0.120" holes across the block at an angle of 55 degrees from vertical. Two holes are drilled in three locations on each bank of the block. These holes should be drilled by an experienced machine shop using a mill. This is because they are tough to drill at the correct angle, and the drill may break in the middle where they intersect with each other.

These cross-drilled holes allow extra water flow and cooling between the bores on a Siamese bore block. Drill vertical holes up into the cylinder head in the same locations (if they are not already there). Use the same head gasket as a template to show where the holes should be located.

Cylinder Head Modification

With aluminum cylinder heads, a small passage should be drilled across the deck of the head between the two exhaust valves in the center of the head. The purpose of this hole is to allow a little coolant flow in this very hot area of the head. The coolant flow is needed to cool the head so the aluminum does not lose its heat treatment. Most aluminum engine castings (including cylinder heads) are heat treated before they are machined. Excessive heat from combustion can make the aluminum soft and weak.

A small 0.106" hole is drilled from the exhaust side of the head into the deck to intersect with the two small vertical holes in the center of the head. This hole is tapped and plugged behind the head bolt with a small allen-head screw. Be sure to apply some sealant on the threads of the plug to ensure it does not leak. This hole should be drilled on a mill or drill press to ensure that it is drilled 0.300" up from the deck and is perfectly parallel with the deck between the two center cylinders on each head. This hole is only needed in one place on each head since the

highest heat area is where the two exhaust valves are right next to each other.

Radiator

Since most stroker engines have the displacement of a big-block engine, use a big-block sized radiator. Many cars had the option of a big-block when they were new, and the larger radiator helps cooling. Some stock radiators don't allow enough coolant flow and can't keep up with the demand of a high-performance water pump. For example, many sprint-car radiators have a bypass in the radiator so that the water pump gets enough volume of coolant. One way to fix this situation is to use a high-performance aluminum radiator. These high-performance radiators have larger-diameter passages inside and allow better coolant flow. An added benefit of aluminum radiators is higher efficiency and better dissipation of heat than the copper/brass radiators.

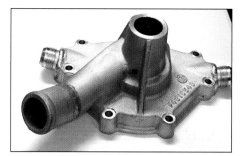

This high-performance water pump P4876548 has been modified for use with external plumbing AN lines. Special aluminum AN fittings are welded onto the water pump. These lines connect to fittings on each side of the engine block. This pump must be used with a motor plate or a special front cover.

Electric Cooling Fan

Install a heavy-duty electric cooling fan. Consider a dual-fan unit with two motors and electronics that turn it on when needed. Install a manual override switch so you can manually turn on the electric fan when desired. Be sure to use a shroud on rear-mounted fans. Fans mounted in front of the radiator should not be used with a shroud since this blocks airflow to the radiator at higher speeds when the fan isn't doing much good.

This water pump has been modified for more clearance to the fuel pump. The tubular portion of the pump is cut off at a slight angle, rotated, and welded back on. Note the bypass and heater hose tubes have been cut off and plugged. Don't plug the bypass tube unless you are not going to use a thermostat in the cooling system.

Oil Cooler

An oil cooler is another way to provide more cooling for your engine. The best way to add an oil cooler is with an

This water pump (Mopar #P5249559) has a special impeller that has eight blades instead of only six. The extra blades give this water pump more flow.

This front cover has been modified for use with a motor plate and water pump P4876548. The cover has been milled to allow room for a motor plate. You should still be able to locate the water pump impeller close to the front cover. If a motor plate is added without milling the front cover, the water pump is not very efficient since the impeller is too far away from the front cover (back of the water pump housing).

High Performance Pulleys

Aluminum HP pulleys are available from several sources. Most water pumps run at about 65% to 75% of crankshaft speed using the stock-size pulleys.

Don't reduce the speed of the water pump for increased performance. Many aftermarket pulley manufacturers advertise increased HP by reducing the speed of the water pump, but this can be a problem with stroker engines. The performance increase is due to the reduction in power that it takes to turn the water pump at a slower speed.

Two common sources for billet aluminum pulleys for Mopar engines are listed in the chart.

The only application in which the speed of the water pump should be reduced is in sustained high-RPM applications (over 6,000 rpm). Stroker engines are not designed for high RPM, so reducing the water pump speed leads to overheating problems.

From 1998-'03, the Magnum 5.9L production engines used a special damper that has the crank pulley cast as part of the damper. This makes it difficult to use an aftermarket pulley since the stock pulley cannot be unbolted from the damper. The only way to use aftermarket pulleys is to swap out the damper with an earlier 1993-'97 5.9L Magnum damper P5007187. This damper has the same external balance but does not have the pulley cast into it. Be sure to use this damper with 5.9L Magnum engines since other dampers may not have the correct external balance. See Chapter 4 for more information on external balance.

Sometimes a higher-pressure radiator cap is enough to keep the coolant from boiling over. The boiling point rises when the coolant pressure is increased. This radiator cap is available from Speedway Motors and has a 28- to 32-lbs. pressure rating.

Manufacturer	Part Number	Description
Champ Pans	JR183	Billet Water Pump Pulley – 2 groove
	JR184	Billet Crankshaft Pulley – 2 groove
March Performance	many options	See www.marchperf.com

oil filter adapter like Moroso #23680. This adapter fits the Magnum, R3, and 340 replacement engine blocks, and screws on instead of the oil filter. Other blocks can use a similar adapter, but the oil filter is a slightly different size. This adapter is for use with AN lines and requires the use of a remote oil filter housing. This adapter also provides more clearance for headers when space is tight.

Water Pump

Consider using a high-performance water pump to increase water flow. In general, the more flow, the more heat can be carried away. Older cooling system theory said to slow down the water flow to pick up more heat, but most experts now agree that increased coolant flow can carry more heat out of the engine. Make sure the rest of the system doesn't restrict coolant flow and can keep up with the water pump. The water inlet side of the water pump is critical (grind to minimize any flow restriction due to sharp edges or other casting defects).

Radiator Cap

Use a 22- to 28-lb. pressure radiator cap. The increase in pressure can significantly increase the boiling temperature of the coolant, and keep it in a liquid form. High-pressure radiator caps are available from Speedway Motors.

Airflow Through the Radiator

An adequate entrance and exit for air that flows through the radiator is needed.

On some cars, the motor plate limits the air exiting through the radiator. Airflow is blocked and bottles up in front of the radiator. Make sure the air doesn't go around the radiator after it enters the grille. Construct ducting to block any open areas where air can bypass the radiator.

Overflow Bottle

Always use a radiator overflow bottle. The best choices are ones that allow the coolant to flow back into the engine. The way to make coolant flow back into the engine is to add a line from the bottom of the coolant bottle to the inlet side of the water pump. This type of system won't let the coolant system run low after it has spit out some coolant into the overflow bottle.

Coolants

50/50 water/anti-freeze is a much better coolant than water alone, and should be used in most engines.

In some severe high-heat situations, Propylene-Glycol can be used as a coolant. It has a much higher boiling point than other coolants. Contact Evans Cooling Systems for more details on this coolant.

Conclusion

With special attention paid to the recommendations shown in this chapter, your stroker engine should handle just about any conditions without overheating. Engines built with Siamese bore blocks require more modifications to the cooling system. Be sure to consider the cooling system when the engine is built. Also consider the cooling system when making modifications to the chassis that may be necessary for the radiator, oil cooler, fan, and other cooling system components.

BUILDING AND BLUEPRINTING

This chapter takes you through the major steps in building a 408-stroker engine. This engine is a mild-performance engine suitable for use in most street rods or muscle cars.

More emphasis is placed on the engine mock-up stage than the actual engine build since this is where special fitting and checking is required. Once all the parts fit correctly and all the issues are resolved, the actual engine assembly process is the same as it would be with any other engine.

This engine uses the following major parts:

- R3 Race Block P4876796AC
- Mopar Cast Crank P5007958
- Magnum R/T Cylinder Heads P5007141
- Mopar M1 Single-Plane Intake Manifold P5007380
- Eagle SIR Rods (6.123")
- KB Hypereutectic Pistons #KB356 (4.030")

Block Preparation / Engine Mockup

The R3 block used in this engine is a non-Siamese bore and has 360 main bearings. The R3 block is used with a standard-style wet-sump oiling system and requires a few modifications.

This 408-ci stroker engine uses the Mopar 4.000" cast crank with 360 mains, 6.123" Eagle SIR rods, and 4.030" KB hypereutectic pistons.

This stroker engine was mocked up (test built) prior to balancing the rotating assembly to make sure everything fit correctly. If the mockup is done prior to balancing the engine, then minor changes don't change the balancing. Just accept the fact that you need to assemble the engine at least twice since it needs to be fully assembled in the mockup stage, and later at final assembly. This is the only way to make sure everything fits correctly and to keep all parts clean after minor machining, grinding, and fitting.

With any stroker engine, minor grinding or machining is needed to provide enough clearance for the longer stroke. Each part should be installed to make sure it fits correctly, especially non-

stock items (i.e., stroker crank, rods, pistons), or where clearance could be a problem with the longer stroke (i.e., oil pan, heads, oil pump, oil pickup).

The piston rings can be omitted in the mockup stage, making the engine a little easier to assemble. Full-floating piston pins also make the engine easier to assemble since the pistons don't need to be pressed onto the rods using special tools only available at a machine shop. The oil galley and water plugs should not be installed yet, since the block is washed after the mockup is complete.

Additional information and a complete bill of materials for this engine are provided in engine package #3 in Chapter 15.

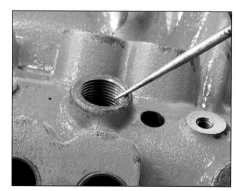

Mopar R3 blocks have a solid valley without slots, unlike production blocks, which do have slots. Do not install plugs in these tapped holes with a flat-tappet camshaft. The flat-tappet cam needs plenty of oil dripping on the cam for lubrication.

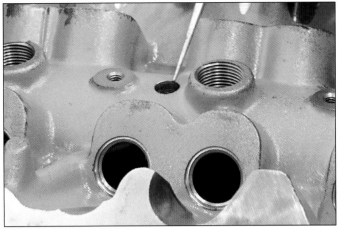

Four or five extra 1/2" holes in the valley are drilled to allow more oil to drip on the cam. These extra holes also minimize the amount of oil that gets trapped in the valley. Be sure to drill these holes in places that don't get into the cam bearings or oil galleys.

The block is filed and de-burred to get rid of any sharp edges that could allow small pieces of the casting to come loose, or where you could cut your hands when working. This block had quite a bit of casting flash that needed to be removed to provide good water flow from the pump into the block.

The distributor bushing is installed using the proper tool. If the tool is not used, the bushing does not fit tightly in the block and won't be burnished to the proper size.

The bushing is driven into the block by tapping on it with a hammer. A wrench is then used to pull the tool through the bushing so that it burnishes it to the proper size as it expands into the block casting at the same time.

The tapped oil-feed hole on the front china wall is not used on this engine, so it must be plugged. This plug was too long and stuck out too far and got in the way of the intake manifold.

The plug was machined shorter so that it did not stick out so far and interfere with the intake manifold. This oil passage could be used for a remote filter or oil cooler in some applications, but it is blocked by the intake on this engine. (Right)

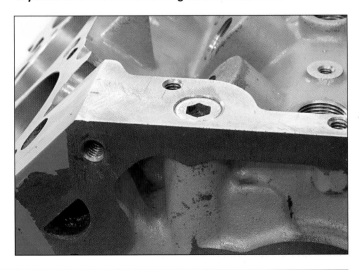

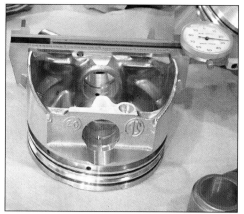

The block has been bored and the machining is checked to make sure the piston-to-bore clearance is correct. The piston-to-bore clearance is correct and within the KB specs.

The two oil passages coming up from the cam are tapped and plugged since they won't be used with Magnum R/T heads. A 5/16" set screw blocks the oil flow since the heads are oiled through the tappets and pushrods. This plug can be removed later if different heads are ever used.

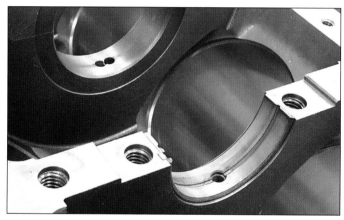

This is what the oil passages look like after grinding away the metal between them to improve oil flow. This allows enough oil flow to all of these passages.

This block did not have adequate oil flow on the two or three oil passages that intersect just above the main bearings. The divider between these passages was ground away to fix the problem (rear bearing saddle requires grinding).

The crank is then measured to calculate the oil clearance by comparing the crank numbers to the bearing measurements. This block is within the desired range and has about 0.0020" to 0.0024" vertical oil clearance on the mains.

The main bearings are measured to calculate the oil clearance. The main caps were installed and torqued to 85 ft-lbs before this measurement was taken.

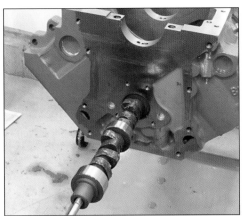

A long 7/16" bolt was used as a handle to help guide the camshaft into place. The cam tunnel is somewhat shrouded in the R3 block, so it must be handled from the front.

The same measurement process was repeated on the rods. The rods were also checked to make sure the edge of the rod bearing doesn't ride too close to the edge of the journal.

A small 1/64" hole was drilled in one of the front oil galley plugs. Dorman plug #555-008 is used on R3 blocks since they have a slightly smaller plug size than stock blocks. Don't install this plug until after the mockup is complete and the block is washed. This small oil hole squirts oil onto the fuel pump eccentric to minimize wear. A small Dremel tool was used to work with this very small drill bit.

The combination timing chain tensioner and thrust plate was also drilled with a larger hole that allows oil to squirt through (goes in front of the plug with the small 1/64" hole). Care was taken to clean up any metal shavings and burrs from this part before assembly.

The timing chain tensioner was installed to hold the camshaft in place. Test fit the timing cover to make sure it fits over the tensioner correctly. Sometimes the tensioner needs some minor adjustment to fit under the cover. Don't install the timing cover at this time.

The timing set was installed temporarily by lining up the two dots using the same procedure as shown in the service manual. Help was needed from an assistant to pry the tensioner out of the way when installing the timing set. Don't remove the retainer pin until the timing set is installed.

A dial indicator was used to check end play on the crank. This crank needed slightly more end play, so the crank was removed and the thrust surfaces of the #3 main bearings were rubbed on a piece of fine emery paper. This took care of the problem and brought the play to about 0.007".

The crank was rotated and clearance checked from the bottom of the pistons to the counterweight on the crank. The KB pistons and Mopar crank fit correctly without any problems (it is close, but there's plenty of room).

The connecting rods were really close to the oil pickup tube, but it still has enough clearance. The Eagle rods provided more clearance here than stock rods.

Each rod-and-piston assembly was installed to check for any interference. The piston rings were omitted to make it easier to install the pistons at this point in the mockup. As expected, the Eagle SIR rods cleared everything without any problems.

The gear on the intermediate shaft hit the block and would not turn. This area had to be ground slightly to provide enough clearance for the gear to correct the problem.

The rod was also very close in this area. Make sure the pickup is not hitting the rods, and that the pickup is located at the correct depth in the oil pan. Moroso says the pickup should be about 3/8" from the bottom of the oil pan. Measure the depth and make sure it is in the correct location. The pickup tube and pump were marked so that they can be installed the same way later on.

This oil pan just touched the outer edge of the three center main caps, but it slipped over them. The holes in the oil pan had to be opened up slightly to fit all bolt holes in the block. The engine was slowly rotated with the oil pan on to listen for any contact between the rods and other parts.

The KB pistons stuck out the top of the deck too far and interfered with the closed chambers on the Magnum R/T heads. The pistons were removed and machined to take about 0.080" off the stepped dome area. The machining process is shown in Chapter 7.

The degree wheel was installed on the crankshaft and a piece of welding wire was used as a temporary pointer. The positive stop was installed in the spark plug hole, and the engine was rotated forward and backward until the #1 piston just touched the positive stop. The degrees were marked at each location and TDC is located halfway between these two locations.

The fuel pump and water pump were mounted on the timing cover to check for clearance. This combination of parts did not allow enough clearance. A fuel pump block-off plate was used to solve the problem since this application can use an electric fuel pump.

A degree wheel and positive stop was used to find the top dead center and confirm the timing marks on the damper and front cover.

A dial indicator was used to measure tappet lift and confirm the proper timing of the camshaft relative to the crankshaft. A one-degree offset camshaft key was used to make a minor adjustment in the camshaft timing. The distributor was also installed at this time. The distributor does not go through the intake manifold like other engines, so it can be installed now and doesn't need to be removed during the rest of the assembly process.

Lightweight valvesprings were installed on the #1 cylinder for use in checking valve-to-piston clearance. These springs make it easier to open the valves by hand in the mockup process.

Minor grinding was needed on the Magnum R/T heads for pushrod clearance. A small die grinder was used to make more clearance for the pushrods.

Disassembly and Cleaning

After the mockup was complete, the engine was completely disassembled and cleaned. All of the minor filing and modifications got the block dirty, and it needed cleaning before final assembly. Several sizes of brushes were used to scrub each passage on the block to get it clean.

The large bottle brush was used to scrub out the bores and remove any metal shavings and dirt from grinding in the mockup. Smaller brushes were used to clean out all other passages on the block.

All water was blown off the block with shop air. Each and every passage must be free of water, or rust forms very quickly on the block.

The block was sprayed with WD-40 to keep it from rusting while the other parts are sent out for balancing.

Final Assembly

The small cup plug was installed in the oil galley just above the oil pump. This plug is easy to forget, but it forces the oil to go through the oil filter.

The rest of the plugs were installed in the water and oil galleys.

This engine was externally balanced to the 360 LA specifications, and it did not require any Mallory metal. The stock 360 damper and torque converter must be used with this externally balanced engine.

The plug that goes in the distributor pocket was also installed. This plug is also easy to forget since you cannot see it without really looking for it. The square head on this plug (and other stock Mopar plugs) uses an odd 5/16" square size. The easiest way to install or remove these plugs is to make a special tool by grinding on a bolt until it fits inside the 5/16" square. This bolt is then used with a wrench to install or remove these plugs.

The oil filter plate, adapter, and gasket were installed. Don't forget to install the plug that goes in the block behind this filter plate.

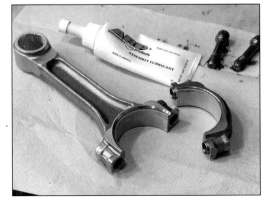

The cap screws in the Eagle rods were lubed with ARP assembly lubricant and prepared for assembly in the engine.

The KB pistons were installed with Spirolocks on each side of the piston pin. These locks take a little practice to install. The locks are rotated around and pushed into the groove of the piston with a small screwdriver.

Check the piston ring gap by installing the ring in each bore. KB recommends more end gap on the top rings. This is because it is subjected to more heat than normal since it is located closer to the top of the piston.

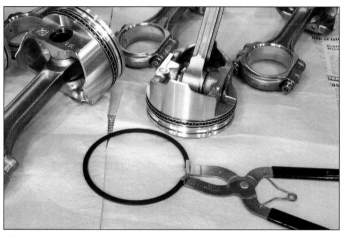

The rings were installed using a Craftsman ring spreader. This tool makes it much easier to install the rings without bending them or spiraling them on.

The pistons are installed in the normal manner with care not to damage the rings.

The dipstick tube was bent slightly to clear the fuel pump mounting base on the front cover. It was also cut down approximately 1.25" to calibrate it for the seven-quart deep sump Moroso oil pan. This is normally done after the engine is assembled and running, since the oil should be drained and refilled with seven quarts to determine where the full mark is at on the dipstick.

The stock Magnum head gasket blocks water flow through the large passages located just under the gasket on the front of each side of the block (see pointer). These holes should be plugged with other gaskets to minimize coolant flow that exits into the heads and intake too quickly without picking up much heat.

The Moly-coated fuel pump eccentric was installed on the front of the timing gear. Note the small hole in the backing plate for the timing chain tensioner (located at about 3 o'clock), this allows a small amount of oil to squirt on the timing change/gears/eccentric.

Grade-8 5/16" x 1.500"-long bolts were used on the rockers arms (use with a lock washer). Magnum R/T heads have large ports so the stock bolts are too long and bottom-out in the tapped holes. The result is bolts that look tight but aren't, and they easily break off. Torque the bolts to 21 ft-lbs.

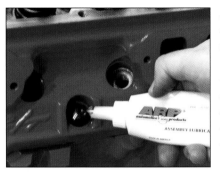

ARP assembly lubricant is also used on the ARP heads studs. These new ARP studs for the Magnum heads feature a small hex on the head that makes them easier to install and remove with an allen wrench.

Fill the unused dowel holes on the bottom ends of the Magnum intakes. These dowel holes are designed to work with some LA blocks, but they often leak when not needed (particularly with gasket set P4876049).

A Holley 0-3310S 750-cfm carb is bolted on with a thin Edelbrock carb adapter plate. The carb plate is needed to fill a small gap at the edge of the carb surface (spread bore shape on intake, but used with square bore carb). The dyno test data for this engine is shown in Chapter 15.

This engine was topped off with a set of Mopar Magnum die-cast valve covers. Heavy-duty reusable valve cover gaskets were used with these covers. These covers provide extra room inside the cover that may be needed with a future upgrade to roller rocker arms. Allen-head screws work best with these valve covers since they have limited wrench clearance around the fasteners.

Additional Information

Stock Production Specifications

Blueprint Specifications	1968-'73 LA 340	1971-'92 LA 360	1993-'03 Magnum 5.9L
Engine Block:			
Cylinder Bore	4.040"-4.042"	4.000"-4.002"	4.000"-4.002"
Max. Overbore	0.040"	0.040"	0.020"
Tappet Bore	0.9050"-0.9058"	0.9051"-0.9059"	0.9051"-0.9059"
Crankshaft Bore Diameter	2.6925"-2.6932"	3.0025"-3.0030"	3.0025"-3.0030"
Pistons:			
Piston Pin Diameter	0.9841"-0.9843"	0.9841"-0.9843"	0.9845"-0.9848"
Piston Pin Type	Full Floater	Press Fit in Rod	Press Fit in Rod
Piston Pin Clearance	0.0000"-0.0005"	0.00025"-0.00075"	0.00023"-0.00074"
Piston Weight	585 grams	584 grams	470 grams
Piston Pin Weight	132 grams	154.6 grams	134 grams
Piston Ring Weight	N/A	56.6 grams	40 grams
Connecting Rods:			
Length	6.123"	Same	Same
Weight	726 grams	758 grams	744 grams
Side Clearance (2 rods)	0.006"-0.014"	Same	Same
Housing Bore - Small End	1.027"-1.039"	0.9829"-0.9834"	.9819"-.9834"
Conn. Rod Bearing Clearance	0.0005"-0.0015"	0.0005"-0.0020"	0.0005"-0.0022"
Max. Allowed	0.0025"	Same	Same
Housing Bore - Big End	2.2500"-2.2507"	Same	Same
Width – Small End	1.200"	1.200"	.9305"
Bushing – Small End	Steel Backed Bronze	None	None
Crankshaft:			
Type	Internally Balanced	Externally Balanced	Externally Balanced
Stroke	3.310"	3.580"	3.580"
Main Bearing Journals	2.4995"-2.5005"	2.8095"-2.8105"	2.8095"-2.8105"
Rod Bearing Journals	2.124"-2.125"	Same	Same
Desired Bearing Clearance	.0005"-.0015"	0.0005"-0.0020"	#1 0.0005"-0.0015", #2-#5 0.0005"-0.0022"
Max. Allowed	0.0025"	0.0025"	#1 0.0015", #2-#5 0.0025"
End Play	0.002"-0.007"	Same	Same
Max. Allowed	0.010"	Same	Same
Camshaft:			
Camshaft Journals (Diameter – Std 59-Degree Tappet Bore)			
#1	1.998"-1.999"	Same	Same
#2	1.982"-1.983"	Same	Same
#3	1.967"-1.968"	Same	Same
#4	1.951"-1.952"	Same	Same
#5	1.5605"-1.5615"	Same	Same

Continued on next page

Stock Production Specifications *continued*

Blueprint Specifications	1968-'73 LA 340	1971-'92 LA 360	1993-'03 Magnum 5.9L
Camshaft Bearings I.D. (Diameter – Std 59-Degree Tappet Bore)			
#1	2.000"-2.001"	Same	Same
#2	1.984"-1.985"	Same	Same
#3	1.969"-1.970"	Same	Same
#4	1.953"-1.954"	Same	Same
#5	1.5625"-1.5635"	Same	Same
Camshaft Bore in Block (Diameter – Std 59-degree Tappet Bore)			
#1	2.1290"-2.1305"	Same	Same
#2	2.1130"-2.1145"	Same	Same
#3	2.0980"-2.0995"	Same	Same
#4	2.0820"-2.0835"	Same	Same
#5	1.6915"-1.6930"	Same	Same
Tappets:			
Diameter	0.904"-0.9045"	0.9035"-0.9040"	0.9035"-0.9040"
Clearance in Block	0.0005"-0.0018"	0.0011"-0.0024"	0.0011"-0.0024"
Tappet Angle	59 degree	Same	Same
Intake Valves:			
Head Diameter	2.020"	1.880"	1.920"
Stem Diameter	0.372"-0.373"	0.372"-0.373"	8mm
Length	4.900"	4.900"	4.969"-4.994"
Stem to Guide Clearance	0.001"-0.002"	0.001"-0.003"	0.001"-0.003"
Exhaust Valves:			
Head Diameter	1.600"	1.600"	1.625"
Stem Diameter	0.371"-0.372"	0.371"-0.372"	8mm
Valve Length	4.900"	4.900"	4.978"-0.5012"
Stem to Guide Clearance	0.002"-0.004"	Same	Same
Valvesprings:			
Installed Height	1.6250"-1.6875"	1.6250"-1.6875"	1.640"

R3 Blocks & Aluminum "A" Blocks – Camshaft Dimensions (48-degree blocks only)

Engine Block	48-degree R3 Block w/ Babbitt Cam Bearings	48-degree Aluminum A & R3 Blocks w/ 50mm Roller Cam Bearings
Camshaft:		
Camshaft Journals		
Journals #1 through #5	1.998"-1.999"	1.967"
Camshaft Bearings I.D.		
Journals #1 through #5	2.000"-2.001"	1.968"
Camshaft Bore in Block		
Journals #1 through #5	2.1290"-2.1305"	2.2817"-2.2822"
Tappet Angle	48 degrees	48 degrees

Torque Specifications

	Thread Size	Torque (Ft-Lbs)	Notes
Bell-Housing Bolts	3/8"-16	30	
	7/16"-14	50	
Camshaft Sprocket Bolt	7/16"-14	50	
Camshaft Thrust Plate	5/16"-18	210 in-lbs	
Connecting Rod Nuts	3/8"-24	45	(Stock Bolt & Nut Only)
Crankshaft Pulley Bolts	5/16"-28	210 in-lbs	
Cylinder Head Bolts	1/2"-13	95	(Stock Bolts Only)
	3/8"-16	45	(w/ 6-Bolt Heads Only)
Damper Bolt	3/4"-16	100	
Distributor Clamp Bolt	5/16"-18	200 in-lbs	
Flywheel Bolts	7/16"-20	55	
Flex Plate Bolts	7/16"-20	55	
Fuel Pump Bolts	3/8"-16	30	
Intake Manifold Bolts	3/8"-16	35	(LA Engines)
	5/16"-18	12	(Magnum Engines)
Header Bolts	5/16"-18	25	(Cast Iron Heads)
	3/8"-16	25	(Aluminum Heads)
Main Bearing Caps	1/2"-13	85	
Oil Pan Bolts	5/16"-18	15	
Oil Pump Cover Bolts	1/4"-20	95 in-lbs	
Oil Pump Mounting Bolts	3/8"-16	30	
Oil Filter Fitting	3/4"-16	50	
Rocker Shaft Bolts	5/16"-18	15	(LA Heads)
Rocker Arm Bolts	5/16"-18	21	(Magnum Heads)
Spark Plugs	14 mm	30	
Starter Bolts	7/16"-14	50	
Timing Cover Bolts	3/8"-16	30	
Valve Cover Bolts	1/4"-20	95 in-lbs	
Water Pump Bolts	3/8"-16	30	

High-Performance Blueprint Recommendations

Main Bearing Clearance	0.002" - 0.003"
Rod Journal Clearance	0.002" - 0.003"
Rod Side Clearance	0.011" - 0.014"
Crankshaft End Play	0.002" - 0.007"
Piston To Bore Clearance	Use Piston Manufacturers Recommendations
Piston Ring End Gap	Use Ring Manufacturers Recommendations

ENGINE PACKAGES

OK, now that we have discussed the details of each component part of the big-inch stroker engine, it's now time to see what some of these engines make on the dyno. Several engine packages are shown in this chapter, ranging from mild show car engines to the monster 476-ci small-block.

Dyno data is shown where available, so you see the power these engines really make.

A few of these packages show very serious racing engines that are not too practical for a street-driven vehicle. But they are good examples of what can be done, and they provide insight on what parts work

together to make good power. Often minor changes to the package like different heads, valvetrain, and camshaft can make the same type of engine very streetable.

It's now time to put one of these engines in your street car or hot rod and rip a little asphalt.

Engine Package 1: 414ci – Bracket Racer

This engine was built for use in a 1965 Plymouth A Body used in drag racing (bracket racing). This engine looks just like the stock 5.9L Magnum with aluminum Magnum heads and M1 intake, but packs 414ci and 523 hp. This car easily rips though a quarter mile in about 10 seconds.

This engine is really only suitable for drag racing due to the aluminum rods. With a change to steel rods, this package would make a great street engine with peak torque at 4,250 rpm and over 400 ft-lbs torque from 3,750 to 6,250 rpm. The camshaft is also a little aggressive for a street engine. But just imagine almost 525 hp at the next stoplight in a lightweight A Body like a Duster, Dart, or your street rod.

Engine:	414ci
Bore / Stroke"	4.060" / 4.000"
Power:	523 hp @ 5,500 and 561 ft-lb @ 4,250
Output per Ci:	1.26 hp/ci and 1.35 ft-lbs/ci
Compression:	10:1
Block:	Magnum 5.9L Block – Modified for 4-bolt mains
Crankshaft:	Forged Mopar #P5007254
Rods:	Bill Miller Engineering – Forged Aluminum
Piston & Rings:	Diamond Racing #51028, Total Seal Rings
Oil Pan & Pump:	Stock Pan, Melling M72HV
Camshaft:	Hydraulic Roller Tappet, COMP Cams #20-000-0 236/243 duration at 0.050", 0.625"/ 0.625" lift, 108 centerline
Tappets:	Hydraulic Roller
Pushrods:	Custom
Rocker Arms:	COMP Cams
Cylinder Heads:	P4876624 w/ extensive porting
Valve Sizes:	Manley, 2.020"/1.625"
Intake Manifold:	Mopar M1 #P5249501 w/ porting
Carburetor:	750-cfm Holley 4-barrel
Ignition:	Mopar Distributor #P3690430
Ignition Timing:	36 degrees
Headers:	1.875" w/ 3.00" exhaust
Engine Builder:	Denny Hummel @ Booth-Arons Inc.

Dyno Test for 414-ci Bracket Racer

RPM	Torque	HP
3500	343	229
3750	403	288
4000	496	378
4250	561	454
4500	557	477
4750	545	493
5000	541	515
5250	520	519
5500	500	523
5750	477	522
6000	454	518
6250	419	498
6500	395	489

Engine Package 2: 414ci – Best of Production

This engine is a concept engine package that uses as many production parts as possible to make the most performance for the least amount of money. The best used production parts are specified to keep the cost low. Since this is a concept engine, I don't have dyno data available, but I estimate that it would make about 425 hp and 450 ft-lbs torque with stock un-ported Magnum heads.

An early 360 block is suggested since it is inexpensive and can be bored to 4.060". The early (1971-'74) 360 block has more stock in the bore walls, and this also provides a better ring seal since the bore is thicker and more stable. A 340 block would allow a few more inches but is more expensive and tough to find in good condition, and this increases the cost of the engine.

Stock production Magnum heads are used since they provide the highest intake airflow of any factory heads. The Magnum rocker arms also provide more lift with a slightly higher rocker arm ratio (1.6:1) than the LA production rocker arms. These heads are available used for a pretty reasonable price, and they can be bought with the rocker arms, valves, springs, keepers, retainers, and valve covers (if possible). The stock Magnum valvesprings are not suitable for a high-lift camshaft and should be replaced with P5249464 valvesprings and P4452032 retainers. Be careful when buying used Magnum heads since they are often cracked on the valve seats. It is recommended that the valves be removed on any used heads for a careful inspection before buying them.

This camshaft shown below has more lift and duration on the exhaust, which is desirable with Magnum heads. This cam is designed for 1.5:1 ratio rocker arms (w/ 0.467"/0.494" lift), but it has more lift with the 1.6:1 Magnum rocker arms (0.498"/0.526"). The exhaust headers are also large to help minimize the exhaust flow restriction with Magnum heads. The intake airflow on these heads stalls at about 0.550" lift, so it doesn't do much good to open the valve more than this without extensive porting on the heads.

The early connecting rods (i.e., 1965-'73 273/318/340) come from the factory with full floating pins (bushed at the small end). This is a very desirable feature that would probably cost $200 to add to any other stock rods. The block requires minor clearancing at the bottom of the bores for these connecting rods.

The Mopar cast pistons are inexpensive and work with the closed chamber Magnum heads without any problems. Another option would be to use Diamond forged pistons, but these are a little more expensive.

If the engine is externally balanced using the stock 360 damper and flywheel or torque converter, the cost is about $200 less for balancing. This package should not require any Mallory for an external balance, and this is why the cost is reduced. Try to get the 360 damper with the used block (if possible).

The only aftermarket parts used in this engine are the 4.000" stroker crankshaft, stroker pistons, camshaft, AMC tappets, pushrods, valvesprings, retainers, oil pan, and intake manifold.

Engine:	414ci
Bore / Stroke:	4.060" / 4.000"
Power:	Estimated 425 hp @ 5,100 and 450 ft-lb @ 4,300
Output per CI:	Estimated 1.03 hp/ci and 1.09 ft-lbs/ci
Compression:	9.5:1
Block:	Used Early 360 Block (1971-'74)
Crankshaft:	Cast Mopar #P5007958 - Externally Balanced
Damper:	Stock 360 w/ External Balance
Rods:	Used (1967-'73) 318 rods w/ stock bushings
Piston & Rings:	Mopar #P5007731, Summit SUM-133-M139-060
Oil Pan & Pump:	Stock 360 Oil Pan and Stock Oil Pump
Camshaft:	Hydraulic Flat tappet LA cam – Crane # 693801, 222/234 duration @ 0.050", 0.498"/0.526" lift
Tappets:	Summit #HT2001 (set of 16)
Pushrods:	Mopar #P5007477 (set of 16)
Rocker Arms:	Used Magnum
Cylinder Heads:	Used 5.2/5.9L Magnum (1993-'03)
Valve Sizes:	Used Magnum – 1.920"/1.625"
Valvesprings/Retainers:	Mopar #P5249464 and P4452032
Intake Manifold:	Mopar #P5007380 Single Plane
Carburetor:	750-cfm Holley
Ignition:	Mopar Electronic Kit w/ Distributor #P3690426
Ignition Timing:	35 degrees
Headers:	1.875" w/ 2.5" exhaust

Engine Package 3: 408 ci – Street Rod

This engine was built by the author for use in a future project car. The full build-up of this engine is shown in Chapter 14.

Dyno Test for 408-ci Street Rod

RPM	Torque	HP	RPM	Torque	HP
2500	447	213	4600	482	422
2600	455	225	4700	482	432
2700	459	236	4800	474	433
2800	464	247	4900	470	439
2900	465	257	5000	466	444
3000	467	267	5100	464	451
3100	463	274	5200	455	450
3200	460	280	5300	444	448
3300	460	289	5400	436	449
3400	466	302	5500	427	448
3500	469	312	5600	421	446
3600	475	326	5700	409	444
3700	481	339			
3800	483	350			
3900	478	355			
4000	475	362			
4100	477	372			
4200	479	383			
4300	483	395			
4400	483	404			
4500	485	415			

Engine:	408ci
Bore / Stroke:	4.030" / 4.000"
Power:	451 hp @ 5,100 and 485 ft-lb @ 4,500
Output per CI:	1.10 hp/ci and 1.18 ft-lbs/ci
Compression:	9.5:1
Block:	Mopar R3 #P4876796AB
Crankshaft:	Cast Mopar #P5007958
Rods:	Forged Eagle SIR I-Beam
Piston & Rings:	KB Hypereutectic #KB356, Speed Pro Moly
Oil Pan & Pump:	Moroso Steet & Strip #20730 w/ pickup #24700, Melling M72HV
Camshaft:	Hydraulic Flat Tappet LA cam, Crane #693801, 222/234 duration @ 0.050", 0.498"/0.526" lift
Tappets:	Summit #HT2001 (set of 16)
Pushrods:	Mopar #P5007477 (set of 16)
Rocker Arms:	Mopar #P4876050 (8 pieces)
Cylinder Heads:	Mopar Magnum R/T #P5007141
Valve Sizes:	2.020"/1.625"
Intake Manifold:	Mopar #P5007380 Single Plane
Carborator:	750-cfm Holley 4-barrel
Ignition:	Mopar Electronic Kit w/ Distributor #P3690426
Ignition Timing:	35 degrees
Headers:	1.750" w/ 2.5" exhaust

Engine Package 4: 408 ci – Magnum Muscle Car

This engine was built using a used 5.9L Magnum block that was recovered from a Dodge van that had an engine fire. The fire didn't hurt the engine, and many of the parts were re-used. The big-valve Magnum R/T heads were ported, and this really shows in the performance numbers. The torque was never below 425 ft-lbs for the entire dyno run from 3,000 to 6,200 rpm.

This is a good example of some pretty impressive performance without spending a fortune. This engine was built for use in a Dodge Dart muscle car. This car already had a small-block in it from the factory, so installation was a snap. This car is street driven but has also run a 10.40 in the quarter mile.

Engine:	408ci
Bore / Stroke:	4.030" / 4.000"
Power:	505 hp @ 5,900 and 525 ft-lb @ 3,800
Output per CI:	1.24 hp/ci and 1.29 ft-lbs/ci
Compression:	9.0:1
Block:	Magnum 5.9L
Crankshaft:	Forged Mopar #P5007254 – Internally Balanced
Damper:	Stock 318 w/ Neutral Balance
Rods:	Eagle SIR
Piston & Rings:	Diamond #51405, Speed Pro Moly
Oil Pan & Pump:	Moroso Deep Sump #20730 and pickup #24700, Mopar #P4286589
Camshaft:	Hydraulic Roller Cam – Mopar #P4876348 230/234 duration @ 0.050", 0.501"/0.513" lift, 108-Degree Centerline

Engine Package 4: 408 ci – Magnum Muscle Car *continued*

Tappets:	Hydraulic Roller – Included w/ Cam
Pushrods:	Stock Magnum
Rocker Arms:	Stock Magnum
Cylinder Heads:	Mopar Magnum R/T - Big Valve #P5007141 w/ porting
Valve Sizes:	2.020"/1.625"
Intake Manifold:	Mopar M1 Single Plane #P5007380
Carburetor:	750-cfm Holley 4-barrel
Ignition:	Mopar #P3690426
Ignition Timing:	35 degrees
Headers:	1.875" w/ 2.5" dual exhaust
Engine Builder:	Ron Beauchamp, Beauchamp Motorsports, Inc.

Dyno Test for 408-ci Magnum Muscle Car Engine

RPM	Torque	HP	RPM	Torque	HP
3000	466	266	4700	500	447
3100	470	277	4800	494	451
3200	487	297	4900	491	458
3300	492	309	5000	490	466
3400	502	325	5100	483	469
3500	500	333	5200	482	477
3600	515	353	5300	477	481
3700	525	370	5400	469	482
3800	525	380	5500	466	488
3900	519	386	5600	466	497
4000	512	390	5700	459	498
4100	508	396	5800	451	498
4200	509	407	5900	449	505
4300	510	418	6000	436	498
4400	512	429	6100	431	501
4500	505	433	6200	427	503
4600	501	439			

Engine Package 5: 371 – Late Model Race Engine

This engine package is used in the CASCAR Super Series. Owned by NASCAR, CASCAR is the premier Late Model touring series in Canada.

The CASCAR rules allow a 360 stroke with a 0.060" overbore. The best way to get to the 0.060" overbore size is to use a 340 block with a 360 stroke and 4.060" bore size. This combination allows a larger displacement with more stock in the bores and the smaller 340 main journals on the crank. The small main journals reduce bearing friction and reduce the crankshaft weight.

The CASCAR rules require the use of a 390-cfm 4-barrel carburetor, so the key to performance is to build an efficient package that can make good power with the small carb. This engine would make much more power with a larger 650- or 750-cfm carb.

The W2 cylinder heads are very efficient, and the 1.44 hp per cubic inch is pretty impressive (especially with the small carburetor). This package also works well in street applications.

The 371 stroker is probably the easiest street-stroker engine to build. This is because the parts are all readily available and no grinding or special fitting is required. All that's needed is a 340 block, crank with 340 mains, and 360 stroke (i.e., P5007253), and 0.060" oversize 360 pistons.

Engine Package 5 continued on page 130

Engine Package 5: 371ci – Late Model Race Engine *continued*

Engine:	371ci
Bore / Stroke:	4.060" / 3.580"
Power:	521 hp @ 6,400 rpm and 472 ft-lb @ 5,100
Output per CI:	1.44 hp/ci and 1.27 ft-lbs/ci
Compression:	Approximately 10:1
Block:	Mopar 340 Replacement Block #P5007552
Crankshaft:	Forged Mopar #P5007253AB
Rods:	Manley 6.123" w/ 2.100" rod journal
Piston & Rings:	Diamond Forged
Oil Pan & Pump:	Dry Sump w/ Razor Pump
Camshaft:	Mechanical Flat Tappet Mopar #P4529972 252/252 duration @ 0.050", 0.555"/ 0.555" lift, 106-degree Centerline
Tappets:	COMP Cams #801-16
Pushrods:	Custom
Rocker Arms:	T&D w/ 0.700" offset
Cylinder Heads:	Mopar W2 #P5007355
Valve Sizes:	2.020"/1.600"
Intake Manifold:	Mopar #P4529408
Carburetor:	390-cfm Holley 4-barrel
Ignition:	Mopar #P4876735 and P4876729
Ignition Timing:	35 degrees
Headers:	1.750" Headers
Engine Builder:	Ron Beauchamp, Beauchamp Motorsport Inc.

RPM	Torque	HP	RPM	Torque	HP	RPM	Torque	HP
			Dyno Test for 371-ci Late Race Engine					
4000	427	326	5100	472	458	6200	439	518
4100	431	336	5200	472	467	6300	433	519
4200	434	347	5300	471	475	6400	427	521
4300	438	359	5400	470	483	6500	419	519
4400	447	375	5500	468	490	6600	411	517
4500	452	387	5600	466	497	6700	404	515
4600	458	401	5700	462	501	6800	397	514
4700	461	412	5800	456	504	6900	386	507
4800	466	426	5900	454	510	7000	380	507
4900	471	439	6000	450	514			
5000	470	448	6100	443	515			

Engine Package 6: 476 ci – Monster Small Block

The largest Mopar stroker small-block that I have ever seen was 455 inches, but every part is available to build one with up to 476 inches. Although the 476 has not been built yet, every piece is available now and can be bought "off the shelf." The only custom-order part is the piston, since no one currently stocks the piston for this engine. Most custom-piston suppliers can easily make this piston with a special order since it is very close in size to a Mopar big-block Wedge piston (slightly smaller bore size). Diamond and Wiseco would be good sources for these pistons.

Other brand (GM and Ford) small-blocks would require special deck plates, a raised cam, and taller-than-stock deck height to get anywhere near this displacement. These changes make it difficult and expensive to build the engine since non-standard parts are needed for the timing set. Also, the intake manifold needs to be spaced upward with a deck plate. A 4.250" stroke would also be a challenge to fit into GM and Ford blocks since they need extensive machining for clearance on shorter stroke cranks.

With the Mopar R3 Siamese P4876673, the stock timing set fits and the intake manifold P4876162 is a "bolt on" without any modifications (use with W9 heads). The W9 heads are recommended since they flow really well right out of the box and have wide valve centers that allow very large valves.

The suggested parts package shown below lists all the parts needed to build one of these monster stroker engines. The HP and torque numbers are estimated and are probably conservative since the 455 engine made this much power with ported heads and intake. The photos below show what this engine looks like (mockup showing these heads, intake, and valley tray on an R3 block).

Engine Package 6: 476ci – Monster Small Block *continued*

476 ci Monster Small-Block (w/ 48 Degree Roller Cam)

Engine:	476ci
Bore / Stroke:	4.220" / 4.250"
Power:	Estimated 750 to 800 hp @ 7,000 and 660 to 690 ft-lb @ 5,600
Compression:	Approximately 10.0:1
Block:	Mopar R3 #P4876673AC – Tall Deck Siamese Bore w/ 48-degree tappet bore
Crankshaft:	Forged Callies Magnum Plus 4.250" with 2.100" Generic Rod Journals
Rods:	Oliver, Manley, or Carrillo 6.000" Generic Rods
Piston & Rings:	Custom Diamond Forged Flat Top w/ Generic Piston Pin
Oil Pan & Pump:	Moroso Street & Strip #20730 w/ pickup #24700, Melling M72HV
Camshaft:	Mopar UGL #P4876633 w/ custom grind 256/256 duration @ 0.050", 0.650"/0.650" lift, 108-degree Centerline
Cam Bearings:	Mopar #P4876372
Tappets:	Mechanical Roller Tappet Crane #69552-16
Timing Set:	Stock Mopar small-block
Pushrods:	Trend – Hollow Tube 3/8" – Custom Order
Rocker Arms:	Mopar #P5007470 (2 sets)
Cylinder Heads:	Mopar W9 #P5007065AB
Valve Covers:	Mopar #P4876124 and stud kit P4876676
Head Gasket:	Mopar #P4876830 (with 4.250" gasket bore)
Head Stud Set:	Mopar #P4876083
Valve Sizes:	Manley #11468T-8, and 11767-8 (2.180"/1.600") Valvesprings Isky #9945 (check with cam grinder for suitability)
Retainers:	Del West (CV Products) #LTW-550
Keepers:	Manley #13062-16
Valve Seals:	CV Products #752
Valvespring Seats:	CV Products #3330-16
Intake Manifold:	Mopar Single Plane #P4876162
Valley Tray:	Mopar #P4510327 or Fabricated Aluminum
Carburetor:	850-cfm Holley 4-barrel
Ignition:	Mopar Electronic Kit w/ Distributor #P3690426
Ignition Timing:	34 degrees
Headers:	1.875" w/ 3.00" Collector

This part listing shows the 48-degree roller cam setup. A mechanical flat tappet camshaft could also be used with a change to the cam, tappets, and valvesprings. Flat-tappet engines would use UGL cam core P4876634 and COMP Cams tappets #801-16. Softer valvesprings are also needed with a flat tappet cam. The engine output would be slightly lower, but the cam and tappets will be less expensive.

Another lower-cost alternative would be to use the 59-degree R3 block and stock-style Mopar flat tappet camshaft. The drawback with this plan is that the valvetrain is not as reliable at higher RPM, and the intake ports won't have as much material left for porting (notches machined in outside of intake ports for pushrod clearance).

The following parts would need to be changed for a 59-degree tappet bore version of this engine:

Block:	Mopar R3 #P4876793AC
Heads:	Mopar W9 #P4510324
Camshaft:	Stock-Style Mechanical Flat Tappet Cam
Tappets:	COMP Cams #801-16
Cam Bearings:	Stock Mopar Cam Bearings
Valvesprings:	Softer Valvesprings (2.000" installed height w/ 1.580" – 1.62" diameter)
Valves:	Mopar #P4876580 (2.150" intake), and P5249886 (1.600 exhaust)
Valve Seals:	Mopar #P3690963
Retainers/Keepers:	3/8" stem – use what is recommended with the spring

(all other parts are the same as shown above)

STROKER KITS

349ci

Flatlander Racing
24 Elm St.
Plaistow, NH 03865
(603) 378-0090
www.flatlanderracing.com
Bore: . . . . 3.940"
Stroke: . . . . 3.580"
Crankshaft: . . . . Mopar Performance cast crank #P5007257
Main Size: 318/340
Rod Type: . . . . Pro-Line 4340 H-Beam
Rod Length: . . . . 6.123"
Rod Ratio: 1.71:1
Pistons: . . . . JE/SRP/Wiseco/Probe/
. . . . Ross forged pistons
Rings: . . . . -
Bearings: . . . . -
Approx. Price: $1,499
Recommended Block: . . . . LA 318 or 5.2L Magnum Production Block
Comments: . . . . + $379 for rings, bearings and SFI balancer

349ci

RPM Machine
9529 South 500 West
Sandy, UT 84070
(877) 354-3812
www.rpmmachine.com
Bore: . . . . 3.940"
Stroke: . . . . 3.580"
Crankshaft: . . . . Mopar Performance cast crank #P5007257

Main Size: 318/340
Rod Type: . . . . Pro-Line 4340 H-Beam
Rod Length: . . . . 6.123"
Rod Ratio: 1.71:1
Pistons: . . . . JE/SRP/Wiseco/Probe/ Ross forged pistons
Rings: . . . . -
Bearings: . . . . -
Approx. Price: $1,499
Recommended Block: . . . . LA 318 or 5.2L Magnum Production Block
Comments: . . . . price w/ flat top pistons

350ci

Speed-O-Motive Inc.
131 North Lang Ave.
West Covina, CA 91790
(626) 869-0270
www.speedomotive.com
Bore: . . . . 3.910", 3.920", 3.930", or 3.940"
Stroke: . . . . 3.580"
Crankshaft: . . . . Mopar Performance cast crank #P5007257
Main Size: 318/340
Rod Type: . . . . Stage I rods w/ ARP wave loc bolts
Rod Length: . . . . 6.123"
Rod Ratio: 1.71:1
Pistons: . . . . Custom machined cast pistons
Rings: . . . . Sealed Power cast rings
Bearings: . . . . Clevite main and rod bearings

Approx. Price: . . . . $795 w/ free shipping
Recommended Block: . . . . LA 318 or 5.2L Magnum
Production Block
Comments: . . . . + $150 for balancing
+$284 for TRW forged
pistons
+$15 Moly rings
+$125 harmonic balancer
damper
+$35 radius and polish
crankshaft
+$95 cross drill crankshaft
+$125 heat treat crankshaft
+$160 coat piston tops and
skirts

370ci
RPM Machine
9529 South 500 West
Sandy, UT 84070
(877) 354-3812
www.rpmmachine.com
Bore: . . . . 4.060"
Stroke: . . . . 3.580"
Crankshaft: . . . . Mopar Performance cast
crank # P5007257
Main Size: 318/340
Rod Type: . . . . Pro-Line 4340 H-Beam
Rod Length: . . . . 6.123"
Rod Ratio: 1.71:1
Pistons: . . . . JE/SRP/Wiseco/Probe/
Ross forged pistons
Rings: . . . . -
Bearings: . . . . -
Approx. Price: $1,449
Recommended Block: . . . . LA 318 or 5.2L Magnum
Production Block
Comments: . . . . all prices w/ flat top pistons

372ci
Flatlander Racing
24 Elm St.
Plaistow, NH 03865
(603) 378-0090
www.flatlanderracing.com
Bore: . . . . 4.070"
Stroke: . . . . 3.580"
Crankshaft: . . . . Mopar Performance cast
crank # P5007257
Main Size: 318/340
Rod Type: . . . . Pro-Line H-Beam
Rod Length: . . . . 6.123"
Rod Ratio: 1.71:1
Pistons: . . . . JE/SRP/Wiseco/Probe/
Ross forged pistons

Rings: . . . . -
Bearings: . . . . -
Approx. Price: $1,449
Recommended Block: LA 340 or 340 replacement
block
Comments: . . . . + $159 for rings and bearings
+ $640 for forged crankshaft

390ci
Hughes Engines
23334 Wiegand Lane
Washington, IL 61571
(309) 745-9558
www.hughesengines.com
Bore: . . . . 3.940"
Stroke: . . . . 4.000"
Crankshaft: . . . . Cast Steel
Main Size: 318/340
Rod Type: . . . . Forged, I-Beam. 5140
Chrome Moly Steel w/ ARP
Wave Loc bolts & Bronze
wrist pin bushings
Rod Length: . . . . 6.123"
Rod Ratio: 1.53:1
Pistons: . . . . Diamond Racing Forged
Pistons (630 grams w/ pin) –
(suitable for nitrous use up to
125 hp – call if you want to
run more)
Rings: . . . . Moly Piston Rings (file fit)
Bearings: . . . . Federal Mogul Main and
Rod Bearings
Approx. Price: $1,905
Recommended Block: . . . . LA 318 or 5.2L Magnum
Production Block
Comments: . . . . Crankshaft assembly is
dynamically, internally
balanced.
The finished assembly
does not require balance
weights on the torque
converter or flywheel /
flexplate
8.9:1 compression
ratio w/ 65cc head w/ 0.039"
compressed gasket
9.4:1 compression ratio w/
60cc Magnum head w/ 0.039"
compressed gasket
+$240 w/ H-Beam, billet
4340 steel connecting rods
(requires slight notching at
the bottom of the cylinder
bores.)

390ci

Speed-O-Motive Inc.
131 North Lang Ave.
West Covina, CA 91790
(626) 869-0270
www.speedomotive.com

Bore:.....................................3.940", 3.950", or 3.970"
Stroke:...................................4.000"
Crankshaft:..........................Hi-Nodular Cast Crank
Main Size:...........................318/340
Rod Type:............................5140 Forged w/ ARP Wave Loc bolts
Rod Length:...........6.123"
Rod Ratio:.............1.53:1
Pistons:...............Custom forged pistons – design your own compression ratio, allow 4 weeks for completion
Rings:...............Total Seal Max Moly Rings
Bearings:.............Clevite Tri-Metal Main and Rod Bearings
Approx. Price:.........$1,550
Recommended Block:....LA 318 or 5.2L Magnum Production Block
Comments:...........+ $150 for balance crank kit external
+$28 Chrysler flexplate
+$79 Chrysler 7.1" diam. damper
+$270 4340 Forged H-Beam rods
+$150 Total Seal TS1 Race Rings Set

392ci

Speed-O-Motive Inc.
131 North Lang Ave.
West Covina, CA 91790
(626) 869-0270
www.speedomotive.com

Bore:.................4.060"
Stroke:................3.790"
Crankshaft:............Forged
Main Size:.............318/340
Rod Type:.............340 Steel Rods w/ ARP Bolts — Resized & Balanced
Rod Length:............6.123"
Rod Ratio:.............1.61:1
Pistons:...............Lightweight Custom Ross Forged Pistons & Pins
Rings:.................Speed Pro Plasma Moly Rings
Bearings:..............Clevite 77 bearings
Approx. Price:.........$2,525 w/ free shipping
Recommended Block:....LA 340 or 340 Replacement Block

Comments:............+$150 for dynamic balancing
+$399 Eagle H-Beam Rods
+$60 dome or dish pistons

402ci

Muscle Motors
2085 Glenn St.
Lansing, MI 48906
(888) 482-4900
www.musclemotorsracing.com

Bore: ....4.000"
Stroke:................4.000"
Crankshaft: ....Mopar Performance cast crank
Main Size:.............360
Rod Type:.............Eagle I-Beam
Rod Length: ....6.123"
Rod Ratio: 1.53:1
Pistons:...............Keith Black Hypereutetic Pistons
Rings:.................Sealed Power Moly
Bearings:..............Michigan 77 full groove-mains, radius rod bearings
Approx. Price:.........$1,599
Recommended Block:....LA 360 or 5.9L Block
Comments:.............Competition balanced with weighted balancer and flexplate
+$400 for forged crankshaft
+$150 for custom pistons
Oversize pistons up to 0.060" – but some blocks may not allow 0.060" oversize

408ci

Allied Motors Inc.
700 First Capital Drive St.
St. Charles, MO 63301
(636) 946-4747
www.strokerkits.com

Bore: ....4.030"
Stroke:................4.000"
Crankshaft:............HD SCAT cast steel
Main Size:.............360
Rod Type:.............I-Beam 4340 Chrome Moly Rods (140 grams lighter than stock)
Rod Length:...........6.123"
Rod Ratio: 1.53:1
Pistons:...............Custom-forged dished pistons (for pump gas engines)
Rings: ....Speed-Pro Moly
Bearings:..............Clevite 77 or Federal Mogul Bearings
Approx. Price:.........$1,550

Recommended Block:. . . . LA 360 or 5.9L Magnum
Production Block
Comments:. . . . . + $200 for H-Beam Rods

408ci

Flatlander Racing
24 Elm St.
Plaistow, NH 03865
(603) 378-0090
www.flatlanderracing.com
Bore: . . . . 4.030"
Stroke:. . . . . 4.000"
Crankshaft:. . . . . Mopar Performance
cast crank
Main Size:. 360
Rod Type:. . . . . Pro-Line H-Beam
Rod Length:. . . . . 6.123"
Rod Ratio: 1.53:1
Pistons:. . . . . JE/SRP/Wiseco/Probe/Ross/
Venolia forged pistons
Rings: . . . . -
Bearings:. . . . . -
Approx. Price: $1,429
Recommended Block:. . . . LA 360 or 5.9L Magnum
Production Block
Comments:. . . . . + $169 for rings, and bearings

408ci

Hughes Engines
23334 Wiegand Lane
Washington, IL 61571
(309) 745-9558
www.hughesengines.com
Bore: . . . . 4.030"
Stroke:. . . . . 4.000"
Crankshaft:. . . . . Cast Steel
Main Size:. 318/340
Rod Type:. . . . . Forged, I-Beam. 5140
Chrome Moly Steel w/ ARP
Wave Loc bolts
Rod Length:. . . . . 6.123"
Rod Ratio: 1.53:1
Pistons:. . . . . Keith Black Hypereutectic
Pistons w/ quench dome
(quench dome must be milled
to achieve the proper head
clearance when using closed
chamber heads)
Rings: . . . . Sealed Power Moly Piston
Rings (file fit)
Bearings:. . . . . Federal Mogul Main and Rod
Bearings
Approx. Price: . . . . $1,495 - $1,565
Recommended Block:. . . . LA 360 or 5.9L Production
Block

Comments:. . . . . Crankshaft assembly is
dynamically, internally
balanced.
The finished assembly does
not require balance weights
on the torque converter or
flywheel / flexplate
9.4:1 compression ratio
(based on 0.030" oversize w/
65cc head w/ 0.039" com-
pressed gasket)
10.0:1 compression ratio
(based on 0.030" oversize w/
60cc Magnum head w/ 0.039"
compressed gasket)
+$270 w/ H-Beam, billet 4340
steel connecting rods
(requires slight notching
at the bottom of the
cylinder bores.)
Optional Diamond forged
pistons available w/
extra cost.

408ci

Mancini Racing Inc.
33524 Kelly Rd.
Clinton Twp, MI 48035
(586) 790-4100
www.manciniracing.com
Bore: . . . . 4.030"
Stroke:. . . . . 4.000"
Crankshaft:. . . . . Mopar Performance
Cast Steel
Main Size:. 360
Rod Type:. . . . . Eagle SR Performance Rods
Rod Length:. . . . . 6.123"
Rod Ratio: 1.53:1
Pistons:. . . . . Diamond — Forged w/Pins
Rings: . . . . Speed-Pro Performance
Bearings:. . . . . Clevite 77 Rod and Main
Bearings
Approx. Price: $1,325
Recommended Block:. . . . LA 360 or 5.9L
Magnum Production Block
Comments:. . . . . + $400 for forged crankshaft
+ $300 for Eagle H-Beam
Rods

408ci

Muscle Motors
2085 Glenn St.
Lansing, MI 48906
(888) 482-4900
www.musclemotorsracing.com

Bore:.................4.030"
Stroke:...............4.000"
Crankshaft:..........Mopar Performance Cast Crank
Main Size:...........318/340
Rod Type:............CAT 4340 H-Beam
Rod Length:..........6.123"
Rod Ratio:...........1.53:1
Pistons:.............Ross forged lightweight pistons
Rings:...............Childs & Albert (filed to fit)
Bearings:............Michigan 77 full groove mains, full radius rod bearings
Approx. Price:.......$1,999
Recommended Block:...LA 360 or 5.9L Block
Comments:............Competition balanced, internally and ready to install
+$400 for forged crankshaft
+$150 for custom pistons

408ci

Speed-O-Motive Inc.
131 North Lang Ave.
West Covina, CA 91790
(626) 869-0270
www.speedomotive.com

Bore:.................4.030"
Stroke:...............4.000"
Crankshaft:..........High-Nodular Cast 4.00" Stroker Crank
Main Size:...........360
Rod Type:............5140 Forged I-Beam Rods w/ ARP 3/8" Wave Loc Bolts & Full Floater Pins
Rod Length:..........6.123"
Rod Ratio:...........1.53:1
Pistons:.............Keith Black Dish Hypereutectic Pistons
Rings:...............Total Seal Max Moly Rings
Bearings:............Clevite Main and Rod Bearings
Approx. Price:.......$1,175
Recommended Block:...LA 360 or 5.9L Production Block

Comments:............+ $150 for external balancing
+$28 for Chrysler flexplate
+$79 Chrysler new 7.10" dis. damper
+$270 4340 Forged H-Beam Rods
+$150 Total Seal TS1 race ring set
+375 w/ custom forged pistons - design your own compression ratio (allow 4 weeks for completion)

416ci

Flatlander Racing
24 Elm St.
Plaistow, NH 03865
(603) 378-0090
www.flatlanderracing.com

Bore:.................4.070"
Stroke:...............4.000"
Crankshaft:..........Mopar cast crank # P5007256
Main Size:...........318/340
Rod Type:............Pro-Line H-Beam
Rod Length:..........6.123"
Rod Ratio:...........1.53:1
Pistons:.............JE/SRP/Wiseco/Probe/Ross/ Venolia forged pistons
Rings:...............-
Bearings:............-
Approx. Price:.......$1,599
Recommended Block:...LA 340 or 340 replacement block
Comments:............+ $159 for rings, and bearings

416ci

Hughes Engines
23334 Wiegand Lane
Washington, IL 61571
(309) 745-9558
www.hughesengines.com

Bore:.................4.040", 4.060", and 4.070"
Stroke:...............4.000"
Crankshaft:..........Cast Steel
Main Size:...........318/340
Rod Type:............Forged, I-Beam. 5140 Chrome Moly Steel w/ ARP Wave Loc bolts
Rod Length:..........6.123"
Rod Ratio:...........1.53:1
Pistons:.............Keith Black Hypereutectic

Pistons w/ quench dome
(quench dome must be milled
to achieve the proper head
clearance when using closed
chamber heads)

Rings: . . . . Sealed Power Moly Piston
Rings (file fit)

Bearings: . . . . Federal Mogul Main and Rod
Bearings

Approx. Price: . . . . $1,505 - $1,645

Recommended Block: . . . . LA 340 or 340 Replacement
Block

Comments: . . . . Crankshaft assembly is
dynamically, internally
balanced.
The finished assembly does
not require balance weights
on the torque converter or
flywheel / flexplate
9.55:1 compression ratio
(based on 0.020" w/ 65cc
head w/ 0.039" compressed
gasket)
10.1:1 compression ratio
(based on 0.020" w/ 60cc
Magnum head w/ 0.039"
compressed gasket)
+$270 w/ H-Beam, billet 4340
steel connecting rods
(requires slight notching
at the bottom of the
cylinder bores.)
Optional Diamond forged
pistons available w/
extra cost.

416ci

Mancini Racing Inc.
33524 Kelly Rd.
Clinton Twp, MI 48035
(586) 790-4100
www.manciniracing.com

Bore: . . . . 4.070"
Stroke: . . . . 4.000"
Crankshaft: . . . . Mopar Performance
Cast Steel
Main Size: 340
Rod Type: . . . . Eagle SR Performance Rods
Rod Length: . . . . 6.123"
Rod Ratio: 1.53:1
Pistons: . . . . Diamond - Forged w/ Pins
Rings: . . . . Speed-Pro Performance
Bearings: . . . . Clevite 77 Rod and Main
Bearings
Approx. Price: $1,325
Recommended Block: . . . . 340 Production or
340 Replacement Block
Comments: . . . . + $400 for forged crankshaft
+ $300 for Eagle H-Beam
Rods

416ci

Muscle Motors
2085 Glenn St.
Lansing, MI 48906
(888) 482-4900
www.musclemotorsracing.com

Bore: . . . . 4.070"
Stroke: . . . . 4.000"
Crankshaft: . . . . Mopar Performance cast
crank
Main Size: 318/340
Rod Type: . . . . CAT 4340 H-Beam
Rod Length: . . . . 6.123"
Rod Ratio: 1.53:1
Pistons: . . . . Ross forged lightweight
pistons
Rings: . . . . Childs & Albert (filed to fit)
Bearings: . . . . Michigan 77 full groove
mains, full radius rod
bearings
Approx. Price: $1,999
Recommended Block: . . . . LA 340 or 340 Replacement
Block
Comments: . . . . Competition balanced,
internally and ready to install
+$400 for forged crankshaft
+$150 for custom pistons

416ci

RPM Machine
9529 South 500 West
Sandy, UT 84070
(877) 354-3812
www.rpmmachine.com

Bore: . . . . .4.070"
Stroke:. . . . . .4.000"
Crankshaft:. . . . . Mopar Performance cast
crank #P5007256
Main Size:. 318/340
Rod Type:. . . . . Pro-Line 4340 H-Beam Rods
Rod Length:. . . . . 6.123"
Rod Ratio: 1.53:1
Pistons:. . . . . JE/SRP/Wiseco/Probe/Ross
forged pistons
Rings: . . . . -
Bearings:. . . . . -
Approx. Price: $2,099
Recommended Block:. . . . LA 340 or 340 Replacement
Block
Comments:. . . . . all prices w/ flat top pistons

416ci

Speed-O-Motive Inc.
131 North Lang Ave.
West Covina, CA 91790
(626) 869-0270
www.speedomotive.com

Bore: . . . . .4.040" or 4.060"
Stroke:. . . . . .4.000"
Crankshaft:. . . . . High-Nodular Cast 4.00"
Stroker Crank
Main Size:. 318/340
Rod Type:. . . . . 5140 Forged I-Beam Rods w/
ARP 3/8" Wave Loc Bolts &
Full Floater Pins
Rod Length:. . . . . 6.123"
Rod Ratio: 1.53:1
Pistons:. . . . . Keith Black Dish
Hypereutectic Pistons
Rings: . . . . Total Seal Max Moly Rings
Bearings:. . . . . Clevite Tri-Metal Main
and Rod Bearings
Approx. Price: $1,436
Recommended Block:. . . . LA 340 or 340
Replacement Block
Comments:. . . . . + $150 for balancing
+$12 for new flexplate
+$125 harmonic
balancer damper
+175 SFI harmonic damper
+$30 ARP main bolt kit
+$59 ARP head bolt kit
+$280 4340 Forged
H-Beam Rods
+$267 forged Ross dish
top pistons (.030" only)
+$150 Total Seal TSI race
ring set

SOURCE GUIDE

Allied Motors Inc.
700 First Capital Drive St.
St. Charles, MO 63301
(636) 946-4747
www.strokerkits.com

Arias Pistons
13420 S. Normandie Ave.
Gardena, CA 90249
(310) 532-9737
www.ariaspistons.com

ARP Inc.
1863 Eastman Ave.
Ventura, CA 93003
(800) 826-3045
www.arp-bolts.com

Arrow Racing Engines, Inc.
3811 Industrial Drive
Rochester Hills, MI 48309-3116
(248) 852-5151

Automotive Machine
32250 Garfield
Fraser, MI 48026
(586) 296-6501

B&M Racing & Performance
Products
9142 Independence Ave.
Chatsworth, CA 91311-5902
(818) 882-6422
www.bmracing.com

Beauchamp Motorsports, Inc.
Ron Beauchamp
9124 Walker Rd.
McGregor, ON, Canada
N0R1J0
(519) 726-9600

BHJ Products, Inc.
37530 Enterprise Ct.
Newark, CA 94560
(510) 797-6780
www.bhjinc.com

Bill Miller Engineering (BME)
4895 Convair Drive
Carson City, NV 89706
(775) 887-1299

Booth-Arons
Engine Division
3861 West 12 Mile Road
Berkley, MI 48072
(248) 398-2730

Brodix, Inc.
P.O. Box 1347
Mena, AR 71953-1347
(479) 394-1075

Bryant Crankshafts
1600 E. Winston Rd.
Anaheim, CA 92805
(714) 535-4387

Brzezinski Racing Products, Inc.
N50 West 23001 Betker Dr.
Pewaukee, WI 53072
(262) 246-8577
www.castheads.com

Carrillo Industries, Inc.
990 Calle Amanecer
San Clemente, CA 92673-6211
(949) 498-1800
www.carrilloindustries.com

C.A.T. Power Engine Parts
345 Cloverleaf Dr.
Suite C
Baldwin Park, CA 91706-6502
(866) 228-7374
www.catpep.com

Callies Performance Products
P.O. Box 926
Fostoria, OH 44830
(419) 435-2711

Champ Pans / JR Manufacturing, Inc.
6198 Hwy 12 East
Eau Claire, WI 54701
(715) 834-7748
www.champpans.com

Chapman Racing Heads
2261 S. 1560 West
Woods Cross, UT 84087-2366
(801) 292-3909
www.chapmanracingheads.com

Cometic Gasket
8090 Auburn Rd.
Concord, OH 44077
(800) 752-9850
www.cometic.com

COMP Cams
3406 Democrat Rd.
Memphis, TN 38118
(800) 999-0853
www.compcams.com

CP Pistons
1902 McGaw
Irvine, CA 92614
(949) 567-9000
www.pankl.com

Crane Cams, Inc.
530 Fentress Blvd.
Daytona Beach, FL 32114-1200
(386) 252-1151
www.cranecams.com

Crower Cams & Equipment Co.
6180 Business Center Ct.
San Diego, CA 93154-5604
(619) 661-6477
www.crower.com

CV Products
42 High Tech Blvd.
Thomasville, NC 27360-5560
(800) 448-1223
www.cvproducts.com

Demon Carburetion / Barry Grant
1450 McDonald Rd.
Dahlonega, GA 30533
(706) 864-8544
www.barrygrant.com

Diamond Racing Products, Inc.
23003 Diamond Dr.
Clinton Twp, MI 48035
(586) 792-6620

Eagle Specialty Products
P.O. Box 1079
Southhaven, MS 38671-0011
(662) 796-7373
www.eaglerod.com

Earl's Performance Products
189 West Victoria St.
Long Beach, CA 90805
(310) 609-1602
www.earlsplumbing.com

Edelbrock Corp.
P.O. Box 2936
Torrance, CA 90509
(800) 739-3737
www.edelbrock.com

Evans Cooling Systems
255 Rt 41North
Sharon, CT 06069
(888) 990-2665
www.evanscooling.com

Evernham Performance Parts
7100 Weddinton Rd.
Concord, NC 28027
(704) 786-1909

Flatlander Racing
24 Elm St.
Plaistow, NH 03865
(603) 378-0090
www.flatlanderracing.com

Holley Performance Products
P.O. Box 10360
Bowling Green, KY 42102
(270) 782-2900
www.holley.com

Hughes Engines
23334 Wiegand Lane
Washington, IL 61571
(309) 745-9558
www.hughesengines.com

Indy Cylinder Head, Inc.
8621 Southeastern Ave.
Indianapolis, IN 46239-1352
(317) 862-3724
www.indyheads.com

Isky Racing Cams
16020 S. Broadway
Gardena, CA 90247
(323) 770-0930
www.iskycams.com

Jesel Inc.
1985 Cedarbridge Ave.
Lakewood, NJ 08701
(732) 901-1800
www.jesel.com

KB Performance Pistons
4909 Goni Rd.
Carson City, NV 89706-0351
(800) 648-7970

Kinsler Fuel Injection Inc.
1834 Thunderbird Street
Troy, MI, 48084
(238) 362-1156
www.kinsler.com

LA Enterprises / Pankle
Crankshaft
16615 Edwards Road
Cerritos, CA 90703
(562) 926-0434
www.pankl.com

Lokar Performance Products,
Inc.
10924 Murdock Drive
Knoxville, TN 37932
(865) 966-2269
www.lokar.com

Mancini Racing Inc.
33524 Kelly Rd.
Clinton Twp, MI 48035
(586) 790-4100
www.manciniracing.com

Manley Performance
1960 Swarthmore Ave.
Lakewood, NJ 08701
(732) 905-3366
www.manleyperformance.com

March Performance
6020 N. Hix Rd.
Westland, MI 48185
(734) 729-9070
www.marchperf.com

Melling Engine Parts
P.O. Box 1188
Jackson, MI 49204
(517) 787-8172

Miller Special Tools
OTC Division, SPX
Corporation
23400 Industrial Park Court
Farmington Hills, MI 48335
Phone (800) 801-5420

Milodon, Inc.
20716 Plummer St.
Chatsworth, CA 91311-5006
(818) 407-1211

Mopar Performance Parts
P.O. Box 559
Oxford, MI 48371
Techline: (248) 969-1690
www.mopar.com

Moparts Connection
3363 Cleveland Highway
Gainsville, GA 30506
(770) 533-9770
www.mopartsracing.com

Moroso Performance Products
80 Carter Drive
Gulford, CT 06437
(203) 453-6571
www.moroso.com

Mr. Gasket Performance Group
10601 Memphis Ave.
Unit 12
Cleveland, OH 44144
(216) 688-8300

Muscle Motors
2085 Glenn St.
Lansing, MI 48906
(888) 482-4900
www.musclemotorsracing.com

Ohio Crankshaft
5453 S.R. 49
Greenville, OH 45331
www.ohiocrank.com

Oliver Racing Parts
1025 Clancy Ave. NE
Grand Rapids, MI 49503-1082
(800) 253-8108
www.oliver-rods.com

Performance Automotive Warehouse (PAW)
21001 Nordhoff St.
Chatsworth, CA 91311-5911
(818) 678-3000

Pro-Gram Engineering Corp.
P.O. Box 217
Barberton, OH 44203
(330) 745-1004
www.pro-gram.com

Probe Industries
2555 West 237th St.
Torrance, CA 90505
(310) 784-2877
www.probeindustries.com

Professional Products
12705 South Van Ness Ave.
Hawthorne, CA 90250
(323) 779-2020
www.professional-products.com

Ross Racing Pistons
625 S. Douglas St.
El Segundo, CA 90245-4812
(310) 536-0100

RPM Machine
9529 South 500 West
Sandy, UT 84070
(877) 354-3812
www.rpmmachine.com

Scat Enterprises, Inc.
1400 Kingsdale Ave.
Redondo Beach, CA 90278-3983
(310) 370-5501
www.scatenterprises.com

Schoenfeld Headers
605 S. 40th Street
Van Buren, AR 72956
Phone (479) 474-7529
www.schoenfeldheaders.com

Smith Brothers Pushrods
62968 Layton Ave.
Suite 1
Bend, OR 97701
(800) 367-1533
www.pushrods.net

Specialty Products Design, Inc.
11252 Sunco Drive
Rancho Cordova, CA
95742-6515
(916) 635-8108
www.spdexhaust.com

Speed-O-Motive Inc.
131 North Lang Ave.
West Covina, CA 91790
(626) 869-0270
www.speedomotive.com

Speedway Motors
P.O. Box 81906
Lincoln, NE 68501-1906
(402) 323-3200
www.speedwaymotors.com

Summit Racing Equipment
1200 Southeast Ave.
Tallmadge, OH 44278
(800) 230-3030
www.SummitRacing.com

Tex Racing Enterprises
P.O. Box 126
Ether, NC 27247
(910) 428-9522
www.texracing.com

T&D Machine Products
4859 Convair Drive
Carson City, NV 89706-0492
(775) 884-2292

Trend Performance Products
23444 Schoenherr Rd.
Warren, MI 48089
(586) 447-0400

Ultra Pro Machining
6350 Brookshire Blvd.
Charlotte, NC 28216
(704) 392-1715
www.ultrapromachining.com

Weld Tech
1789 S. Green St.
Brownsburg, IN 46112
(317) 852-4450
www.weldtech.com

Wilson Manifolds
4700 NE 11th Ave.
Ft Lauderdale, FL 33334
(854) 771-6216
www.wilsonmanifolds.com

Winberg Crankshafts
2201 W. Cornell Ave.
Englewood, CO 80110
(303) 783-2234

Wiseco Piston Company, Inc.
7201 Industrial Park Blvd.
Mentor, OH 44060
(800) 321-1364
www.wiseco.com

Source by Type of Product

Accessory Drive:
CV Products
Mancini Racing
Moroso Performance Products
March Performance Products
Champ Pans / JR Manufacturing, Inc.

Camshafts / Valvetrain:
COMP Cams
Crane Cams
Crower Cams & Equipment Co.
Hughes Engines
Isky Racing Cams
Jesel Inc.
Mancini Racing
Manley Performance
Melling Engine Parts
Mopar Performance Parts
Smith Brothers Pushrods
T&D Machine
Trend Performance Products

Cooling System Parts:
Champ Pans / JR Manufacturing, Inc.
CV Products
Evans Cooling Systems
Mancini Racing
March Performance
Mopar Performance Parts

Connecting Rods:
Bill Miller Engineering (BME)
Carrillo Industries, Inc
C.A.T. Power Engine Parts
Eagle Specialty Products
Hughes Engines
Mancini Racing
Manley Performance
Oliver Racing Parts
SCAT Enterprises, Inc.

Crankshafts:
Bryant Crankshafts
C.A.T. Power Engine Parts
Callies Performance Products
Crower Cams & Equipment Co.
Eagle Specialty Products
Evernham Performance Parts
Hughes Engines
LA Enterprises / Pankle Crankshaft
Mancini Racing
Mopar Performance Parts
Moparts Connection
Ohio Crankshaft
Oliver Racing Parts
SCAT Enterprises, Inc.
Winberg Crankshafts

Cylinder Heads:
Brodix, Inc.
Edelbrock Corp.
Hughes Engines
Indy Cylinder Heads, Inc.
Mancini Racing
Mopar Performance Parts
Moparts Connection

Cylinder Head Porting:
Brzezinski Racing Products, Inc.
Chapman Racing Heads
Hughes Engines
Ultra Pro Machining
Weld Tech

Engine Blocks:
Evernham Performance Parts
Hughes Engines
Indy Cylinder Heads, Inc.
Mancini Racing
Mopar Performance Parts
Moparts Connection

Fasteners:
ARP
Hughes Engines
Mancini Racing
Mopar Performance Parts
Mr. Gasket Performance Group

Gaskets:
Cometic Gasket
Mopar Performance Parts
Mr. Gasket Performance Group

Headers:
Mancini Racing
Mopar Performance Parts
Schoenfeld Headers

Induction Systems:
Demon Carburetion / Barry Grant
Edelbrock Corp.
Evernham Performance Parts
Holley Performance Products
Hughes Engines
Indy Cylinder Heads, Inc.
Kinsler Fuel Injection, Inc.
Mancini Racing
Mopar Performance Parts
Moparts Connection
Pro-Gram Engineering Corp.
Professional Products
Wilson Manifolds

Machining Services:
Automotive Machine
Arrow Racing Engines, Inc.
Beauchamp Motorsports, Inc.
Booth-Arons
Hughes Engines
Indy Cylinder Heads, Inc.

Main Caps:
Pro-Gram Engineering Corp.

Motor Plates:
Arrow Racing Engines

Oil Pans / Oil Pumps:
Champ Pans / JR Manufacturing, Inc
Mancini Racing
Melling Engine Parts
Milodon, Inc.
Moroso Performance Products

Plumbing:
Earl's Performance Products

Short Blocks:
Beauchamp Motorsports, Inc.
Hughes Engines
Mancini Racing
Mopar Performance Parts

Stroker Pistons:
Arias Pistons
Bill Miller Engineering (BME)
CP Pistons
Diamond Racing Products, Inc.
Hughes Engines
KB Performance Pistons
Mancini Racing
Probe Industries
Ross Racing Pistons
Wiseco Piston Company, Inc.

Stroker Engines:
Beauchamp Motorsports, Inc.
Booth-Arons
Hughes Engines
Indy Cylinder Heads
Mancini Racing
Mopar Performance Parts
Muscle Motors
Speed-O-Motive Inc.

Stroker Kits:
See Appendix A

Tools:
BHJ Products, Inc.
Hughes Engines
Miller Special Tools

Transmission Parts:
B&M Racing & Performance Products
Beauchamp Motorsports, Inc.
Lokar Performance Products, Inc.
Mr. Gasket Performance Group
Speedway Motors
Tex Racing Enterprises

Valley Trays:
Arrow Racing Engines
Mopar Performance Parts

Valve Covers:
Mancini Racing
Mopar Performance Parts
Moroso Performance Products

Engine Build Sheet

Photocopy this form and keep it in a file for each engine

Engine Blueprint Record

Engine Type	
Build Date	
Displacement	
Special Notes:	

Block

Material	
Manuf./PN	
Bore Size	
Cam Location	
Main Bearing Dia.	
Special Mods:	

Piston Diameter and Bore Clearance

Cylinder #	1	3	5	7
Bore Dia.				
Piston Dia.				
Clearance				
Cylinder #	2	4	6	8
Bore Dia.				
Piston Dia.				
Clearance				
Width				

Piston

Piston Brand/PN	
Compression Height	
Wrist Pin Brand/PN	
Wrist Pin Dia./Length	
Wrist Pin Clearance	
Wrist Pin Retainer	

Piston Ring

Ring Brand/PN	
Top Ring Type	
Width	
Side Clearance	
End Gap	
2nd Ring Type	
Width	
Side Clearance	
End Gap	
Oil Ring Type	
Side Clearance	
Gap	

Piston Deck Height

Cylinder #	1	3	5	7
Deck Height				
Cylinder #	2	4	6	8
Deck Height				

Notes

Rod and Main Bearings

Main Bearing Brand/PN	
Rod Bearing Brand/PN	
Camshaft Bearing Brand/PN	

Crankshaft

Crankshaft Brand/PN					
Stroke					
End Play					

Main	1	2	3	4	5
Main Bore					
Main Bore w/bearing					
Crank Main Journal					
Main Bearing Clearance					

Conn. Rod	1	3	5	7
Big End Dia.				
Big End Dia. w/bearing				
Crank Journal Dia.				
Rod Bearing Clearance				

Conn. Rod	2	4	6	8
Big End Dia.				
Big End Dia. w/bearing				
Crank Journal Dia.				
Rod Bearing Clearance				

Connecting Rods

Rod Brand/PN				
Length (Center to Center)				
Side Clearance	1-2	3-4	5-6	7-8
Wrist Pin/Piston Clearance				
Wrist Pin/Rod Clearance				
Rod Bolt Brand/PN				
Rod Bolt Torque				
Rod Bolt Stretch				

Valvetrain Data

Rocker Arms:	
Make	
PN	
Material	
Offset	
Rocker Arm Ratio:	
Intake	
Exhaust	
Intake Valve Lift	
Exhaust Valve Lift	
Pushrod:	
Length	
Diameter	
Wall Thickness	
Lifter:	
Make/PN	
Diameter	
Offset	
Rev Kit Make	
PN	

Crankshaft

Make of Style/Brand	
Cam PN	
Material	
Intake Duration @.050"	
Exhaust Duration @.050"	
Intake Installed at Centerline	
Lobe Separation Angle	
Intake Lobe Lift	
Exhaust Lobe Lift	
Intake Valve-to-Piston Clearance @ 10° ATDC	
Exhaust Valve-to-Piston Clearance @ 10° BTDC	
Intake Valve Lash	
Exhaust Valve Lash	

Cylinder Head

Brand/PN	
Chamber Volume	
Intake Port Volume (cc)	
Intake Valve Type/PN	
Intake Valve Size	
Exhaust Valve Type/PN	
Exhaust Valve Size	
Valvespring Brand/PN	
Valvespring	
Inside Diameter	
Outside Diameter	
Installed Height	
Intake/Exhaust	
Valvespring Seat Pressure	
Valvespring Open Pressure	
Coil Bind Height	
Retainer Make/PN	
Keeper Make/PN	
Head Gasket Thickness	

Engine Balancing

Piston Weight (grams)	
Wrist Pin	
Pin Locks	
Ring Set (1 Piston)	
Rod, Small End	
Total Reciprocating Weight	
Rod, Big End	
Rod Bearing (1 Pair)	
Oil	
Total Rotating Weight	

Balance Percent* 0.50 for V-8 90-degree

Bob Weight = 2 x (Reciprocating Wt. x .50 + Rotating Weight)

Cylinder Head Flow

Modifications	
Flow Bench	
Test Pressure	
Bore Fixture Dia.	
Intake Valve Dia.	
Exhaust Valve Dia.	

Intake Flow

Lift	CFM
.100	
.200	
.300	
.400	
.500	
.600	
.700	

Exhaust Flow

Lift	CFM	Exh. to Int. %
.100		
.200		
.300		
.400		
.500		
.600		
.700		

Compression Ratio

Swept Volume*	
Dome (-) or Dish (+) Volume	
Ring Land Volume	
Deck Volume	
Head Gasket Volume	
Chamber Volume	
Total Volume	

$$CR = \frac{\text{Total Volume}}{\text{Total} - \text{Swept Volume}}$$

$$CR = \underline{\hspace{2cm}} : 1$$

*Swept Volume (cc) = Bore^2 x Stroke x 12.87